# Creation and Emotion
## *in the*
# Old Testament

D1522668

# Creation and Emotion
## *in the*
## Old Testament

DAVID A. BOSWORTH

Fortress Press
Minneapolis

CREATION AND EMOTION IN THE OLD TESTAMENT

Library of Congress Control Number: 2023008314 (Print)

Cover image: Jene Stephaniuk on Unsplash
Cover design: Savanah N. Landerholm

Print ISBN: 978-1-5064-9103-5
eBook ISBN: 978-1-5064-9104-2

*To Frostburg, Maryland, my Zion*

# CONTENTS

# ACKNOWLEDGMENTS

Several people and institutions have made this work possible. The project began as a presentation at the Society of Biblical Literature Annual Meeting in Denver in 2018. The session was jointly hosted by the Trauma in the Bible section and Emotions and the Ecological Hermeneutics section. I presented on the role of creation in the divine–human relationship in Isaiah 13–27. A second presentation expanded the scope to Isaiah 1–39 at a presentation to the Catholic Biblical Association Annual Meeting at Walsh University in North Canton, OH, in 2019. At the Society of Biblical Literature annual meeting that year, I included analysis of nature in Akkadian prophetic texts, but this work dropped from the project. The major finding is that Akkadian prophetic texts make far fewer references to nature than Isaiah. It did not provide enough data to incorporate into this study. I presented part of chapter 1 at the Society of Biblical Literature Annual Meeting in the Nature Imagery and Conceptions of Nature consultation in San Antonio in 2021. The project has grown and evolved over the years into something more and different from what I started with. It has been a long and difficult path with several unexpected turns. I have learned much along the way and have many people to thank for helping me get this far. Progress toward the book was accelerated by a grant from the Catholic Biblical Association and Confraternity for Christian Doctrine of the United States Conference of Catholic Bishops that, among other things, funded my research leave in fall 2020. The School of Theology and Religious Studies at the Catholic University of America provided supplementary funding that paid for a research assistant in spring 2021. This research assistant merits particular thanks. Lucia Tosatto entered into the project with interest and understood exactly what I needed. Conversations with her helped me clarify the scope and nature of the project, and she provided invaluable research help in a host of areas. With more funding from the School, Lucia became my research assistant again in summer 2022 as I completed this book. I may not have met my deadline without her outstanding help. Special thanks to Dean Mark Morozowich for making the funding for her possible. The present work represents a further development of my science-engaged biblical scholarship. The Dialogue on Science, Ethics, and Religion (DoSER) of the American Association for the Advancement of Science (AAAS) assisted my initial progress on this research path. My colleague Robert Miller and I oversaw a Science for Seminaries grant administered by DoSER with Templeton Foundation funds from 2013 to 2015. That grant accelerated my learning and connected me to several people with a common interest in science and theology from both sides of the dialogue. One such connection led me to become a Sinai and Synapses Fellow in 2015–17. Rabbi Geoff Mittelman of the National Jewish Center for Leadership and Learning develops community among fellows from a variety of fields and walks of life (not all academic). The bibliography reflects my indebtedness to some of the scholars working in fields related to Scripture, psychology, emotion, and the environment. My family provides a safe harbor during storms and a secure base from which to set sail. Special thanks to Britt Silkey and Alex Bosworth, who top the list of people I am grateful for. As the content of the book clarifies, places matter. Frostburg, Maryland, has afforded an outstanding environment for the life of our family. The natural beauty and social life of the town have afforded many happy memories. The dedication reflects my place attachment to the Mountain City.

# INTRODUCTION

CREATION CONJURES EMOTION.[1] Natural landscapes, plants, and animals shape our lives in ways that escape our attention. Even subtle environmental cues have a significant impact on emotion and behavior.[2] Speakers use language to tap into place-based emotions. A psalmist accesses widely shared fears of dark and confined spaces to express deep anxiety: "You plunge me into the bottom of the pit, into the darkness of the abyss . . . caged in, I cannot escape." (Ps 88:7–9) Home, by contrast, affords safety and security as a place of peace and rest (Ruth 1:9; 1 Sam 25:35; 1 Kgs 22:17; Isa 55:17). The proverb "Like a bird far from the nest, so is anyone far from home" (Prov 17:8) reflects the anxiety and vulnerability of migrants and the importance of place in human life (Gen 12:11–12; 26:6–7; Ps 137; cf. Isa 16:2; Ps 11:1). Places contain objects and features that shape their emotional salience. Isaiah construes the arid Negeb as a "distressed and troubled land" inhabited by lions and snakes (Isa 30:6). The vision of desert lands transformed by flowing water and cleansed of predatory animals evokes joy (Isa 35). Any creature might have ruined Eden, but the narrative gives this role to an animal that inspires dread and fascination in humans across cultures.[3] Indeed, the story seeks to explain the widespread fear of snakes even as it amplifies that fear. This book explores how biblical writers recruit creation to elicit emotions.

Creation encompasses culture. YHWH not only makes the universe but institutes marriage and forms nations. Israel emerges as the most important entity YHWH creates (e.g., Ps 77:17–21).[4] The Israelites still distinguished nature and culture. For example, the book of Isaiah includes a thematic distinction between cultivated land and wilderness, and the divine speeches in Job 38–41 indicate a similar category distinction between human culture and the natural world. The Hebrew word pair "heaven and earth" profiles a concept similar to the modern concept profiled by the terms *cosmos* or *nature*.[5] Evidence points to the ancient wisdom that culture arises from nature.[6]

Israelites understood creation as personal and relational, in contrast to modern Western people who think of nature as impersonal and mechanistic. This difference in conceptualization creates differences in the emotional salience of nature. YHWH establishes an order in the natural and social worlds. Humans can violate the social order and cause ecological catastrophes (Isa 24:1–6, 18–23; Jer 4:22–28; Hos 4:1–3). YHWH as creator can reestablish the proper order of creation, understood as nature and culture (Ps 85:11–13; Hos 2:23–25).[7] Natural events have an ethical meaning. YHWH sends plagues to punish people (Gen 12:17; Num 11:33; 17:11–15; 25:1–9; 2 Sam 24). Many modern people, by contrast, understand nature more scientifically and do not recognize these kinds of connections between natural events and human behaviors. Hurricanes disproportionately strike the Caribbean for reasons of geography rather than the sinfulness of the people who live there, and the severity of the cyclones is determined by factors such as ocean temperature rather than the severity of sin. For the ancients, however, the natural world was loaded with cultural meaning and moral significance. Drought and other natural disasters signify a sinful social order, while fertility and peace reward justice (Deut 28; Isa 19:5–10; 24:3–23). A relational creation affords emotional depth and variety. Drought elicits guilt or shame for wrongdoing in addition to grief over lost harvests (Jer 14:1–13). Creation triggers a wide range of emotions within the biblical worldview.[8]

"An experience without emotion is like a day without weather."[9] Emotion infuses all aspects of life. Fear permeated my being after I almost stepped on a rattlesnake while hiking in the woods. Fear increased my heart rate and respiration and heightened my sensory perception for snake-like things and my reactivity to them. Every stick along the trail looked like a snake. Fear directed my attention, shaped how I interpreted what I saw, and motivated my retreat from the wilderness. Fear enhanced my memory for the encounter and spawned curiosity about snakes.[10] This episode illustrates the integrative role of emotion. Emotions organize the whole person's response to events, including heartbeat (Jer 4:19), thought, and action. Emotions "assign value to stimuli and events" and infuse attention, memory, and decision-making.[11] Emotions help evaluate, prioritize, and organize responses to internal sensations (e.g., hunger) and the external world (e.g., a rattlesnake). Emotions exist between reflexes and deliberative thinking. Reflexes dictate a narrow range of responses, but deliberation results in a wide range of behaviors. Emotion falls between the two. Specific emotions motivate a wide but finite range of behaviors. We have few reflexes and rarely deliberate, so we operate by emotion through the bulk of our lives.[12] Emotions coordinate diverse aspects of the whole person. Emotions encompass feelings (the subjective experience of the emotional state).[13]

Emotions exist independently of language, but words still matter because people need to talk about emotions. We need to recognize the emotions that we and others experience and name them, so we can better regulate emotion and engage in relationships.[14] Our ability to understand the mental states of ourselves and others enables good social functioning, while deficiencies in these skills correlate with a range of mental health problems and poor relationships.[15] People therefore need linguistic expressions for emotions, and children acquire these expressions as they acquire the language and culture of their communities. Emotion terms evoke the conceptual content related to the emotion. This content includes knowledge of situations that elicit the emotion, associated feelings and behaviors, and cultural values influencing whether or how the emotion may be expressed.[16] Speakers more readily conceptualize and regulate their emotions in adaptive ways when they can talk about them. Differences in emotion vocabulary across languages reflect diverse cultural emphases.[17] For example, the Japanese term *amae* profiles the "sensation of temporary surrender in perfect safety" in the care of loved ones.[18] It may be felt in the context of many relationships, from family to the workplace. "Children may be accused of behaving in an *amaeru* way" if they seem to be hoping that others will do things for them.[19] The word is sometimes translated as "behaving like a spoiled child" or "relying on another's good will," but it is not regarded as a negative emotion to be blamed or avoided, but a deep trust that evokes an infant in its mother's arms. Something like *amae* can be felt by people who are not Japanese, but most cultures have not associated a term with the emotion for purposes of readily conceptualizing the experience. In English, people may speak about *trust* or *dependence* because it can be useful to identify this emotional reality that resembles *amae*, but the Japanese term enables a culturally supported conceptualization not found in English. Efforts to match linguistic terms and emotions across languages find that some terms translate well into many languages. Terms that do not readily translate across languages, like *amae*, can still be explained because the experiences and situations can be accessed across cultural divides with appropriate cultural explanation.[20] Language helps us infer the mental states of others. Humans could not create language or culture without this "mind-reading" skill.[21] Mind reading, therefore, is not an ability we switch on when we need it but a default mode of operating.[22]

We can use language to evoke or shape emotion. "Linguistic acts are social acts that one person intentionally directs at another . . . in order to direct her attention and imagination in particular ways so that she will do, know, or feel what he wants her to."[23] We can use language to influence the minds of others because language taps in to the general structures of human mental life.[24] Commonalities across human languages result from the fact that we are all one species. People speaking in any language conceptualize the world in terms of agents acting on objects, objects moving from place to place, people interacting with one another, and perceiving, thinking, and feeling things. Similarly, people speaking in any language have common communicative motivations such as requesting things of others, informing others, and sharing experiences—especially emotional ones.[25] People speaking in any language shape the attention of others in similar ways, such as distinguishing information already in the attentional frame from new information. People speaking any language process information in similar ways, through common features of visual perception, categorization, analogy, and other features of human cognition that shape and constrain language.[26]

For all the commonalities among humans, cultures vary enormously and influence conceptualizations, including how people think about emotions.[27] Cultures also offer ethical evaluations of emotions and normative rules about who may express what emotions under what circumstances. These cultural rules and values become part of a person's conceptualization of emotion. Language directs attention to concepts that derive from culturally shaped understandings of the physical and social worlds.[28] Speakers use linguistic expressions to evoke a conceptual understanding that the hearer must work out based on shared culture and context. Words, then, are not containers carrying packages of meaning, but gestures that point toward concepts. I will therefore speak of linguistic expressions "profiling" concepts rather than words "referring" to things.[29] Words can have multiple meanings and concepts can be elicited with many expressions, so there is no one-to-one correspondence between words and concepts.[30] The present study explores how biblical writers combine creation and emotion. It includes the study of words and modern research on emotion within a cognitive linguistic framework that can hold all this material together.[31] Creation and emotion are not fully separable domains, but entirely overlap. Emotion colors creation. Every word that profiles creation elicits emotion.

This project began as a limited study of the natural world within the book of Isaiah. My sidewise glances beyond Isaiah led to the larger scope of this work. Isaiah still appears prominently and disproportionately in this book as a canon within the canon. Or better, a corpus within the corpus. I developed a spreadsheet of all nominal references to the natural world in Isaiah to pursue a corpus linguistic approach. Corpus linguistics provides a helpful correction to our biases. We notice evidence that tends to support our arguments while ignoring or underestimating contrary evidence. Corpus linguistic methods can illuminate how differences in frequency of expressions can shape attention.[32] Rare expressions capture our attention due to their rarity, while more frequent constructions may not register as strongly. For example, we may be struck at the seeming frequency with which Isaiah construes the earth as a person (Isa 1:2; 24:20; 26:21; 34:1; 44:23; 48:5; 49:13; 62:4 twice).[33] A corpus linguistic analysis, however, shows that 116 passages in Isaiah construe earth as a place, most often as a container. Earth metonymically profiles inhabitants in an additional thirty-one examples. The ten personifications of earth capture attention because they are rare. Hebrew writers frequently construe humans as agents who can think, feel, and speak, so these expressions do not draw attention as forcefully as the earth speaking.[34] Cognitive biases operate more freely in a corpus as large as the entire Old Testament.[35] The present work, therefore, is based in part on a spreadsheet listing all nominal references to the natural world in Isaiah in an effort to achieve a relatively full picture of nonhuman creation in one substantial book. This close attention to a corpus within the corpus helps limit the biases that have more room to operate outside corpus linguistic constraints. Cognitive biases pervade and pervert our thinking. They cannot be eliminated, but corpus linguistic methods and publicly shared data can identify them and limit their effects.[36]

Biblical quotes are taken from the *New American Bible (Revised Edition)* (NABRE), but I have changed *the LORD* to YHWH. I indicate more significant changes in the notes.

# 1

## LOVE AND GRIEF

GRIEF IS THE price we pay for love. We grieve most over those we love most. Jacob cannot stop mourning when he believes his favorite son Joseph has died (Gen 37:35). Grief reminds us that we depend on others. Emotional attachments give rise to grief when pets die, objects break or become lost, and familiar places become strange. Some of our favorite places involve memories of shared activities with family and friends. Development overruns natural habitats and old buildings may be replaced, renovated beyond recognition, or abandoned to decay.[1] Our love for places leads to sorrow when we see how the location is changed. The emotion resembles homesickness.[2] Place-based love and grief appear in biblical literature.[3] People who love Jerusalem mourn over the devastated city and rejoice at its restoration (Isa 66:10). Psalm 42–43 blends longing for God with longing for the temple where God resides. The speaker weeps and repeatedly describes himself as downcast (42:6, 7, 12; 43:5), groaning (42:6, 12; 43:5), and mourning (42:10; 43:2) due to separation from the source of joy (43:4). The love of Jerusalem derives from memories of public festivals (42:5). Hebrew has no word for homesickness, but the prayer expresses this emotion eloquently. Those who witnessed the destruction of Jerusalem reflect grief over the loss of the loved place without being removed from the location. The speaker in Psalm 74 describes how invaders attack the temple with picks and axes, smashing it and setting the wreckage on fire. The prayer construes the catastrophe as a consequence of God's wrath and communicates the grief of the people. Psalm 79 similarly depicts the devastation of Jerusalem, including the land littered with corpses. The beautiful and beloved Zion becomes a dystopian hellscape that provokes grief over the negative transformation of a loved place. One does not need to be absent from home to mourn its loss. Biblical authors speak of places as objects of love ("May those who love you [Jerusalem] prosper," Ps 122:6), but often express this love in other ways, as in Psalms 42–43; 74;

79 (cf. 46; 48). The absence of emotion words does not indicate the absence of emotion.

## Love Zion as Your Mother
### *Isaiah 49:13–21*

Isaiah 49 focuses on Jerusalem's transition from empty and ruined city to populated and reconstructed city. The text construes Zion as a mother to heighten the emotions involved in the transformation of the city. The blend overlays the love between mother and child on the love between city and inhabitants.

YHWH proclaims that the nations will bring Zion's children back to her and serve her, continuing the theme of comfort for the people from Isa 40:1 (see comfort in 49:13).[4] The text offers comfort by blending place and parent, Zion and mother, and promising a happy restoration. Loved places can offer a sense of security and safety similar to the embrace of family. The term "place attachment" highlights how love of place relies on the same emotional and relational dynamics at work in parent–child bonds.[5] Shared love of place "exerts the most positive influence of any single force on the design of community."[6] Biblical writers contribute to the conceptual architecture of Jerusalem by building up cultural meanings that reinforce love for Zion.[7]

YHWH prompts the hearer to open up a mental space and fill it with knowledge about mothers.[8] The text does not use the term *mother*, but *woman*. It then introduces *her infant*, which makes the woman a mother. The domain MOTHER encompasses everything that the hearer knows about mothers and motherhood.[9] The text prompts the hearer to create a mental space "online," meaning that the language evokes certain aspects of the domain that the hearer brings into working memory. The totality of knowledge about mothers does not fit into the mental space. In this case, YHWH highlights a mother's reliable love and care for a vulnerable newborn, construing YHWH as mother-like and Zion as infant-like.[10] YHWH's love for Zion is more reliable than a mother's love for her infant. The text then enlists Zion in the role of mother and demonstrates YHWH's love for her by restoring her children to her. The context clarifies the focus of the

Mother-Zion blend: Zion loves her inhabitants as a mother loves her children, and YHWH loves Zion as a daughter.[11] Mother-Zion is not a mother
or a city, but a blend of both. Cities do not have natural gender, palms,
or children, and they do not love or experience grief; and mothers do not
have walls and gates. Mother-Zion combines all of these features. This passage construes Zion as a devastated place and grieving mother who receives
comfort from YHWH's promise of restoration. Blends seek to reduce things
to human scale or make them conceptually accessible.[12] The blend reduces
the city to human scale, making it more conceptually accessible by construing it as a woman.[13] People depend on their mothers for survival as cities
similarly provide for their inhabitants. All humans are born into a community that precedes them.[14] The Mother-Zion blend shifts between maternal
and geographic language as the text requires in the moment. Zion's level-
ers leave her as her children come to her, blending Zion's bereaved status
with her devastated architecture. Zion's children blend with the jewels of a
bride. The bereft Mother-Zion experiences a wondrous restoration of children.[15] The return of children raises the question of who bore them and
reared them. Zion's questions indicate that she enjoys the status of mother
without the agony of giving birth or the work of rearing children. Leaders
of the nations bring her children home so that the gift of motherhood
comes to Zion suddenly and without effort. The leaders did the work of
guarding and nursing them, giving Zion the benefit of children without
the cost. YHWH acts out of love for Zion, not for the people directly. The
people benefit because Mother-Zion mediates divine love and restoration.
Mother-Zion thereby emerges as the source of the people's new life and,
along with YHWH, the target of their gratitude. The blend recruits the love
people have for their mothers to enhance their love of Zion. A ruined and
empty Zion may appear unloved and unlovable, and the exiled people may
have no living recollection of its former grandeur (cf. Ps 46) or experience
of its festivals (Isa 33:20). These descendants of exiles were strangers to
Zion.[16] The exiles may have retained a concept of "the place that was," or an
"image of how and where to live" that can be transmitted generationally.[17]
This concept of Zion as it was may have survived for the exiles in some
texts now included as Scripture—such as Psalms 46, 48, 132, and 137. The
author of Isaiah 49 had some existing concepts about Zion to recruit into

the blend of Mother-Zion to rekindle or reinforce the exiles' love for Zion based on their love for their mothers.

The Mother-Zion blend reflects the similarity between love of mother and love of place. In Isaiah, personified Zion represents a place, not the community of people who live there.[18] In the Isaiah blend, the people are the children of Mother-Zion, thereby separating the people and city conceptually. The conceptual separation clarifies that love of Zion is attachment to a place, not only to a community. The text presents Jerusalem as the true home of the diaspora Jews in order to construct a coherent group identity.

The similarity between attachment to a parent and attachment to a place emerges in the four signs of attachment. These four behaviors appear in both interpersonal relationships with nonparents and attachment to places, including place attachment in the Bible.[19] First, children seek to stay close to their caregiver. This behavior can be observed in infants crawling after a caregiver, the desire to return home from work or a journey, or families returning repeatedly to a favorite vacation spot. In Isa 49:17, YHWH tells Zion "your children hasten," meaning that they are returning to her. Their haste suggests a sense of urgency and desire to be with their mother Zion. YHWH also describes them as "gathering and coming to you" (49:18). The human audience know themselves loved by Zion as by a mother. They reciprocate her love and desire to be with her. Mother-Zion mediates the restoration of community since she motivates YHWH's saving action and provides the shared place that makes community possible. The blend upholds Zion as home (see also Pss 42–43; 122; 137; 148).

Second, mothers provide a safe haven to their children in times of distress. When small children experience fear or pain (e.g., appearance of a stranger, hunger, injury), they return to their caregivers for help regulating out of negative emotions. Loved places provide a similar function. People who are sick or anxious desire to be at home. Isa 66:13 explicitly blends the safe haven function of mothers and Zion: "As a mother comforts her child, so I will comfort you. In Jerusalem you will find your comfort." The simile blends the spaces of YHWH and mother. YHWH comforts the people like a mother comforting her children. Similes limit or constrain blends, making them less vivid than metaphors.[20] The text imposes no such constraints in the Mother-Zion blend as Zion is fully personified, giving birth and nursing children. The Mother-YHWH simile may limit YHWH's motherhood in order to allow full range for the motherhood of Zion. Jerusalem can be a source of comfort and safe haven because YHWH protects and provides for the city. The Mother-Zion passages in Isaiah 40–66 seek to reestablish this sense of safety following the catastrophe of conquest and exile (cf. Ps 89). God will again defend Zion and offer comfort to its frightened inhabitants.

Third, caregivers provide children with a secure base from which to explore the world and enter into new relationships. YHWH's speeches to Zion in Isaiah 40–66 seek to fill her with confidence in her safety and security. YHWH will oppose Zion's enemies and save her children (49:24). The speech concludes with the affirmation that "all flesh will know" that YHWH is the savior and redeemer of Zion (49:26). In Isaiah 52, YHWH identifies Jerusalem as a holy city and affirms that "never again shall the uncircumcised or the unclean enter you" (52:1). YHWH returns to the city as her king to protect her (52:7–10) and urges her to not be afraid or discouraged (54:4). YHWH evokes the constancy of creation to instill a sense of safety and confidence: "Though the mountains fall away and the hills be shaken, my love shall never fall away from you nor my covenant of peace be shaken." (Isa 54:10) The prophetic voice assures Zion that her children will be taught by YHWH and enjoy peace and justice (54:13–14). The Psalms of Zion (Pss 46; 48; 132) similarly manifest the secure base function of the city. Psalm 46:3–4 echoes Isaiah's creation language: "Thus we do not fear, though the earth be shaken and mountains quake to the depths of the sea, though its waters rage and foam and mountains totter at its surging." Creation affords a model of reliability that blends with YHWH's love. These texts seek to reestablish trust in YHWH as protector and in Zion as secure base. Despite its past devastation (Ps 89), Zion will become home again.

Fourth, grief or protest at separation reveals attachment. The people rejoice with Zion in her joy as they mourned over her in her devastation (66:10). She is waste, desolate, bereft, and alone (49:19–21) without her children. The emotional pain of Mother-Zion reflects the reciprocal pain of the people who experience separation from her. Psalm 137 expresses the sorrow of forced migration. Weeping by the waters of Babylon signals grief. The memory of the city, its destruction, and their forced migration engender intense sorrow over the loss of a loved place. Their lack of joy makes it

impossible to sing the songs of their homeland. The remembrance of Zion
provokes grief, but the exiles refuse to let go of their attachment to the city.
They invite curses on themselves if they should forget Jerusalem and fail to
uphold it as their greatest delight. The people experience the destruction
of Jerusalem as the death of their mother. The Mother-Zion blend reflects
the same love and grief manifested in Psalms 42–43, 74, 79, and 137. The
blend draws on the emotional power of bereaved mothers to unify the people around their shared love of the city.[21]

The Mother-Zion blend places the human audience in the position
of child, but the occasional reference to "daughter Zion" places the human
audience in the role of parent to a daughter. The title *daughter*, however,
does not introduce any elaboration of Zion as a daughter in relationship to
anyone else. The label elicits the concept of daughter as "desired, vulnerable,
endangered femininity."[22] The expression "daughter Zion" occurs in contexts
involving the suffering of the people and place (Isa 1:8; 47:1; Jer 50:42; Lam
1:6; 2:1), or happy contexts that recall prior suffering (Isa 52:2; 62:11).[23]
Ancient Israelite daughters lived in a family system that both valued and
devalued them.[24] The culture motivated parents to prefer male to female
children (1 Sam 1:11). Fathers still cared for their daughters, and one motive
to reject monarchy was that the king would take daughters to serve his court
(1 Sam 8:13). The expression "my daughter" appears outside parental contexts to indicate love and care (Ps 45:11; Ruth 2:2, 8, 22; 3:1, 10, 16, 18;
cf. "my son" in 1 Sam 26:21, 25; 2 Sam 19:1; Prov 1:8, 10). When Nathan
wants to illustrate the close emotional bond between the poor man and the
lamb, he says the man treated it "like a daughter" (2 Sam 12:3). The endear-
ing aspect of daughter Zion derives from the domain of daughter, which
involves bonds of kinship, parental care, and vulnerability in a patriarchal
social order. The daughter-Zion blend evokes a desire to care for and protect
a vulnerable female child. Biblical literature works the powerful emotions of
the parent–child bond from both ends of the dyad. Biblical writers prefer
the term Zion over other labels for the location (e.g., Jerusalem, Ariel, city of
David) when blending the city with a mother or daughter.[25]

Zion profiles the mountain more reliably than other terms. It seems
to have applied first to the earliest settlement that David conquered (2 Sam
5:7; 1 Kgs 8:1), but then shifted or extended to the Temple Mount north of

the city of David when the temple was constructed there (Isa 8:18; 10:12). The term may have this fluidity because the topography does not clearly delimit these locations. Steep slopes impose the boundary of the mountain to the south, east, and west, but "the city's northern border has no clear-cut topographical demarcation."[26] The ridge east of the Kidron Valley can be construed as a single extended ridge with variations in elevation. The Temple Mount and city of David may have been construed as a single formation, facilitating flexibility in the profile of Zion.[27] The physical geography of Zion possesses features that make it an appealing place for human habitation. Its mountaintop location affords a defensible position, and the Gihon Spring affords a reliable source of water. These features attracted human settlement. Early inhabitants constructed a water system and built walls to enhance its defensibility.[28] The features of Zion make the location desirable for human habitation and lay the natural foundations for cultural constructions.

Place attachment enhances community cohesion and social capital. People more readily coordinate their values and activities toward common ends.[29] The architects of the community used place attachment to Zion as a central piece of a theological schema that connected the dynasty of David and the temple of YHWH in a singular and special location where both would endure forever.[30] Multiple biblical texts contribute to the construction of Zion as a central place in the hearts of the Judeans. The narrative of David's conquest of the city places the origins of Zion theology in a divine oracle (1 Sam 7:8–17), which is recollected in Psalms 89 and 132. This "Zion theology" shaped how the people interpreted subsequent events that dramatically altered the Judean landscape and shaped Judean attachment to Zion. Several cultic complexes in different towns competed with Jerusalem's temple in the tenth to eighth centuries. These sites were destroyed and the temple in Jerusalem became the only cultic complex in the seventh century.[31] Jerusalem became a pilgrimage destination, reflecting attachment to it as a holy city.[32] Hezekiah massively expanded the city and built a tunnel to bring water from the Gihon Spring to a pool within the walls of the city, which enhanced its defensibility in advance of Sennacherib's invasion.[33] The biblical tradition, represented in both 2 Kings 18–19 and Isaiah 36–37, narrates the wondrous salvation of Jerusalem from Sennacherib's invasion through the agency of YHWH. This event reinforced the belief that the city was invincible because of YHWH's protection. The centrality of Jerusalem emerged as other locations faded, but the biblical stories about Jerusalem present it as unique from the beginning. Deuteronomy speaks of the place that YHWH will choose. That place is Jerusalem (e.g., Deut 12:5; Ps 78:68).[34] YHWH's choice of the city makes it prosperous (Ps 132:13–17), and YHWH protects the city and its inhabitants (Ps 46:6–8). The community's love for Zion manifests as care for its physical infrastructure. YHWH tells Mother-Zion "your walls are ever before me" (Isa 49:16). Psalm 48 instructs its audience to walk around Zion and observe its towers, ramparts, and citadel (Ps 48:13–14). Psalm 51 asks YHWH to "treat Zion kindly according to your good will; build up the walls of Zion" (51:20). Love for the city should motivate its reconstruction (Hag 1–2; Neh 1). Zion hosts multiple public festivals that endear the city to people who enjoy these community traditions (Pss 42:5; 48:10–12; 55:15; 84:2–5; 118:26–27; 122:1–5; 135:1–3; Isa 33:20). Some texts illustrate the social and emotional attachments that these activities elicited (Pss 48:2–3; 13–15; 84:6, 11). Happy memories formed in specific places engender love for those places.[35] The speaker of Psalm 122 associates Zion with joyful communion in "Jerusalem, built as a city, walled round about" (122:2–3) and invites the audience to "pray for the peace of Jerusalem." The psalmist addresses the city itself: "May those who love you prosper! May peace be within your ramparts, prosperity within your towers." (Ps 122:6–7)

"Jerusalem is emphatically a mountain city."[36] Passages that engender love for the city often profile the mountain because of the association between mountains and divinity. Psalm 48 describes Zion as "his holy mountain, fairest of heights, the joy of all the earth, Mount Zion, the heights of Zaphon, the city of the great king" (48:2–3). Some mountains serve as locations for divine presence, as Mount Olympus, Mount Zaphon, or Mount Sinai/ Horeb. Mount Zion joins the ranks of these divinely chosen mountains, and Psalm 48:3 identifies Zion as Zaphon.[37] Several expressions profile the mountain together with the temple (Isa 2:2; 56:7), and the mountain and city are often called holy (mountain in Isa 11:9; 27:13; 57:13; 65:11, 25; 66:20; city in 48:2; 52:1). The elevation of the mountain appears in contexts that emphasize the need for ethical conduct. The speaker of Psalm 24 asks, "Who may go up the mountain of YHWH? Who can stand in his holy place? The clean of hand and pure of heart, who has not given his soul to useless things, what is vain" (24:3–4). Similarly, trembling sinners in Jerusalem ask "Who of us can live with consuming fire?" (Isa 33:14) and are told "Whoever walks righteously and speaks honestly" (33:15) and lives ethically "shall dwell on the heights, with fortresses of rock for stronghold, food and drink in steady supply" (Isa 33:16). YHWH's presence in the city imposes ethical demands on the community. Ideally, the people live according to YHWH's instructions and enjoy peace and prosperity. Isaiah laments the degradation of the city caused by the wickedness of its inhabitants (Isa 1:21–28). The text draws on shared love of Zion to motivate ethical conduct in light of YHWH's presence in the city. When the people obey the law, they build social trust.

Isaiah 2:2–4 imagines universal peace and justice when love for Zion encompasses the whole world.[38] The passage emphasizes the mountain and its connection to ethical conduct as the place where the nations receive YHWH's instruction (2:34). Zion is not the highest mountain within its local region (Ps 125:2), but slightly shorter than the mountains on either side at 2,438 feet (743 meters) compared to the Mount of Olives at 2,533 feet (772 meters) to the east and Old City at 2,503 feet (763 meters) to the west. Mountains like Zaphon and Hermon are much higher, but their snow-capped peaks are not suitable for human habitation. Mount Hermon includes the highest location in modern Israel at 7,336 feet (2236 meters) and Mt Zaphon is 5,509 feet (1,679 meters) high. The oracle envisions Zion becoming the "head" (2:2) of all the mountains. This language highlights the social status of the mountain, and the remainder of the oracle focuses on its social significance rather than its physical elevation.[39] Its increased elevation reflects its greater political and theological significance as the center of authority exercised for the good of all. All the nations will "stream" (2:2) to Jerusalem. The speaker construes the nations generically. There are no named nations (e.g., Moabites, Ammonites, etc.), but a collective totality of "all nations" followed by "many peoples" who go up the mountain. The lack of specific names opens the passage to the widest possible interpretation, encompassing the whole world, not only near neighbors of Israel. The text then presents the perspective and thought of these incoming peoples with use of *walk*, a verb of motion that blends with ethical conduct and relationship with God.[40] They say "Come, let us ascend" the mountain with the temple as their ultimate goal in order that "we may walk in his paths." They expect to receive instruction (v. 3) in language that enhances the ethical and relational sense of *walk* through collocation with *instruction*. As a result, YHWH will mediate disputes between the nations and there will be no war. In sum, the many nations of the world will unify as one people attached to Mount Zion and loyal to YHWH, so conflicts will be resolved peacefully rather than through war. This image of universal peace appears in the parallel passage in Micah 4:1–4 and in Psalms 46:9–10; 47:8–10; 50:1–2; 76:2–3. The expansion of love for Zion from Judah to the whole world will create a global community with shared ethics and common goals. The vision of peace appears in Isaiah 40–66, including the passages in which Zion appears as a mother. Isaiah 60, for example, depicts the nations coming to Zion to bring her their wealth, rebuild her infrastructure, and serve her. Nations that do not serve Zion will perish. The imperialistic tone of these passages contrasts with Isaiah 2:2–5 where the nations rejoice in their pilgrimage to Jerusalem.

Biblical texts reflect and reinforce Judean love for Jerusalem. Zion theology binds the city to the temple and the dynasty of David and places the city at the center of Judean identity. Isaiah employs the Mother-Zion blend to rekindle love for the city in a population of exiles who may find the ruined site hard to love. By depicting the ruin as a bereaved mother, the texts strive to elicit love and concern for the city and a desire to return and rebuild. The renewed city becomes the center of the renewed community. This central site affords a unifying figure for the whole community, even those who do not live in Jerusalem. Love for the place, however, extends beyond Zion to the surrounding countryside and the land more generally.[41] Texts assume and encourage love for the region and its agricultural lands, and grief when the lands suffer drought or other ecological disaster. Grief and loss may be expressed through the transformation of landscape as well as the devastation of cities. In a healthy ecology, vibrant cities thrive on the fertile farmland that surrounds and nourishes them. Drought, like foreign invasion, devastates the fields with dire consequences for the city.

## Grieve for Zion and Her Land
### Jeremiah 14:1–7

The prophets prompt grief by leveraging human emotional responses to drought. People form attachments to their land, and some biblical texts reflect the joy and communal celebration that accompanied the harvest (Isa 30:18–26; 32:9–20). These festivities build place attachment analogous to the festivals associated with Jerusalem and the temple. By contrast, drought endangers this happy hope of harvest and generates anxiety about the future. Drought represents a loss that provokes grief. Drying vegetation appears also as a source domain in conceptual blends that elicit grief. Indeed, the blend of drying and mortality led to the development of the two meanings of one Hebrew verb: *to dry up* and *to mourn*.[42] Biblical descriptions of drought offer insight into how drought was experienced as a reality that shapes audience reactions to prophetic predictions of drought. The connection between a drying earth and human grief emerges in Jeremiah's description of a drought. Jeremiah 14 shows how the environment can shape emotion and behavior. The passage focuses on the emotional reactions of the people and their attempts to persuade yhwh to end the drought (14:1).[43] Judah profiles the inhabitants of Judah who mourn, not the land. The gates participate in mourning through their own sadness, depicted with a verb that may mean *to dry out* or *to wither away*, applied to plants or people.[44] The personified gates and city represent the people crying out to God. The young servants who can find no water, like the farmers in the countryside, feel shame and humiliation and cover their heads. The text describes self-abnegation and distraught emotions as the people seek to gain sympathy from God with awareness of their guilt (Jer 14:7). The drought is so severe that deer abandon their young. Wild donkeys, which survive in arid wastelands (Jer 2:24; Job 39:5–8), suffer thirst and hunger.[45] The drying of the land impacts humans and animals. The description of the land itself is limited to its physical condition: it is desiccated and there is no water or grass.[46] Jeremiah 14:1–7 illustrates how a catastrophe-like drought leads to emotional distress and appeals to God for salvation. The ritual mourning reflects an emotional experience of grief and remorse directly tied to the desiccated land. God tells Jeremiah, "if they fast, I will not listen to their supplication" (v. 12). Ritual behaviors like fasting and self-abnegation seek to gain the attention, empathy, and help of the deity.[47] The ritual interventions of the people will fail. Jeremiah depicts Judean reactions to drought.[48]

Joel 1 also describes a grief reaction to crop failure that closely resembles the description in Jeremiah 14. The failure results from a locust plague and drought that defoliated the vegetation and left the vines and trees unable to produce fruit, resulting in an ecological catastrophe.[49] The prophet calls on the priests and ministers to mourn because of the disaster (Joel 1:9).[50] The same verb describes the land as dried up, shifting its meaning and providing a thematic wordplay that connects mourning people to desiccated land. The passage calls on the priests to mourn *because* the land is dried up.[51] By the same logic, the speaker calls on agricultural workers to be ashamed and wail *because* the vegetation has dried up and the harvest failed (1:11–12).[52] The passage ends with a renewed call for the priests to lead the people in fasting and prayer to end the drought. The emotional language describes human responses to the ecological crisis. The land and vegetation are not pictured in emotional terms. Rather, many lexemes depict the dried-out landscape, while the emotional language applies to humans who react to the drought with grief and shame, including wordplays involving the *mourning* priests and *drying* land, and the *drying* vegetation and *shamed* inhabitants.[53]

Prophets threatened drought and desiccated vegetation to induce emotional responses like those described in the actual catastrophes in Jeremiah 14:13–21 and Joel 1:9–14. The prophetic motif of drying vegetation seeks to elicit grief from the audience and motivate the petitionary behavior described in Jeremiah 14 and Joel 1. The connection between drying and grief motivates metaphorical uses of drying plants. I located examples of the motif by searching for verbs that profile drying.[54] The analysis discovered twenty-three examples of a motif of drying vegetation limited to the prophets.[55] The prophetic motif of drying vegetation typically presents drought as a punishment. Moab (Isa 15:5; 16:8–9), Egypt (Isa 19:5–9; Zech 10:11), Babylon (Jer 50:38; 51:36), and Nineveh (Nah 1:4) will suffer drought as punishment for their pride and violence. The apocalypse of Isaiah expands this punishment to the whole world (Isa 24:4–7; 27:10–11). The most common target of punishment, however, is Israel/Judah (Isa 33:9; Jer 4:23–28; 8:13; 12:1–4, 7–13; 23:9–12; Hos 4:1–3; Amos 1:2; 4:7; Hag 1:11).[56] The land suffers for the sins of its inhabitants, who experience grief, fear, and shame. Seen in this wider context, *to dry up* emerges as another meaning for the verb *to mourn*. The land dries in these passages, but does not mourn. Other passages use drying vegetation as a metaphor for mortality, frailty, and sometimes emotional enervation. These metaphors may have led speakers to extend the meaning of the verb from drying to mourning. The metaphoric uses of drying vegetation cluster in Isaiah, Psalms, and Job.[57]

The frequency of the prophetic motif of drying vegetation may correspond to Israelite familiarity with drought and its consequences. The Israelites lived in a region with many different ecological niches, but none receive much rainfall. The Negeb receives almost no rain (less than one cm per year), with average rainfall increasing as one moves north toward Lebanon (60–70 cm in Jerusalem to over 100 cm in the extreme north of modern Israel). The fertile coastal plains receive much more rain (40–60 cm) than the arid Jordan Rift Valley. The Dead Sea region is desert (less than 10 cm) and southern Galilee is semi-arid (up to 30 cm).[58] Jerusalem perches on a mountain ridge parallel to the coast and situated close to both the east–west and north–south divide between arid and fertile regions. Israelites in and near Jerusalem had direct experience both of the dry Jordan Valley and Negeb to the south and west and the greener hills and coast plains to the north and west. People relying on dry farming in an arid land show a heightened sensitivity to desiccated vegetation, especially considering their experience of drought (Gen 12:10; 26:1; 42:5; Ruth 1:1; 1 Kgs 17:1, 7). The proximity of arid regions served as a constant reminder of what a prolonged drought could do to their fields. In short, the Judeans lived between fertile and desolate landscapes, so the prophetic claim that God would dry out their land seemed plausible and terrifying. Such a prophetic motif would not have developed if Israel lived in a rainforest (over 200 cm of rainfall per year, sometimes over 500 cm).

Isaiah 33 reflects on the relationship between the social and natural order as created by YHWH. The people's prayer asks YHWH to save them from the attacker, whose army gathers spoil like caterpillars and locusts (33:4).[59] The speaker grounds the plea for YHWH to save the people in YHWH's special relationship with Zion. The text first restates this special relationship, concisely identifying its multiple facets. YHWH dwells on Zion and ensures the prosperity and safety of the city and its territory by bringing the seasons that make the agricultural cycle work. YHWH builds up the wealth of the city (33:5–6). YHWH also protects and provides for the city. The people must fear YHWH and live ethically. In this way, YHWH fills Zion with justice. This happy picture of normalcy, however, contrasts with the present situation. The

Hebrew particle *look!* at the start of 33:7 introduces the surprising contrast between the prior description and the present reality. The men of the city cry out and its messengers weep bitterly. The mention of empty highways and roads expands the crisis from the city to its territory and region. People do not fulfill their obligations, attend to witnesses, or care about the collapse of social trust.[60] Parallel to this social collapse, the ecosystem also fails.

Isaiah 33:9 describes Sharon as a desert and Bashan and Carmel as losing their foliage. They dry out, but do not mourn. The passage includes Lebanon feeling shame.[61] If land can feel shame, then it may also feel grief. Indeed, land can be said to grieve (furrows weep in Job 31:38), but the land does not mourn here. Fruitful land can be characterized as proud (Nah 2:3) or glorious (Isa 21:16; 35:2), so a drying and withering land may be characterized as its opposite: ashamed. More specifically, Lebanon represents pride due to its famous trees and lush old-growth forests (Isa 2:13; 10:34; 35:2; 60:13), and the majesty of Lebanon provides a means for kings to manifest their own pride and power (14:8; 37:24). Lebanon is here humbled and shamed by its drying (cf. 10:34; 29:17). The pride of Bashan emerges in Amos's denunciation of the women of Samaria, whom he calls "cows of Bashan" (Amos 4:1). Amos's comparison relies on the glory of Bashan as an analogy for the glory of Samaria. Bashan, Carmel, and Lebanon were all renowned as green pasture lands (Isa 35:2; Jer 50:19; 1 Chr 5:16; 27:29) that symbolize fruitfulness, but may wither in divine judgment as Nahum 1:4 makes clear:[62] "He rebukes the sea and dries it up, all the rivers he dries up, Bashan and Carmel desiccate, the bloom of Lebanon desiccates." Note this example from Nahum describes the drying of vegetation in a passage closely parallel to Isaiah 33:9. The language of God rebuking the sea expresses an idea similar to shame (Isa 50:2; Nah 1:4; Ps 106:9). Both the dried sea and desiccated landscapes appear shamed in contrast to their normal state. The connection between desiccated landscapes and nakedness elsewhere reinforces the connection between dried land and shame. Joseph accuses his brothers of coming to Egypt to see "the nakedness of the land" at a time of failed agricultural productivity (Gen 42:9, 12). Nakedness is associated with shame and humiliation (e.g., Gen 2:25; 3:7–11; Deut 28:48; Isa 20:3–4). Hosea 2:10–12 makes explicit the connection between human nakedness and desiccated land. God will take back the clothing from personified Israel, which represents depriving the land of the produce of flax and wool (materials for making clothing), leaving Israel naked and ashamed. The image of a dried-up land, therefore, does not summon images of a mourning land but of a shamed and naked land.

Examples of the verb *dry up/mourn* in the prophetic motif of drying vegetation likewise reflect a drying rather than a mourning land. The passages focus on the emotionality of the people. The prophetic motif presents drought as a consequence of human sin because the social order influences the natural order. Desiccated land triggers grief and shame in the inhabitants in Jeremiah 14:1–7 and Joel 1:5–14, which describe actual ecological catastrophes as experienced by the Judeans. YHWH establishes the regularity of seasons that create the wealth of Judah, but broken covenants lead to drought (Isa 33:3–9). Similarly, Isaiah 24 describes a universal drought caused by people breaking an ancient covenant and laws.[63] The wickedness of the people polluted the land so that it is consumed by a curse that punishes the guilt of the people.[64] The ecological devastation described in Jeremiah 4:22–28 flows from the people who "are wise at evil, but they do not know how to do good" (4:22) and includes desiccation of the land (4:23, 27–28). The withering vegetation in Jeremiah 8:13 likewise happens "because we have sinned against YHWH" (8:14). The connection between human sin and drought emerges clearly and concisely in Jeremiah 12:4: "How long must the land dry out, the grass of the whole countryside wither because of the wickedness of those who dwell in it?"[65] Hosea similarly states the relationship clearly while drawing on language reminiscent of the decalogue: "Swearing, lying, murder, stealing, and adultery break out; bloodshed follows bloodshed. Therefore the land dries up, and everything that dwells in it languishes. The beast of the field, the birds of the air, and even the fish of the sea perish" (Hos 4:2–3). Jeremiah 23:10 connects adultery (meaning idolatry) with drought: "The land is filled with adulterers; because of the curse, the land dries out, the pastures of the wilderness are withered."[66] Haggai connects a drought to the failure to rebuild the temple (Hag 1:8–11). Desiccated land has a meaning and purpose. Ecological disaster punishes people for their sins and induces grief, fear, and shame, which may motivate repentance, good behavior, and restoration of the ecosystem. In Isaiah 33:3–9, the people cry out, weep, and abandon their normal routines because the drought disrupts their lives. Isaiah 24 focuses on the disappearance of joy, Jeremiah 8:13–14 on fleeing, and Jeremiah 12:11–13 on shame. As Jeremiah 14:1–7 and Joel 1 make clear, people should repent and petition YHWH when confronted with ecological disaster. Prophets use the threat of drought to capture the attention of the audience and evoke grief to motivate the people to change their behavior.

The connection between drought and grief may motivate metaphorical uses of desiccated plants within the established conventional plant-people blend.[67] The plant-people may be said to wither, through a metaphorical extension of drying language, from withering plants to dying people. Withering plants also blend with the emotional exhaustion of people. The two blends share an emotional relationship. The grief experienced in bereavement also emerges in times of drought, which raises the prospect of death by starvation. Drying vegetation blends with human mortality nineteen times.[68] It blends with emotional exhaustion four times (1 Sam 2:5; Ps 18:46; Jer 15:9; reading Isa 64:5 as mortality rather than emotional enervation, but it is ambiguous). The common human experience of drying and wilting vegetation in the Levantine climate lends itself to blends with frail and fading humans.

Grasses and flowers afford an image of humans as ephemeral, small, and frail (Job 14:2; Ps 102:12). Psalm 90, for example, reflects on the frailty, mortality, and smallness of all humans: "[Humans] sleep, and in the morning they sprout again like an herb. In the morning it blooms only to pass away, in the evening it is wilted and withered" (90:5–6). Psalm 90 construes humans as fast-growing but short-lived grasses in contrast to the eternal life of YHWH. The image seeks to elicit divine sympathy for humans in their suffering, as the lament asks YHWH for relief from pain. The psalmist asks to know the duration of YHWH's anger, that the community may have hope.[69] The prayer resembles Psalm 102. Both psalmists see the contrast between YHWH's eternity and human frailty, and both use this observation to move YHWH to grant mercy.

Isaiah 40 construes humans as grass to draw attention to their smallness and frailty in contrast to YHWH's grandeur and majesty. Instead of lament as in Psalm 90, however, Isaiah seeks to comfort the plant-people by presenting YHWH as powerful and willing to help them. The first passage focuses on the brevity of human life in general: "A voice says, 'Proclaim!' I answer, 'What shall I proclaim?' 'All flesh is grass and all their loyalty like the flower of the field. The grass withers, the flower wilts, when the breath of YHWH blows upon it. Yes, the people is grass!'[70] The grass withers, the flower wilts, but the word of our God stands forever' " (Isa 40:6–8). The message affirms the centrality of the word of God over any human speaker of that word.[71] The word will stand forever, while humans fade like grass and flowers. The text identifies God's agency in human mortality since the vegetation withers under the "wind/breath of God." People themselves are like grass, and their loyalty is like flowers.[72] The text highlights human loyalty or social commitment as something lovely, but frail and ephemeral.[73] It may imply that human loyalty dies because people are mortal, or suggest that even while they survive, people are fickle in their commitments. God, by contrast, is reliable and eternal. The plant-people blend highlights the transience of humans as distinct from the eternity of the word of God. Alternatively, it may contrast the unreliability of human commitments with the reliability of the word of God, as parallel to the brevity of human life in contrast to the eternity of God.

The plant-people blend occurs again in Isaiah 40:22–24 where it applies specifically to the princes and rulers of the earth who are brought to nothing (40:23) when YHWH breathes on them and they wither. No specific species of plant is named here, but the thought continues the image of grass and flowers from earlier in the chapter since these types of plants do not endure long. The plants provide an accessible image of the small and ephemeral rulers extinguished by YHWH. The terms *nothing* and *naught* profile a hard concept to understand, but the withering and decay of plants recall a common experience. Both passages present the death of humans as a result of divine action associated with wind. The dying people thereby become like chaff driven away by a strong wind, an image of insubstantiality (Isa 41:2).[74] The plant-people blend highlights mortality also in Psalms 37:2, 90:6; Job 14:2, 18:16, 24:24 (and maybe Ps 58:8).

Drying plants metaphorically describe the mental distress and sense of shame and helplessness of the Judean population before the advancing Assyrian army in Isaiah 37:27. God's response to Hezekiah's prayer of distress concerning the invasion of Sennacherib includes the use of drying vegetation to describe human communities. In this part of the response, God is speaking to Sennacherib about Judah, but Hezekiah is the real audience: "Their people are powerless [lit. short of hand], dismayed and distraught, they are plants of the field, green growth, grass on the rooftops scorched by the east wind."[75] (37:27) God depicts the people of Judah as terrified of the Assyrian army advancing into their territory. The vegetation image elaborates on the emotional description of the people. They are "short of hand," meaning *powerless* or *helpless.* They are also *dismayed,* a verb seen above in Jeremiah 14:2 in reference to land that can also mean *broken* or *shattered* of physical objects (Jer 50:2). Hebrew speakers, like speakers of many other languages, can construe emotional pain as physical breakage (Pss 34:19, 51:9, 69:21, 147:3; Prov 15:4, 22:9; Isa 61:1, 64:14; Jer 23:9). The third term, *distraught,* commonly describes a sense of shame or mental distress. These emotions correlate with plants, young shoots, and grasses that briefly grow on rooftops but are "scorched by the east wind."[76] The expression instantiates the plant-people blend to imply that the Assyrian army is as impossible to resist as the wind. The blend presents a complex mix of fear, helplessness, and shame. The passivity of the people appears as emotional enervation (distress would suggest more activity, such as fight or flight). The plants envisioned here are grasses rather than trees. They depend on water for their vitality and ability to grow upward. As they are deprived of water, they change color, wilt, and collapse to the ground in weakness and death. The withering grasses serve as an apt description of people losing courage. The Judeans do not respond to Assyrian aggression with anger and the will to resist, but with fear and shame, which are emotions that motivate retreat and surrender.

The image of drying in Jeremiah 15:9 likewise combines fading courage with failing vitality: "The one who bore seven wilts, breathing out her life; her sun sets in full day, she is ashamed and abashed" (Jer 15:9).[77] The passage blends the water that plants need with the breath that humans need. The woman's fertility ends as a plant withers and collapses. A further solar metaphor clarifies that her end is untimely and not a consequence of old age, implying the death of her children. The emotional terms echo the shame language found in Jeremiah 14 and Isaiah 37:27. The wider context resembles the Isaiah passage in its focus on helplessness before military invasion. The image of a mother wilting appears also in 1 Samuel 2:5 where Hannah says that the mother of many will wilt, while the barren woman has many children. This reversal blends fruitful plants with fertile women (e.g., Ps 128:3). There is no indication in 1 Samuel 2:5 that the mother will lose her children as there is in Jeremiah 15:9 (cf. v. 8), so her lack of more children does not create as much emotional distress as loss of children. The mother wilts in the sense that she becomes a plant that no longer bears fruit, and that transition may be emotionally painful. Fertile plants blend with fertile women (Pss 127:3, 128:3). The emotional pain of not being fertile combines with the blend of emotional exhaustion and wilted plants. Drying vegetation blends human mortality nineteen times and with emotional exhaustion four times.[78] The blend with emotional exhaustion likely developed for the blend with mortality. Thoughts of death kindle emotions like fear, disgust, and shame, so drying vegetation may have extended its reach from mortality to emotion.

## Conclusion

Biblical texts reflect the love ancient Judeans held for Jerusalem and its countryside and the grief they experienced when the city was destroyed or when the fields desiccated during drought. These texts develop and reinforce place attachment to Jerusalem by investing the city with meaning and personifying it as a mother. Biblical discourse thereby reflects the place attachment felt by those in the community that created the Bible and were created by it. The texts show how drought caused Judeans to grieve over desiccated arable land. They extended the plant-people blend to correlate withered vegetation with human mortality and emotional exhaustion. The plant-people blend shows how creation and emotion overlap in the Judean mind.

# 2

## SURPRISE AND FEAR

THE NATURAL WORLD generates surprise through violated expectations like earthquakes.[1] Surprise is a short-lived emotion, lasting at most a few seconds before it quickly transitions to another emotion, such as fear, joy, disgust, or anger.[2] Sudden events or violations of the natural order surprise us and focus our attention on the novel phenomenon. A burning bush causes Moses to say, "I must turn aside to look at this remarkable sight. Why does the bush not burn up?"[3] (3:3) The unexpected sight captures Moses's attention and motivates him to approach and encounter God. The burning bush inspires no fear, but the encounter with God does: "Moses hid his face for he was afraid to look at God" (Exod 3:6). Surprising developments in creation may elicit fear if the unexpected change endangers life and well-being. Fear shapes attention, leading one to think about frightening things, real and imagined. My fear after seeing a rattlesnake, for example, kept my mind focused on potential serpentine dangers well after any actual danger had passed. Fear reminds us that we are mortal. Our sense of mortality motivates us to cling to our cultural traditions and communities that have a life larger and longer than our own. Biblical prophets often seek to capture attention through surprise and direct that attention to fear-inspiring stimuli in order to motivate repentance and fidelity to cultural traditions. Creation affords many opportunities to elicit surprise and fear.

## Creation Triggers Surprise and Fear
### Isaiah 13

Surprising natural events often manifest YHWH's anger and elicit human fear. Isaiah 13 includes several unexpected phenomena. The poem includes many indications that the whole world will suffer punishment before Babylon emerges near the end as the specific target of attack. The darkening of the luminaries and shaking of the earth afflict the whole world, and the invading army attacks the whole land (13:5).[4] The traces of widespread destruction cohere with the theme of the day of YHWH, which represents a day of universal judgment. The passage paints a vivid picture of divine wrath and human fear using creation to achieve its ends.

Surprise arises from violated expectations, and Isaiah 13 is full of surprises. The passage calls the audience to direct their attention to an army that is about to execute YHWH's anger (13:3, 5). Divine anger leads directly to human fear (*therefore* in 13:7). The prophet piles seven depictions of fear into vv. 7–8: "all hands fall helpless, every human heart melts, and they are terrified, pangs and sorrows take hold of them, like a woman in labor they writhe. They look at each other astounded, their faces aflame."[5] Only two emotion words appear in this series: *terrified* and *astounded*, although Hebrew has many words for fear.[6] The term *terrified* profiles both fear and haste.[7] It indicates an intense fear mixed with surprise at an unexpected turn of events. The author of Judges 20 uses the verb to profile the surprise and fear of the Benjaminite warriors. They repeatedly win in the fighting against the other tribes, so the ambush and trap laid by the Israelites takes them by surprise. They immediately see they are lost. The passage sets up the Benjaminite expectation of victory: "they thought 'Surely they have fled before us as in the earlier fighting' " (Judg 20:39, see also 32). The Hebrew particle *behold* marks their surprise when they look back and see the smoke rising from their burning city ("behold, the whole city was going up into the sky" 20:40).[8] When the retreating Israelites wheel around to attack, "the Bejaminites were terrified because they realized that disaster had overtaken them."[9] (20:41) The Benjaminites experience surprise and fear, and *terrified* profiles this experience better than the prototypical Hebrew word for fear, which does not involve surprise.[10] The verbs *terrified* and *astounded* appear together in Psalm 48 when the kings assembled against Zion: "When they looked they were *astounded*, *terrified*, they were put to flight. Trembling seized them there, anguish like a woman's labor, as when the east wind wrecks the ships of Tarshish." (Ps 48:6–8) The shipwreck is a surprising event that serves as an analogy to the surprise experienced by the kings who attack Zion. God's presence inspires shock and fear profiled by both *terrified* and *astounded*. Habakkuk 1:5 captures the surprise profiled by *astounded*: "Be utterly astounded for a work is being done in your days that you would not believe were it told." Other surprising events that inspire fear include the death of Abner (2 Sam 4:1) and the destruction of Pharaoh's army in the exodus (Exod 15:15).[11]

The prophetic speech in Isaiah 13:7–8 describes Babylon's impending doom as a surprising turn of events. The verbs *terrified* and *astounded* individually and together profile surprise and fear. In Isaiah 13:8, the image of faces aflame unpacks the surprise and fear evoked by *astounded*. Strong emotions induce blushing, and the surprise and fear of the people cause them to blush and turn to each other in dismay.[12] The passage also likens the people to a woman in labor, writhing and suffering labor pains. The description of hands fallen and hearts melted also appear in the context of childbirth but more widely profile fear and failing courage. The childbirth metaphor in biblical literature does not include the happy conclusion of new life. Infant mortality was high and many women died in labor, so labor did not immediately evoke the prospect of a healthy baby. Instead, the birth metaphor blends the female experience of birth with the wider (male and female) experience of crisis. Both events involve surprise and fear, and people may feel powerless because both "are events in which God is in control and the human being helplessly awaits the next step."[13] Isaiah 13:7–8 explicitly clarifies the intense surprise and fear that the people feel.

Natural catastrophes elaborate on the life-threatening crisis of the day of YHWH. This focus on fear has a purpose. Some passages clarify why the prophet speaks of the day of YHWH. Joel 2:12–17 calls on the audience to repent and return to YHWH, who is merciful. Zephaniah 2:1–3 likewise offers hope of salvation through seeking YHWH, justice, and humility. Humans use cultural constructions to cope with the anxiety arising from their knowledge that they will die.[14] Consequently, reminders of mortality create an increased need to associate with the cultural constructions that stave off the fear of death. Real and imagined catastrophes elicit the desire to draw close to the community and its values and traditions. The speaker of Psalm 102, for example, suffers illness that triggers anxiety about his mortality ("I wither like the grass," 102:12) but finds solace in the eternity of YHWH, the perpetuity of his community, and the continuity of his personal dynasty. The prayer reflects the human need for culturally defined self-esteem as a means of deflecting thoughts about death. Frightened Judeans might turn to the worship of other gods or illegitimate forms of YHWH worship. The prophets channel behavior along orthodox paths by identifying YHWH as the angered deity and proclaiming that idols provoke YHWH to anger. The strategy does not always work because speakers cannot fully control where audiences find comfort. Jeremiah attacked the Judean faith in the impregnability of Zion in an effort to convince the people to accept Babylonian conquest as YHWH's punishment. They responded angrily to this assault on their source of comfort in time of danger. Jeremiah was nearly killed for his oracle and denounced as a traitor for his larger message (Jer 26:7–11). Undermining confidence in culture can evoke increased anxiety about death. Jeremiah's audience attacked the prophet in order to defend their faith in Zion, which eased their anxiety about death as the Babylonians approached. Isaiah 13 uses the day of YHWH to induce fear of death by depicting creation unraveling and leaving the people no safety. The oracle assumes the reliability and stability of creation in order to provoke surprise and fear by depicting natural catastrophes that manifest a dangerously destabilized cosmos.

The predictable patterns and enduring structure of creation build trust. The reliability of creation reflects the reliability of YHWH's love, fidelity, and law.[15] Psalm 93 connects them: "YHWH is king, robed with majesty; YHWH is robed, girded with might. The world will surely stand in place, never to be moved. Your throne stands firm from of old; you are from everlasting" (93:1–2). The stability of YHWH's throne parallels the stability of creation, and the threat of the chaos waters cannot overturn creation or creator (Ps 93:3–5). YHWH holds creation steady and holds human societies to a reliable ethical standard. Similarly, Psalm 96: "The world will surely stand fast, never to be shaken. He rules the peoples with fairness" (96:10). All creation, therefore, rejoices before God's just governance of the world (96:11–12). Psalm 104 celebrates God's government of creation, including God's maintenance of reliable patterns on which all creatures depend: "You fixed the earth on its foundations, so it can never be moved" (104:5). They also rely on the alternation of night and day and the change of seasons (104:19–23). YHWH maintains patterns in creation with limited variation (104:27–30). Creation is so completely dependent on the creator that the normally stable earth trembles under God's watch (104:32). Psalm 75:4 implies that though the earth shakes, it will not totally collapse because God steadies its pillars.

Likewise, YHWH "set the moon and sun in place," establishing night and day and the seasons (Ps 74:15–16). Psalm 19 offers a meditation on the luminaires as silent proclaimers of the glory of YHWH. It then praises YHWH's reliable law, which "gives wisdom to the simple" (19:8), "enlightening the eye" (19:9). Those too simple to understand the structure of the cosmos, and thereby discern how to live their lives, may turn to the laws of YHWH to guide their conduct. These laws distill how to live in harmony with the creation YHWH has made and thereby have a good life. God has joined human behaviors and natural events. The stability of creation depends on the good behavior of humans. Isaiah 13 depicts the unraveling of the natural order as a consequence of human sin (13:10–11). The shaking earth and darkened luminaires signal God's involvement in the military invasion and heighten the terror inspired by the army. It compounds military defeat with cosmic catastrophe.

Human fear falls into four major categories: place-based fears, animal fears, blood fears, and social fears.[16] These categories structure analysis of how Isaiah 13 prompts fear. First, place-based fears include fear of open spaces, closed spaces, dark places, and places lacking exits, such as bridges and tunnels. Isaiah 13 draws heavily on place-based fears, especially earthquakes and darkness. The shaking of heaven and earth triggers surprise and fear because they contrast with the assumed norm of cosmic stability. Earthquakes follow no fixed predictable pattern and can be fatal. The shaking cosmos signifies divine anger and triggers human fear. Passages that draw attention to the stability of the cosmos instill quiet and trust (e.g., Ps 19), but texts that depict instability inspire fear (e.g., Isa 13). Like the cosmos, people can also be shaken.[17] The human experience of being shaken corresponds to fear (e.g., Ps 30:7). The overlap in vocabulary profiling a shaking earth and trembling, frightened people highlights the correspondence between the natural and social order. The sun, moon, and stars provide reliable light on which people depend. Sunlight is most critical to survival, but the moon and stars provide reliable indications of times and seasons (Gen 1:14–19).[18] No one expects sudden loss of all heavenly lights. This extraordinary phenomenon reinforces the claim that YHWH sent the attacking army (Isa 13:2–3). When the sun stands still in Joshua 10, the narrator underscores the surprising nature of the event: "Never before or since was there a day like this, when YHWH obeyed the voice of a man, for YHWH fought for Israel" (10:14). The unique day of YHWH involves surprising celestial events. People fear darkness. Sometimes this fear disrupts normal functioning and requires therapeutic intervention. More often, the intense fear of dark that many children experience lessens as they become adults who show heightened nervousness or alertness in dark environments.[19] People do not fear darkness itself but the dangers that it may conceal. Humans have poor eyesight in darkness and when light falls below a certain threshold, the brain can no longer fill in the blind spot at the center of human vision. Biblical writers use this fear of the dark to infuse texts with emotion. The penultimate plague on Egypt is darkness. The darkness is almost tangible ("one can feel it" in Exod 10:21). A dense darkness (10:22) settled over Egypt, but the Hebrews still had light (10:23). The Egyptians could not move or see one another for the three days of the darkness. This description emphasizes the power of darkness to limit movement by limiting vision. The next and last plague of the firstborn happens at midnight (11:4; 12:29). The horror of widespread death seems most suitable in the middle of the night when bad things happen. Job 24:13–17 represents darkness as the time when murderers and adulterers go about their crimes while staying at home in the daytime. Proverbs 7:9 contrasts the ways of the just and the wicked as light and darkness, respectively. The wicked stumble for lack of light. Darkness provides cover for crime (Isa 29:15; Ps 74:20). The darkening of the luminaries in Isaiah 13:13 resembles the plague of darkness in Exodus 10 except that Isaiah offers no time limit on the darkness, which might persist indefinitely. This sudden and unexpected change in the heavens provokes surprise and fear in a passage that piles terror upon terror.

Second, fear of animals relates directly to the natural world. Snakes, spiders, bears, lions, dogs, horses, and other creatures induce fear. These fears respond to the potential dangers presented by fellow creatures. Isaiah 13 does not focus on danger posed by animals. People will be killed by the army, not by lions or bears as in 2 Kings 17:25; Isaiah 15:9; Jeremiah 5:6. The passage ends with a depiction of Babylon in ruins and inhabited by a range of animals that may be found in abandoned places, like owls and the small mammals they hunt. The motif of ruins combines animal and place fears by profiling animals that make spooky noises in places that people avoid. Isaiah 13:21–22 includes wild dogs and jackals, which present some danger to humans, along with terms that may profile demonic crea-tures to be avoided (e.g., *desert demons* and *satyrs* in NABRE).[20] The ruined city is like Sodom and Gomorrah (13:19), cities associated with disaster and wasteland. The oracle draws on animal imagery to depict human fear through animal-human blends. Sheep and gazelles live in fear of being killed and eaten. Isaiah 13:14 blends frightened humans with sheep with-out a shepherd and with hunted gazelles. Like these animals, the people will flee danger and seek the comfort of their own people and their homelands. People will seek a sense of security in their traditions to shield themselves from terror of mortality.

Third, blood fears involve anxieties about illness, injury, death, and sur-gical procedures. Blood fears include natural phenomena (e.g., pathogens) and can overlap with animal fears (e.g., mauled by a lion) or place fears (e.g., suffering injury or death from falling from a height). The passage offers vivid specifics that elicit blood fears. The childbirth metaphor discussed above dwells on the dangerous and fearsome process of birth as a metaphor for human fear on the day of YHWH. It profiles rape as a literal female experience common in war, eliciting both women's fear of rape and men's fear of their wives being raped. The word used is so vulgar and provocative that the scribes replaced it with an alternative term in every place it appears (Deut 28:30; Isa 13:16; Jer 3:2; Zech 14:2).[21] The author selected the vulgar term to shock the audience and maximize fear. The same context depicts people penetrated with the sword and their children dashed to pieces. These vivid expressions summon fears of violent penetration that amplify the more generic threats of destruction and depopulation. The oracle evokes the value and rarity of gold to depict the depopulation of the world. The verse uses unusual vocabulary for humans and for gold. The terms *mortals* and *humans* most often profile humans as a collective. They appear together in poetic contexts to highlight the mortality of humans (Isa 13:12; Pss 8:5; 90:3; 103:15). The text con-strues humanity as a collective entity like gold construed as a substance. The terms for gold are unusual, both emphasizing the rarity of the metal.[22] Gold is rare and precious, and *refined gold* and *gold of Ophir* (a distant and exotic place) emphasize this rarity that the text blends with humanity to present the depopulation of the land. The army will slaughter so many people that humans will be hard to find.

Fourth, social phobias involve fear elicited by social situations such as public speaking, criticism, rejection, or interpersonal conflict. Since humans are hypersocial, relationships and reputations are critical to survival and well-being. People can also be a direct source of danger. Far more people are killed by other people than by animals and natural disasters. The passage describes the day of YHWH in terms of a military assault. YHWH has summoned a large and noisy army from the end of the heavens (13:5). Once they are identified as Medes, they are described as relentless killers. They cannot be bribed into sparing populations because they have no regard for silver or gold, which makes them unlike a typical army. They also do not spare the fruit of the womb nor pity children (13:18). The oracle depicts the Medes as ruthless killers, evoking social fears that transition into blood fears based on the specifics of how the Medes will kill and rape.

The text enhances surprise and fear by using language to direct the audience's attention toward some aspects of the invasion and away from others through what it includes and excludes. The oracle depicts the ominous mobilization of troops and the army overrunning the territory, including details on the pillage, rape, and murder inflicted on the population and the attempted escape of various unspecified peoples. The oracle omits any mention of the maneuvers of the army, its clash with opposing forces, or any hint of defensive preparations or resistance. It also withholds the identity of the invading army and its target until 13:17–19. The text excludes any mention of military occupation and consequent survival. It depicts instead the empty and ruined place identified as Babylon in 13:19. The text focuses the audience's attention on their own mortality by including only frightening aspects of the invasion while omitting anything that might offer hope of survival through resistance, escape, bribery, compassion, or surrender.

The language of Isaiah 13 amplifies the surprising nature of the events it describes by employing language that expresses surprise and captures attention. YHWH uses three attention-grabbing imperative verbs (*set up, cry out, beckon* in 13:2) directed at those who are mustering the army. The opening of the oracle draws attention to impending war. The imperative *howl* demands attention to bad news that justifies the desperate cry the verb demands. It occurs in contexts of mourning (Isa 15:2–3, 8; 16:7; 23:1, 6, 14; 65:14) and petition (Isa 52:5; Hos 7:4). The Hebrew particle *for* clarifies the reason for wailing: the day of YHWH is coming and it means destruction (13:6). The Hebrew particles *behold!* and *hark!* have an imperative force calling for the audience's attention and representing the surprise of a character or speaker.[23] The prophetic voice in 13:4 twice repeats the particle *hark!*, which calls attention to auditory information, as distinct from the more visually oriented *behold!* (Gen 4:10; Isa 40:3, 6; 52:8; 66:6; Jer 3:21; 8:19; 10:22; 25:36; 31:15; 50:28; 51:54; Mic 6:9; Zeph 1:14; 2:14; Song 2:8; 5:2). The particle *behold!* appears at the start of 13:9 again to draw attention to the day of YHWH as a day of divine anger and destruction. The particle occurs again in 13:17, which identifies the attacking army as the Medes and emphasizes their mercilessness.[24]

The prophetic depiction of the day of YHWH involves surprise and fear. It appears in Amos 5:18–19 where Amos contradicts his audience's expectation of what the day of YHWH will be. Amos's audience expects the day of YHWH to be a good day full of light, but Amos corrects this illusion by first capturing attention with an exclamation (*Woe!*) and a question (What will the day of YHWH mean for you?, 5:18). The attention-grabbing exclamation leads to a question that arouses interest. The unexpected answer generates surprise. The passage compares the day to two stories.[25] The first describes two back-to-back unlikely encounters with dangerous animals. Encountering a lion or a bear must have been an unlikely event, but encountering both in immediate succession is extremely unlikely. In the second story, a man thinks he is safe at home but is bitten by a snake. The gesture of resting a hand on the wall implies a relaxed position of a person who expects home to be a safe haven from the dangers of the world. Precisely in this moment of relaxation in safety, the person is bitten by a snake. Both scenarios express surprise and fear through the use of unexpected encounters with dangerous animals. The fear and surprise of these encounters cohere with the depiction of the day of YHWH as a day of darkness and gloom instead of light. Amos's description of the day of YHWH coheres with the emphasis on surprise and darkness in Isaiah 13, although it is not clear whether the darkness represents a cosmic change as in Isaiah 13:10 or a more metaphorical description in which a dark day is a bad day. Either way, it elicits fear of darkness to challenge the audience's misunderstanding of the day of YHWH as a good day.

Joel likewise depicts the day of YHWH as extraordinarily surprising. Joel 2:1–14 describes the invasion of a human army analogous to the locust swarm that devasted the land in Joel 1:2–20. The juxtaposition "demonstrates the inseparable link between natural and human events."[26] The beginning and end of the oracle involve creation motifs. The passage paradoxically compares the darkness of the day of YHWH to dawn breaking over mountains (2:2). The dissonance of the comparison mimics the surprise that it seeks to express. The day of YHWH stands out as surprising. It is unique among all days that have ever been or ever will be (2:2). The land before the invasion is like the Garden of Eden, but the day of YHWH transforms it into a desolate wilderness through fire (2:3). The sudden and surprising transformation triggers fear and grief over the lost garden land. The end of the oracle reflects on the enormous size of the army and the great and terrifying (Joel 2:11) day of YHWH, which involves shaking and darkness: "before them the earth trembles, the heavens shake; sun and moon are darkened, and the stars withhold their brightness." (2:10) The cosmic correlates of the day of YHWH match the description in Isaiah. The normally stable cosmos shakes, and the normally reliable light of the luminaries fades to darkness.

Zephaniah draws on some of the same creation motifs used in other passages about the day of YHWH to illustrate its surprising and fearsome nature. Like Isaiah 13, Zephaniah 1 focuses on the alarming noises of war (1:10, 14, 16) and the inability of gold and silver to buy safety (1:18). Blood and bowels pour out of pierced bodies (1:17). YHWH's wrath will consume the earth with fire (1:18). The passage associates the day with darkness (1:15) and depicts the people as blind and hemmed in (1:17), kindling fear of darkness, confinement, and enclosed spaces. All these passages (Isa 13; Amos 5:18–19; Joel 2; Zeph 1) present the day of YHWH as filled with surprising and terrifying events. They depict the day as terrifying by prompting a range of human fears. These include various mixes of place fears (darkness, inescapability), animal fears (lions), blood fears (bodies pierced), and social fears (military invasion).

# The Amazing Wisdom of Animals and Folly of Humans
## *Jeremiah 8:4–9*

Violations of the regular patterns of creation trigger surprise. Creation can also induce surprise by contrast with the irregularity of human behavior. The contrast relies on conceptualizing the natural and social orders as connected. YHWH punishes human sin with darkness and instability on the day of YHWH and uses drought to punish communities for their injustice. Jeremiah 8:4–9 presents human misbehavior in violation of the natural order. The author conceptualizes human action as a result of human knowing. The wicked behavior of the Judeans implies a defect in their minds and their understanding of the natural order. The oracle rhetorically asks whether someone who falls gets up again, and whether someone who strays returns (8:4). The first expression contrasts two verbs: *fall* and *rise*. People do not stay down when they fall unless they are too injured to get up again. The next contrast appears not to be a contrast at all since the verb is identical. The Hebrew root that means *to turn* appears six times in these three verses (8:4–6).[27] The first pair of verbs draws on the context to clarify the divergent senses of the root as *turn away* and *turn back* toward a goal or path. The verb profiles the process of turning around, especially 180 degrees. It thereby mirrors the prior contrast of falling and rising. These lines present the regular patterns of fallen people getting up and people who turn down a wrong path turning back. The rhetorical questions emphasize the predictable and regular nature of these behaviors to prepare for the surprisingly unexpected persistence of the Judeans in the wrong path. Jeremiah uses a similar question about people changing their gods (Jer 2:10–11) to elicit surprise from heaven and earth at Israel's apostasy (2:12).

The next verse (8:5) takes up the turning theme and applies it to ethical conduct. Hebrew includes a conventional metaphor of ethical conduct and relationship with YHWH as following a path.[28] A speaker may call the people to turn and correct their behavior. The path can be omitted, however, and only the goal remain. In verse 5, YHWH wonders why the people turn with persistent turning, meaning they turn away from YHWH and right conduct and steadfastly maintain this incorrect orientation. YHWH specifically identifies deceit as the object the people have grasped. They should turn away from their deceit but prefer to hold tightly to it. YHWH knows their deceit because YHWH has listened attentively and heard that they do not speak rightly. The expression encompasses both factual and ethical correctness. Through this close surveillance, YHWH also knows that no one repents. Instead of repenting, each one turns into his path like a horse plunging into battle. The verb *plunging* typically profiles overflowing or gushing water.[29]

The verse here blends rushing water with a horse charging into an enemy formation on the battlefield. In another context, this behavior might be evaluated as courageous (Job 39:19–25). In this context of apostasy, however, the behavior of the cavalry horse appears unnatural and foolish. Horses have no reason to engage in human wars. They are prey animals that spook easily and instinctively flee from danger. In a trained warhorse, however, this instinct to flee at speed was converted into a motivation "to explode onto the battle scene."[30] The spirited charge of the warhorse could be a liability on the battlefield unless the horse was trained for war so that its competing desires to flee and charge could be controlled by a rider or charioteer. A further method of control may lie behind Jeremiah's blend of cavalry horse and unrepentant people. Horses have a nearly 360-degree field of view, and the many sights on a battlefield could inspire a horse to flee and overrule its rider. Consequently, cavalrymen have used blinders since ancient times to drastically limit a horse's field of view so that it would be blind to the many frightening things taking place around it and thus be more controllable. With blinders, the horse might see only a 20–30-degree field.[31] In Hebrew, like many other languages, words for visual perception can profile intellectual knowing.[32] The horse that plunges into battle is almost totally blind like the person who persists in sin. The blend of warhorse and sinner captures both the enthusiasm and unnaturalness of a horse fighting a human battle. The horse must be specially trained and partially blinded in order to charge into battle. The person must be similarly habituated and blinded to persist in an unnatural course that leads to doom. The blend of warhorse and deceitful sinner creates an analogy between the habituation and training required for cavalry horses and the education in deceit that the scribes and priests provide to the people in Jeremiah 8:8.

In Jeremiah 8:7, the oracle establishes a new mental space for different animals that contrast with the sinners. Four nouns profile four different migratory birds. The first is likely the white stork (*Ciconia ciconia*), an unclean bird (Lev 11:19; Deut 14:18) that builds nests in high places (Ps 104:17). It migrates between Europe and Africa without flying over the Mediterranean Sea, which lacks the thermal updrafts they need for their high, gliding flight. The birds fly instead over the Levant or the Strait of Gibraltar. Unlike the black stork (*Ciconia nigra*), it congregates in flocks and is not shy of people.

Large flocks of white storks can be seen in Israel during their passage south in the fall and north in the spring. As with other birds, the stork migration is a regular and predictable behavior. The stork "knows" its seasons, meaning that it knows when to migrate and return. The text groups the other three bird species together as joint subjects of keeping the time of their coming. The first is almost certainly the turtledove. Turtledoves appear in the spring (Song 2:12) and reside in Israel during the summer, flying south in November. The next two appear only here and in Isaiah 38:14 and in the same order. They may be the swallow and the thrush.[33] Hundreds of species of migratory birds stop in modern Israel, making identification uncertain.

The stork knows its seasons and the other three birds keep the time of their return, meaning that all four birds return at the same time each year. The verb *keep* appears in contexts of keeping YHWH's commandments, which is the sense here.[34] The regular pattern of migratory bird behavior reflects a command of YHWH that the birds obey. The stork *knowing* and the other birds *keeping* construe the same reality in different ways. The verb *know* profiles the mental state that shapes the behavior profiled by the verb *keep*. The objects of these verbs likewise reflect similar realities. The stork knows its *appointed times*, a term also used of divinely commanded festival times (Lev 23:2, 4; Num 10:10).[35] The other birds keep *the time of their coming*, indicating that they are supposed to come at a specific time and they are not early or late. Ornithologists would describe these migratory behaviors as instincts. The shifting balance of daylight and night triggers the urge to migrate. The oracle construes this bird behavior as reliable obedience to a natural order ordained by YHWH. The birds do not need to be trained like the warhorse. This conceptualization of bird migration shapes the meaning of "my people does not know the order of YHWH." The noun *order* here profiles the law or command of YHWH that the people do not observe. People do not observe the order of YHWH because they do not know it. They do not know it because the lying pen of the scribes has altered the law of YHWH (8:8). Moreover, they have been trained to persist in behavior contrary to the cosmic order, like the horse trained to fight human wars. Jeremiah objects that the scribal textualization of law misrepresents the law.[36] The wise will be shown to be fools when they come to shame, dismay, and capture. Their capture means becoming captives of the Babylonians. The unwillingness of the wise to accept Jeremiah's message reveals their lack of wisdom and inability to perceive YHWH's law and plan. As a result, they will be *dismayed*, using a term that profiles emotional distress, brokenness of objects, and the dried land in Jeremiah 14:4.

The contrast between the birds that know their times and the people who do not know the order of YHWH evokes surprise and amazement. The people resemble warhorses trained to act in ways contrary to their nature and best interests. In this blend of warhorse and human, the scribes and wise men correspond to those who train the horses for battle. The scribes train the people to lie and deceive, inculcating habits that bring them to ruin. The remainder of the chapter describes punishments of the fraudulent priest and prophets (9:10–12) who have misled the nation to its doom (9:13–17). As a result of the disobedience of the people, YHWH will bring foreign invasion of cavalry (9:16) and ecological catastrophe (9:13). The amazement elicited by the contrast between obedient birds and disobedient humans emerges in the manner of expression as well as the content of the blend. The rhetorical questions at the start of the oracle express a clear expectation that sets up the surprise encoded in the next two questions, which ask why the people fail to behave as expected. YHWH has listened closely (Jer 8:6) to verify the surprising information that the people persist in their wickedness without regret. The emphatic Hebrew particle *even* introduces the striking contrast with migratory birds. Questions continue to express amazement with the particle *how*, which often introduces rhetorical or (as here; Gen 26:9) incredulous questions (How can you say "We are wise?" 8:8a). Jeremiah expresses surprise (*see!*) as he points to the fact that the scribes have lied and misrepresented the law of YHWH (8:8b).[37]

The people's wicked behavior derives from the flawed knowledge they learned from the lying scribes. They should reliably do good like birds that reliably migrate. If they make a mistake, they should correct themselves like someone who has fallen or walked down the wrong path. Instead their perverse behavior resembles that of the warhorse that must be trained to charge into dangers that it would otherwise avoid. In other words, the behavior of the people is so perverse it can only be explained as the result of significant miseducation. Jeremiah similarly describes the people in Jeremiah 23:8 as *accustomed to evil,* using a term that means "trained" or "taught," like the warhorse.

## Isaiah 1:2–3

The book of Isaiah opens with surprise to capture the attention of the audience. It introduces the infidelity of the people (Isa 1:2–3). Heaven and earth often appear in biblical Hebrew as hendiadys for the cosmos, perhaps roughly equivalent to the modern English notion of nature (e.g., Gen 1:1, 2:1, 14:22; Ps 69:35, 89:12, 102:26, 115:15, 124:8; Isa 45:12, 65:17).[38] Used together in this way, heaven and earth refer to creation as a whole and are not used metonymically of the host of heaven and the inhabitants of the earth. The speech, therefore, is not directed toward a human audience but to the cosmos itself. The closest parallel is Deuteronomy 32:1, but see also Deuteronomy 30:19, 31:28; Isaiah 44:23, 49:13; Psalm 50:4. Heaven and earth serve as sympathetic listeners. The prophet speaks first to capture the attention of heaven and earth and invite them to listen to the divine speech, which directs attention to Israel's unnatural rebellion against YHWH. The text implicitly assumes that the people can hear the utterance because the prophet's speech, though directed at heaven and earth, must be overheard by the people. Indeed, the people are the "real" audience of the speech, and subsequent oracles will address them directly in ways that unpack the meaning of the speech to heaven and earth. In this arrangement, the topic and audience of the speech are the same: the people of Judah. They are placed in the position of eavesdroppers overhearing what YHWH says about them behind their backs. This framing accomplishes two goals: First, it captures attention since people notice when they are talked about. Second, it creates distance between the topic and the human audience, even though the two are the same. This conceptual distance between the Judean audience and the "children" talked about makes it easier for the audience to enter into YHWH's surprise and amazement at the strange behavior of "my children."[39] If YHWH addresses the people directly and accuses them of rebellion, they may be more defensive and resistant to listening—and less able to see YHWH's perspective. The relatable metaphor of the parent–child bond and the familiar livestock analogy help the human audience understand YHWH's perspective

and see their own behavior in a new light. It prepares them for the indictments that begin in Isaiah 1:4.

YHWH raised and reared children who have rebelled.[40] The human
audience understand themselves to be these children.[41] The vocabulary
draws attention to the effort that YHWH has invested as a parent. The two
verbs occur together only here and in Isaiah 23:4, which assumes motherhood. The verb *raised* has a maternal subject in Isaiah 49:1; 53:18; Hosea
9:12, but nothing in this passage specifies gender.[42] The rebellion of the
children appears through a verb profiling disloyalty and criminality (Isa
1:28; 53:12; 59:13) and a preposition identifying YHWH as the wronged
party. The rebellion contradicts expectation. YHWH magnifies the surprise
through a comparison with the animal kingdom: farm animals know their
masters, but Israel does not know YHWH. Cattle that live in pastoral contexts graze during the day and seek safety from predators at night. When
humans provide them with permanent structures, the cattle return to these
stables at night without prompting. Cattle thereby seek their own safety
and advantage.[43] The historical introduction to a Hittite treaty draws on
bovine behavior to describe humans seeking their own good. The people
of Kizzuwatna shift allegiance between Mittani and Hatti, but the king of
Mittani boasts that they have become loyal to him: "Now, finally, the cattle
have chosen their stable. They have definitely come to my land!"[44] The kings
claims that the people recognize that the protection of Mittani is preferable
to Hatti. Cattle seek safety and security in the structures provided by their
owners, and this self-interested behavior describes the conduct of the people
of Kizzuwatna. The behavior of the people of Judah, however, perversely
diverges from this expected self-interest. They should understand YHWH as
the source of safety and security, but they do not. The term for *owner* profiles
benevolent care, not mere titular ownership (see YHWH as owner in Exod
15:6; Deut 32:6–14; Pss 72:4, 104:24, 139:13; Prov 8:22).[45] This evidence
suggests that the ox knowing its owner reflects more than mere submission
but assumes a bovine response to benevolent treatment. The ox's knowing
therefore has an affective dimension similar to *knowing* in, for example, sexual knowing (Gen 4:1, 19:5, 8; 1 Kgs 1:4) and care-taking (2 Sam 7:20; Ps
144:3; Jer 1:5).[46] In this context, "the animal is completely dependent and
unreservedly trusts the owner."[47] Context shapes the scope of attention, and

its current placement sets no limitations to how the rebellion of YHWH's children may be construed. The rebellion is as surprising as cows wandering into the wilderness at dusk instead of coming home. The bond of livestock to their owner is less emotionally intense than the bond of children to their parents. The contrast makes the perversity of the Judean rebellion against their father YHWH the more striking.

The opening verses of Isaiah draw on a widely shared expectation of the natural order in which children love their parents like domestic animals love their masters. The divine speech describing an unexpected disruption in the natural order enhances the surprise engendered by the prophetic address to heaven and earth. The emphasis on knowing pertains to the divinely ordained cosmological order. The text calls the implied human audience to redirect their attention and reconsider their assumptions by confronting them with surprising phenomena: a call to heaven and earth to listen and a contrast between normal cattle and abnormal Judeans. The language construes the disobedience of the people as a lack of knowing. Actions flow from mental states, so the people's rebellion manifests a disordered mind.

## Isaiah 28:23–29

Perhaps the most surprising thing about Isaiah 28:23–29 is its presence in a prophetic book.[48] The topic shifts from an oracle against leaders in Jerusalem to common farming practices. This detailed description of farming practices points to the correspondence between how God has established the created order and what effective farmers do to achieve bountiful harvests. The text explicitly states that God teaches the farmer the pattern of planting and threshing (28:26, 29). Divinely instructed farmers use appropriate tools and methods at the right times, and God communicates this instruction through creation. Generations of farmers have learned these proper methods through observation and cultural transmission. The text focuses on several specific practices. The first section (28:23–26) concerns planting. Ancient Levantine farmers commonly plowed the ground multiple times. Of the three verbs for plowing in verse 24, the last is least understood. It may refer to making furrows at the edge of the field, which would connect it to the emmer planted as a border in verse 25, or it may be a third plowing, for which Ugaritic has a special term.[49] The rhetorical question indicates that although farmers repeatedly plow their land, the plowing does not go on forever. The plants in verse 25 have been a source of confusion because many languages (ancient and modern) do not adequately distinguish various types of cumin from caraway or *nigella sativa*. The text likely refers to flowering plants whose seeds are used for spices—likely cumin and black cumin that are broadcast in part of the farmer's plot. The terms for *wheat* and *barley* are well-known, but the other two words for grains are more obscure. The words may profile two-rowed barley (so-called because its spike has two ears) and emmer, respectively.[50] Emmer has better weed and disease resistance than most cereals, which explains its placement at the border where fields tend to be invaded by weeds.[51] Of the three verbs of sowing, the last refers to a more careful planting rather than broadcasting. Farmers regulate their plowing and sowing activities according to the needs of the crops, which the farmer has learned from God, as the conclusion to the first section states (28:26). The second section (28:27–29) concerns threshing after harvest and refers to most of the same crops. The spice plants are not threshed with a sledge because the seeds and stems would be crushed together and hard to separate, which would be counterproductive. Instead, farmers use a flail to beat the plants in a more controlled way. Similarly, cultivated wheat comes in two major varieties distinguished by the ease with which they can be threshed.[52] The wheat kernels do not easily break free of the seed cover (called the glume) in the "covered wheats" or "hulled wheats" like emmer, spelt, and einkorn, making the separation of kernel and husk more challenging. These wheats are closely related to wild wheats and produce less grain but grow in marginal soils and resist disease. Modern domesticated wheats (*triticum aestivum*) or "naked wheats" or "free-threshing wheats" like wheat, durum wheat, and club wheat are easier to thresh because the seed cover does not encompass the kernels. In the opening of verse 28 the speaker refers to what the audience already knows: that it would be inappropriate to pound free-threshing wheat as part of the threshing process, although hulled wheats do need this additional processing.[53] This distinction of two major types of wheat may continue the previous note about the several kinds of wheats the farmer planted in verse 25, although here the distinction is implied since only naked wheat is named together with the crushing process reserved for covered wheat. The passage illustrates that the order of creation shapes proper methods of plowing, sowing, and threshing.

The concluding lines of each section (28:26, 29) reveal the main point of the description of agricultural activities, even though it does not apply this lesson to any specific domain. Both verses use unusual language to articulate the connection between the farming practices and divine instruction. The first statement in verse 26 ("His God has taught him this rule, he has instructed him") makes God the subject of two verbs of teaching, one that often profiles *discipline* and one related to the word for *instruction*. These two verbs do not occur together in the same verse except here.[54] The Hebrew term *discipline* profiles an activity that may be presented as a positive or negative experience. A person may plead not to be disciplined (Ps 6:2, 38:2, 39:12) or delight in the gift of divine discipline (Ps 94:12).[55] God teaches the farmer a customary way of doing things (Judg 18:7; 1 Sam 27:11; 1 Kgs 18:28; 2 Kgs 11:4, 17:33). The custom is fitted to creation. Some ancient myths ascribe a divine origin to agriculture, but the biblical traditions do not include such stories. Instead, early humans discover the divinely instituted patterns of nature without special revelation (Cain and Abel in Gen 2:4; Noah in Gen 9:20). The means of God's instruction, therefore, appears to be careful examination of nature for the purpose of shaping human cultural practices. The rhetorical questions of the first section underscore human conformity to nature. The first question asks whether the farmer plows forever, which would make no sense. The next question has a more positive formulation describing the leveling and sowing as implicitly the only rational activity in the context of how God ordered creation. The second section employs statements to describe threshing and ends with a statement (28:29) that develops the divine instruction from 28:26: "this too comes from YHWH of hosts." The verb *comes (forth)* profiles a wide range of processes related to movement away from a source or starting place, including plants coming forth from the ground (Deut 14:22; 1 Kgs 5:13). It connects a newborn to its mother (Gen 25:26; Job 1:21; cf. Gen 10:14; 17:6) and breath to a body (Ps 146:4). The verb here indicates the organic connection between human culture and YHWH. The divine origin of the human practice provides evidence of YHWH's wonderful plan and great wisdom. The term *plan* (or decision, advice, counsel) implies an active role performed by the person producing the plan.[56] Hebrew most often construes a *plan* as belonging to someone, but not as an object that can be transferred from one person to another. Plans may belong to wise (Jer 18:18; Ezek 7:26) or wicked people (Job 21:16, 22:18; Ps 1:1). Plans can be fulfilled (Isa 5:19; 25:1; Prov 19:21; Ps 33:11), confounded (Isa 8:10; 19:3; Ps 33:10), or hidden (Isa 29:15). In the present context, the wondrous plan of YHWH is creation itself and the patterns that make the farmer's practice effective. The term for "wisdom" here is a relatively uncommon term that profiles a happy outcome, success, or the prudence or skill that created the result. In Proverbs 8:14, wisdom proclaims her possession of both a *plan* (or counsel) and *wisdom* along with insight and strength. A successful outcome seems to be built into the concept of wisdom, but this appearance may be a result of the small corpus since Job 26:3 uses the term in parallel with the suggestion that one may offer wisdom without knowledge. In its remaining occurrences, however, it profiles success (Job 5:12; 6:13; 11:6; 12:16; Prov 2:7; 3:21; 8:14 [Mic 6:9 is textually uncertain and Prov 18:1 unclear]). The specific nuance of the great wisdom of YHWH is uncertain, but it supplements the wondrous plan and coheres with the idea that God's creation has an order that the farmer mirrors in his own practice to enjoy success. The conclusion reaffirms the connection between human culture and the natural order stated in 28:26. The passage illustrates how natural processes reflect divine wisdom, and humans can become wise and successful by learning them. It does not offer any specific application of the need to shape human activity according to the created order beyond the farming practices described.

The inclusion of this description of farming practices in the midst of prophetic discourse arouses surprise and leads commentators to look at the passage more closely, like Moses approaching the burning bush. The passage does not explicitly reveal the analogy to other aspects of life, so there is no revelatory surprise as in the vineyard song (Isa 5:1–7) or Nathan's parable (2 Sam 12:1–12). Instead, the pastoral poem appears at the end of one woe passage (28:1–29) immediately before the start of another woe passage (29:1–24). It is delimited with four imperative verbs calling for attention in 28:23 and the concluding refrain on YHWH's wisdom in 28:29. These discourse markers help delimit the farming description from the other material while relating it to Isaiah 28:1–22 rather than 29:1–24.[57] The specific content of the main teachings at issue in chapter 28 appears in 28:14–22. The text affirms that since YHWH is the power behind Assyria, Egypt can offer no help against the Assyrian invasion. Rather, the failure to rely on YHWH will only intensify YHWH's anger against the leadership in Jerusalem who have not shaped their foreign or domestic policy in accordance with the realities of creation. The passage draws on architectural imagery to contrast the danger of relying on Egypt with the security of relying on YHWH. The measuring line and plumb line used in constructing the building are justice and righteousness. The use of a plumb line highlights how buildings must be constructed in ways that accommodate the fact of gravity. Plumb lines ensure that walls are perfectly vertical and therefore stable, and careful measurements of lengths and heights similarly ensure structural integrity. The passage concludes by urging the people to change their ways and trust in YHWH before it is too late. The architectural analogy coheres well with the farming description in 28:23–29. The created order imposes certain constraints and affordances to which humans and animals must conform. Gravity makes buildings possible and requires them to be constructed in certain ways lest they collapse (Isa 28:16–17; 30:13). In the same way, societies are like buildings, with foundations and edifices (Ps 11:3) and they will stand or fall depending on whether or not they are constructed in harmony with justice and gravity, respectively. An unjust order will disintegrate, and a crooked wall will collapse. In this way, YHWH teaches people the right way to do things. The description of farming practices reinforces the connection between creation and culture articulated in the architectural imagery in 28:14–22. The passage is open to interpretation, but readers generally agree about the core point of the text expressed in 28:26, 29: Life is best lived in accordance with the wisdom of YHWH.[58] Isaiah 1:2–3 explicitly contrasts animal behavior with human conduct in ways that make its purpose clear. By contrast, the application of Isaiah 28:23–29 remains mysterious and unexpected.[59] Isaiah 28–33 broadly reflects the time of Sennacherib's invasion and Judah's alliance with Egypt. Throughout these passages, the prophet challenges his audience's sense of reality in an effort to reveal the true structure of the world and thereby correct their poor decision-making. Isaiah criticizes the drunken leaders for their exploitation of the poor and misguided reliance on Egypt for help against Assyrian aggression. They do not realize that their oppressive policies have caused YHWH to use Assyria as a weapon against them to punish their injustice, and they do not see that they intensify their sin by refusing to accept divine punishment and trust in YHWH. If they understood the order of creation, then they would behave differently and enjoy better outcomes, like the farmer in the passage. Instead, they make a "covenant with death" (28:8). They are drunken (28:1, 3, 7), bragging (28:1, 3–4), and mocking (28:14, 22) people who deserve to suffer (28:17–22).

## Isaiah 11:6–8 // 65:25

Isaiah 11:1–5 envisions a Davidic king who will rule with justice and be guided by the spirit of God and not make decisions based on deceptive outward appearances or false claims. He will have *knowledge of YHWH* (11:2), which will be shared by the whole world in verse 9. As a result, he will slay the wicked and give justice to the poor. This vision of justice and peace brought about by the ideal king then transitions to a surprising description of the natural world that has been variously read as a literal eschatological hope and a metaphorical elaboration of the previous vision of justice. The text develops the ideal reign of the Davidic king, employing nature imagery to represent the peaceful coexistence of people. Biblical literature reflects significant discomfort with the harsh reality of predation. Both creation stories in Genesis 1 and 2–3 reflect amity among humans and animals and in Genesis 1:29–30 all creation is vegetarian and only after the flood do animals develop a fear of humans in a world where carnivores roam (Gen 9:2–3). Furthermore, predation appears as a common metaphor for injustice. The wicked are like carnivorous animals who devour the poor (Pss 10:8–9, 14:4; Prov 30:14; Amos 8:4).[60] The transformation of predatory animals contributes to a sense of safety and peace in which Judah suffers no external threat and no internal injustice.

The predatory animals encompass a range of threats. The wolf, though closely related to domestic dogs, remains feared everywhere its range overlaps with humans. Wolves pose a danger to livestock and to humans caught alone in the wilderness. Human fear of the wolf has been dramatically reduced as people have killed wolves to make territory safe for themselves and their domestic animals. Except for Jeremiah 5:6, all biblical references to wolves are metaphorical for people (predatory nobles in Ezek 22:17; cavalry in Hab 1:8; unjust judges in Zeph 3:3; the tribe of Benjamin in Gen 49:27). Leopards similarly pose a danger to humans and livestock (Jer 5:6; Hab 1:8). They live away from cities (in the mountains in Song 4:8), and Jeremiah 13:23 uses the leopard's spots as an analogy to the fixed habit of sin in his audience. Lions and bears frequently appear together in texts, and bears rarely appear without lions. The two animals pose a serious threat to sheep (1 Sam 17:14, 36, 37) and humans (Hos 13:8; Amos 5:19; Lam 3:18; Prov 28:15 [the beasts are metaphorical in the last two passages]). She-bears are especially dangerous when their cubs are threatened (2 Sam 17:8, Hos 13:8, and Prov 17:12). The lion appears frequently in biblical texts, and more than once in this short passage.[61] Snakes occur less often but have a major role in Genesis 3 and Numbers 21:4–9. All these fearsome creatures behave in a surprising way, as demonstrated by their peaceful coexistence with others whom they normally kill. Cattle, sheep, and their young are the most vulnerable and common targets of these predators, but the text shows these nervous prey animals relaxed in the presence of the predators. The passage draws attention to the unexpected interactions between predator and prey. The wolf will be the guest of the lamb and the leopard lay down with the young goat. The specific word choice of *laying down* suggests a high level of mutual comfort as these animals adopt relaxed poses with their defenses down and no thought of flight. The lion and the cow will get fat together grazing on grass. The expression is striking both for the companionship of the lion and the cow and for the image of the lion as an herbivore. The lion will be so docile that a child can lead it around with the domestic cow. The cow and the bear will be friends and their young lie down together. The lion appears again in a more explicit statement of its new herbivorous nature, eating straw "like the ox." In keeping with the prior material, children playing near the snake dens inspires surprise but not fear. Like other fierce creatures, the snake has lost its fearsome nature and poses no threat to the children. The introduction of children into the amity among animals makes the image more immediately salient to a human audience. Not only are the lives of prey animals transformed for the better, but humans too can stop worrying about the safety of their children or themselves. Without this inclusion of humans, people have no clear investment in the vision. The last image in verse 8 isolates the human–snake relationship independent of the snake's connection to any other animal. The normally terrifying image of a baby with a viper appears in a context of calm and safety so that it does not arouse fear.

The text describes scenes that are hard to imagine because of how radically they violate expectations. This extraordinary vision of predator and prey living in harmony finds a summary and explanation in the concluding verse 11:9. The dangerous animals (or the wicked people they represent) "will not harm or destroy on all my holy mountain." The text makes Jerusalem the central location for this happy transformation. The whole earth will be filled with the knowledge of God in an image reminiscent of Isaiah 2:1–4. The just rule of a Davidic king will begin in Jerusalem, but the knowledge of God will expand through the world, bringing peace and justice. The idea that peace with the animal world depends on the knowledge of God appears also in Jeremiah 5:4–5 where the lack of this knowledge means that the lion, the wolf, and the leopard will prey on humans. Also, Leviticus 26:3–6 claims that if people obey YHWH, then they can lie down without fear because YHWH will remove harmful animals from the land.[62]

A later author was similarly taken by this striking text and reworked it at the end of YHWH's description of the new heavens and the new earth in which there will be perpetual joy and no suffering or premature death. The description of social concord and happiness in 65:17–24 concludes with an expansion of this new creation to the natural world. Isaiah 65:25 is "a summary of Isa 11:6–9."[63] The passage repeats the image of the wolf and the lamb that opens 11:6–9, and the seemingly impossible image of the lion eating straw, but drops both references to children. The comity of the wolf and the lamb appears somewhat more intense here as they will "pasture as one."[64] The unity of *one* captures the essence of Isaiah 11:6–9 with a word that does not appear in that text. This passage opens with the wolf and the lamb. Instead of simply dwelling together, they eat *as one*. The statement "the lion will eat straw like the ox" comes directly from Isaiah 11:7. Children do not appear in this summary, although the end of infant mortality appears earlier in the chapter (65:20).[65]

## Conclusion

Biblical writers use creation to prompt surprise and fear in at least two different ways. Most commonly, prophets present major violations of the natural order that threaten human existence. The violated expectations create surprise, capture attention, and direct that attention to terrifying events that trigger fear. The prophets seek to elicit the audience's fear of death so that they recommit themselves to the cultural traditions and values upheld by the prophets. Other texts use the coherence between the social and natural worlds to evoke surprise and amazement by contrasting the order of creation with the disorder of the human mind and society. Human culture should conform to the natural order, but human behavior often violates this expectation. Both uses of the natural order reflect how creation and emotion blend in human experience.

# 3

## DISGUST AND ANGER

BIBLICAL WRITERS USE the natural world to summon anger and disgust. Cosmic catastrophes express divine anger (Isaiah 13). Ahab becomes angry when Naboth refuses to sell him a vineyard (1 Kgs 21:1–4). Ahab is angry at Naboth, not the vineyard, but anger can be directed at nature. Farmers and gardeners struggle against uncooperative weather, invasive weeds, and unwelcome pests. Nature elicits our wrath by interfering with our goals. Jonah becomes angry over the death of the plant that gave him shade (Jon 4:5–11). Disgust arises immediately from creation. Organic matter triggers disgust. The decay of death repels us, along with creatures associated with decay or excrement, like maggots. Disgust triggered by creation can extend to disgust triggered by the misbehavior of other people. Disgust obscures the boundary between the natural and cultural worlds. Moral disgust mixes with anger to make a potentially explosive brew.

## When Disgust Provokes Anger
### Isaiah 5

The vineyard parable (Isa 5:1–7) draws humans into the experience of YHWH's anger and disgust. The story leads the audience to see themselves as YHWH sees them: wicked people who must be punished for their repulsive crimes. Isaiah uses a familiar and accessible human experience of anger at plants in order to draw the audience into an emotional understanding of God's wrath. Disgust appears in the text with the Hebrew word glossed as *sour grapes* in an effort to capture the disgust that this word profiles.[1] The presence of anger emerges from the scenario in which the vintner expects grapes, but the vine frustrates his goal so he attacks the vineyard.[2] Across cultures, "typical triggers of anger include frustration; threats to autonomy, authority, or reputation; disrespect and insult; norm or rule violation; and a sense of injustice."[3] Blocked goals emerge as the common thread through these triggers.[4] People have goals beyond the interpersonal realm and experience anger separate from social relationships. They rage against uncooperative machines and invasive pests. The invitation to the audience to judge between the vintner and the vineyard indicates the vintner's anger and sense of betrayal. The subsequent destructive actions express rage.

People consider anger a negative emotion like fear and shame, yet it involves an approach motivation like joy.[5] Positive emotions elicited by happy scenarios feel subjectively pleasant and motivate people to seek out the stimulus. Negative emotions motivate avoidance because of their association with unhappy circumstances and subjectively unpleasant feelings. Anger arises from negative circumstances but involves pleasant sensations.[6] People commonly experience sensations of power, strength, elevated alertness, invulnerability, and confidence when angry.[7] These positive sensations motivate risk-taking and optimism about the outcome. We pleasantly contemplate our future angry actions but look back on past anger with regret.[8] The vintner in the vineyard song relishes the prospect of destroying the vineyard. Later in the book, YHWH keeps and protects a vineyard (Isa 27:2–5), affirming "I am not angry" (27:4).

Isaiah 5:1–7 narrates the elaborate efforts of the vintner to achieve a fruitful harvest of high-quality grapes. The hillside is a suitable location for a vineyard. The vintner terraforms the site to create a terraced slope ideal for planting. Agricultural terraces provide level ground that inhibits erosion and facilitates good drainage. Constructing these agricultural terraces represents a considerable investment of time and effort in the pursuit of an optimal plantation. Larger stones dug up and removed from the soil could be repurposed for the terrace walls (5:5). In addition to the multiple retaining walls, another wall perpendicular to these may have been constructed to facilitate access to the terraces by laborers.[9] These walls were supplemented by a hedge for added security. The fable of the hedge and the vineyard tells of a foolish man who inherited his father's vineyard and tore down the hedge because it did not bear grapes. As a result, the vines were destroyed by human and animal intruders and the audience learns not to expect grapes from brambles and that protecting a vineyard is as important as possessing it.[10] The man's anger at the hedge resembles the vintner's anger at the vine. The vintner constructs a watchtower as another security measure. Stone structures similar to huts appear often in the archeological record in vineyards. These structures often have Hellenistic and Byzantine dates, but may represent a tradition continued from the Iron Age. Uzziah is said to have constructed agricultural towers (2 Chr 26:10). These simple structures could be constructed from stones dug out of the hillside. The hut served multiple purposes. As a cool and shady location, it afforded a place for laborers to rest, stay overnight to guard the vineyard, and store jars of fermenting wine. These jars could be filled with grape juice from the adjacent winepress, the other major structure described inside the vineyard (5:2). While the terrace walls and tower are built with stones, the winepress was hewn out of the bedrock. Biblical Hebrew has three words for winepresses, and the writer selects the one that profiles a relatively elaborate and complex structure including channels and vats for processing and collecting the juice.[11] The planter invests considerable effort in the vineyard with the hope of reward. He plants the best quality vine available in the expectation of harvesting high-quality grapes to produce the finest wine and fetch the highest price. He plants a shoot or branch from an existing vine because vines grown from seed yield fruit of inferior quality.[12] The vintner plants choice vines (Isa 5:2, 4; also in Jer 2:21; Gen 49:11), which may profile a cutting from the Soreq Valley known for its tree and vine cultivation.[13] The care with which he has prepared the terraced land and selected high-quality vines matches his optimism about the outcome expressed in the construction of the watchtower and a winepress. The speaker asks what more the vintner could have done for the vineyard. The question is rhetorical; there is nothing more he could have done. Isaiah 5:3–4 elaborates on the vinter's blocked goals, which trigger anger and aggression. The passage concludes by identifying the perverse vines as the people of Judah. The high-quality grapes hoped for are acts of judgment and justice, and the disappointing fruit is bloodshed and outcry (Isa 5:7).[14] This passage describes the anger of God at the injustice of the Judeans. Humans can understand effort invested in the hope of harvest and the consequent frustration and anger when this goal is blocked through no fault of their own.

In addition to the anger triggered by frustrated goals, the vineyard elicits disgust through its repulsive fruit. The Hebrew root *stink* profiles a bad smell that triggers disgust.[15] This exact form of the root appears only in Isaiah 5, so its precise meaning is unclear. Some render it as *wild grapes*, capturing the sense that this fruit should not appear in the carefully tended vineyard (NRSV, NJPS). Wild grapes do not taste as sweet as domesticated varieties, but they are edible.[16] The translation *sour grapes* captures the most salient point about the fruit: it is disgusting and inedible.[17] Disgust evolved as a means of helping us avoid pathogens. Disgust triggers show both consistency and variability across cultures. Things widely regarded as disgusting serve as vectors of communicable disease. Bodily products like feces, saliva, mucus, and vomit can carry a wide range of diseases that still sicken and kill millions of people per year. Rats, cockroaches, flies, and other critters carry disease, often as a result of their contact with waste and decay.[18] The danger of pathogens may explain a variety of avoidance behaviors related to disgust. Animals have two primary means of staying safe from pathogens: avoidance and cleaning.[19] They may avoid close contact with members of their own species who show signs of infection. Biblical law, for example, sanctions the isolation of people with visible skin lesions. The biblical purity system also takes particular care concerning the treatment of corpses, blood, and semen as sources of contamination.[20] Animals also avoid other species that may be vectors of disease. Humans avoid cockroaches, mice, and other animals associated with garbage and decay. Animals also avoid locations and things that may be contaminated with pathogens, like places where there is dung or corpses. Humans also track the connections between objects and environments and continue to avoid things that they know to have been in contact with something potentially contaminating.[21] Biblical purity laws, for example, frequently involve concern for contamination that can render an object unclean by contact with something unclean. Cleaning requires approach rather than avoidance. Cleaning removes disgusting material from the self or the environment. Many species across animal kingdoms separate their waste products from their living environments by defecating away from nests or at the perimeters of their territory. Many social insects include workers specifically devoted to cleaning and waste disposal.[22] Humans modify their environments as needed, separate waste from other activities, and maintain cleaning regimes that minimize pathogens. The common efforts of many species to avoid pathogens suggest that disgust has a deep evolutionary history. The diversity of disgust triggers across cultures, however, point to a cultural history and learned variability in humans. People regard taboo foods as disgusting, although the specific target foods vary by culture. The disgusting nature of the vineyard's fruit in Isaiah 5:2 heightens the sense of anger and outrage. It produces a sour grape that is repulsive and worse than nothing.

The human audience can access the frustrated goals and consequent anger in this agricultural scenario. Anger in the Bible typically involves anger at people, not vineyards. Anger appears explicitly in situations where a person of superior status becomes angry at the perceived insubordination of a social inferior.[23] As a result, polite speech in Hebrew often requests that the hearer not become angry (Gen 44:18). Abigail asks David to forgive her for her offense, which is daring to speak to him at all (1 Sam 25:28). Social superiors express anger; inferiors do not. Closer reading with a view to anger reveals that social inferiors may experience anger at superiors, but may not express it.[24] As a result, anger words in Hebrew appear disproportionately with subjects who are more powerful, like kings and YHWH.[25] This anger vocabulary is missing in the vineyard song, but the signs of anger appear clearly. The vintner has no hesitation about violently punishing the plantation since he is superior to it and has nothing to fear from expressing his wrath. The narrator of Isaiah 5:1–7 assumes that the anger of the vintner is fully justified and the violent response appropriate.[26]

The story highlights the disgusting nature of the grapes and ultimately blends food disgust with moral disgust. The grapes represent actions. Hebrew literature has a wider conventional metaphor of fruit as action, the visible result of invisible interior processes (Ps 1:3; Jer 17:8; Hos 10:13).[27] The Hebrew wordplay at the end of the parable contrasts the expected fruit (judgment and justice) with the actual fruit (bloodshed and outcry). The audience becomes vicariously angry at the failed vine and disgusted at its fruit. Then they realize that they are the vine and their behavior is morally repugnant. Isaiah has a wealthy audience in view and does not condemn those too poor to own a vineyard.[28] The remainder of the chapter identifies specific behaviors that make the leading Judeans disgusting to YHWH and motivate YHWH's anger and consequent punishment. They greedily enlarge their own estates at the expense of others (5:8), drink to excess (5:12, 22), pervert justice for bribes (5:23), arrogantly claim wisdom (5:21) to substitute their own preferences for good and evil (5:20), and despise YHWH (5:12, 19, 24). These indictments in Isaiah 5 include references to punishment that will befall the sinful nation, including harvest failure (5:10), drought (5:13), exile (5:13), ruined estates (5:17), military invasion (5:26–30), and widespread death (5:14). Isaiah 5:8–30 unpacks the vineyard parable by specifying the sinful actions represented as sour grapes and the punishments represented by the devastation of the vineyard. The systematic destruction of the whole vineyard communicates the intensity of the vintner's wrath and threatens the devastation of Jerusalem and Judea.[29]

The vineyard song blends food disgust and moral disgust. The vine produces disgusting sour grapes that blend with the morally repugnant behaviors produced by the people of Judah. Moral disgust recruits the disgust evolved for pathogen avoidance and blends it with revulsion at the behavior of others.[30] Behaviors that elicit disgust show both variance and commonality across cultures, as with food disgust.[31] Moral disgust emerges in Leviticus 18:25, 28 where the land vomits out its inhabitants for defiling it.[32] YHWH warns the Israelites to avoid the disgusting practices of the Canaanites lest the same fate await the Israelites.[33] People avoid, ostracize, and isolate those engaged in repulsive behaviors. They may escalate from avoidance to violent attack (cleansing). Biblical texts seek to instill disgust reactions toward lepers as well as criminals and people who engage in practices construed as foreign. Biblical texts do not make a distinction between ritual and moral purity, and both types of taboo involve disgust toward certain substances and behaviors deemed threatening.[34] Similarly, people do not reliably distinguish between what is disgusting and what is immoral.[35]

## Physical and Moral Disgust in Exodus

A thread of physical and moral disgust connects multiple episodes in the exodus narrative. In the beginning, the Egyptians experience the Hebrews as disgusting and therefore mistreat them. YHWH retaliates against Egypt with several disgusting plagues. In some plagues, disgust appears with particular reference to the sense of smell, evoked with the Hebrew root that profiles the stinking grapes in Isaiah 5:2, 4. Disgust begins, however, with the Israelites themselves. At the start of Exodus, "the Israelites were fruitful. They swarmed and multiplied and became so very numerous that the land was filled with them"[36] (Exod 1:7). The language blends people and plants with *fruitful*, but the next verb blends people with animals that swarm. Excessive fecundity triggers disgust, and Leviticus reliably identifies swarming creatures as disgusting.[37] The word choice *swarming* hints at the negative Egyptian reaction to Israelite fecundity.[38] The Hebrews are creepy swarming creatures that multiply like vermin. The verse includes several verbs that profile the remarkable explosive growth in Israelite reproduction to explain Pharaoh's revulsion.[39] The Pharaoh who did not know Joseph "said to his people, 'See, the Israelite people have multiplied and become more numerous than we are!'" (1:9) The Hebrew particle *see!* indicates Pharaoh's surprise, and he decides to treat the Israelites shrewdly by reducing them to slavery. This cruel strategy fails, however, and the more the Hebrews were oppressed, "the more they multiplied and spread, so that the Egyptians were disgusted by the Israelites"[40] (1:12). The expression reuses the verb *multiply* from 1:7, 9, but *spread out* appears here for the first time. It suggests the realization of Pharaoh's fear, as the fecundity of the Hebrews makes them impossible to contain. The verb profiles breaking out in ways that may pose a danger (Exod 19:22, 24; 2 Sam 6:8; 2 Kgs 14:13; Prov 25:28). The Hebrews threaten to break out of containment and pour over boundaries due to their fecundity. The rampant growth of the people leads the Egyptians to share in Pharaoh's disgust for the Israelites. Translators render the verb *disgusted* as "fear" or "loathe" in this context, but it profiles disgust.[41] The Hebrew audience sees the fulfillment of promises of fertility (Gen 46:3–4; 48:3–4), but Egyptians see creepy swarming creatures.[42] Pharaoh's fear and disgust motivate him to command midwives to kill all the male babies born to Hebrew women. When they refuse to kill the infants, Pharaoh asks them why they have let the boys live, and their answer speaks to Pharaoh's disgust at the Israelites: "The Hebrew women are not like the Egyptian women. They are animals and give birth before the midwife arrives."[43] (Exod 1:19) This blend of Hebrew women and animals in the context of birth elicits disgust because the birth process accentuates the animal nature of the women. Birth involves disgusting matter like blood and excrement and is a source of impurity (Lev 12:1–8).[44] Some human-animal blends elicit animal reminder disgust, or the disgust people feel when they face their animal nature and recall that they are not separate from nature, despite the trappings of culture.[45] Our animal nature reminds us that we are mortal. The intrusion of animal activities like sex, birth, and defecation evokes animal reminder disgust.[46]

The Hebrew term for *stinky* can profile moral disgust. It occurs with this moral sense in several passages, including Exodus 5:21. Pharaoh punishes the Hebrews after Moses asks him to let the Hebrews go, citing his concern about their excessive number (Exod 5:5). He compounds their work (5:6–9), and the overseers beat the Hebrew foremen for their failure to do the impossible (5:14). When the foremen complain to Pharaoh, he accuses them of laziness or slackness in their work and will not relent. "Lazy! You are lazy! That is why you keep saying, 'Let us go and offer sacrifice to YHWH!' Now off to work!" (Exod 5:17–18) A close analogue to Pharaoh's complaint appears in Proverbs 18:9: "Those slack in their work are kin to the destroyer."[47] Pharaoh views the Israelites as destroyers because their slackness in work threatens his wealth. He sees them as stealing what is rightfully his.[48] He thinks Moses lies about the reasons for wanting to leave Egypt (Exod 5:14). The Israelite foremen see the injustice of their situation but turn their anger against Moses instead of Pharaoh since anger cannot be expressed to superiors. They fear Pharaoh but not Moses. Pharaoh's speech clarifies that he conceptualizes his behavior as a punishing response to Moses's request. Pharaoh may be intentionally driving a wedge between the Israelites and their would-be leaders, Moses and Aaron. The foremen then *assail* Moses and Aaron (5:20), an action described with a verb that can mean "to encounter" (1 Sam 10:5) or "to attack/kill" (2 Sam 1:15), and say to them: "YHWH look upon you and judge! You have made our scent stinky in the eyes of Pharaoh and his servants, putting a sword into their hands to kill us."[49] (Exod 5:21) The foremen describe Pharaoh's attitude toward them in terms of smell. The olfactory meaning of *stinky* remains salient, but it profiles both bad smell and moral disgust.[50] The inclusion of *odor* and sight (*in the eyes of*) draws attention to the expression through its strange juxtaposition of sensory modalities. The speech emphasizes the foremen's fundamental complaint: Moses and Aaron have done something that affects the way Pharaoh perceives them to the detriment of the foremen and Israelites. Pharaoh sees the Hebrews as slacking off in their work and thereby robbing him of their productivity, so he punishes them with more work. The foremen make sense of Pharaoh's conduct and speech by attributing stinkiness to themselves in the eyes of Pharaoh. Pharaoh's perception of them as smelly and morally repugnant (lazy, slack, deceptive) explains why he compounds their labor by withholding straw.[51] His accusatory speech and punishment signal anger. He wants them to work harder and stop asking to leave. Their complaint violates his goals and expectations. Moses in turn complains to YHWH for treating the people badly and doing nothing to save them. Moses thereby acknowledges the justice of their complaint against him. YHWH, in turn, initiates the plagues (Exod 6).

Five other narratives likewise connect moral disgust to violent treatment with the verb *stink*, and these examples can further clarify the meaning of the expression in Exodus. First, Jacob complains that Simeon and Levi have made him stinky by their genocidal action (Gen 34:30): "You have brought trouble on me by making me stinky to the inhabitants of the land, the Canaanites and the Perizzites. I have so few men that if these people unite against me and attack me I and my household will be wiped out."[52] Their extreme vengeance strikes Jacob as treacherous and wrong (Gen 49:5–7). He imagines that the people surrounding them must be disgusted at the immoral treatment of the Shechemites. As a result, he fears, the Canaanites and Perizzites will do to his household what his sons did to Shechem.[53] Becoming disgusting to others may be dangerous because it may motivate violent attack (Exod 5:21; Isa 5:1–7). Second, Israel becomes stinky to the Philistines due to their own morally repulsive behavior. After Jonathan attacks a Philistine garrison in Gibeon, the people hear the report that "Israel has become stinky to the Philistines."[54] (1 Sam 13:3–4). Unprovoked attack is morally repugnant and leads to retaliation.[55] Saul gets credit or blame for the surprise attack in time of peace. Such a gross violation triggers anger and disgust that motivate Philistine attack. Third, David falsely tells King Achish of Gath that David is raiding Judean villages rather than neighboring Amalekites and others. As a result, "Achish trusted David, thinking, 'He must surely be stinky to his people.[56] I shall have him as a servant forever'" (1 Sam 27:12). Achish assumes that David must be morally repugnant to Israel because of his treacherous attacks on them while in the service of the Philistines. As a result, he can never return to his homeland or be welcomed among the Israelites. Fourth, the Ammonites make themselves repugnant to King David after their king decides that David's messengers are actually spies. King Hanun humiliates them by shaving half their beards and cutting away the lower part of their clothes at the buttocks: "When the Ammonites realized that they were stinky to David,[57] they sent for and hired" mercenaries to help them defend against David's attack (2 Sam 10:4–6). As with Jonathan's surprise attack on the Philistines, Hanun's mistreatment of David's messengers represents a violation of international ethical norms. Both offenses appear treacherous to the wronged party, motivating violent retaliation. David attacks them without mercy. He takes the capital, pillages it, deports the population, and sets them to work making bricks (2 Sam 12:26–31). This extreme punishment indicates David's disgust and anger. Fifth, David experiences betrayal when Absalom tries to seize the throne. After he captures Jerusalem, Ahitophel advises Absalom to have sex openly with the concubines David left behind in Jerusalem to take care of the palace. "When all Israel hears how stinky you have made yourself to your father[58] all those on your side will take courage." Absalom had sex with his father's concubines in view of all Israel (2 Sam 16:20–22). Absalom's sexual seizure of his father's concubines creates an unbridgeable rift between himself and his father. His supporters know that Absalom cannot possibly reconcile with David. Absalom claims the throne in a way that makes him repugnant to David both for the treason and for the incest (1 Kgs 2:13–25; Lev 18:8; Amos 2:7). David secludes these concubines and never has sex with them again (2 Sam 20:3).

In all the narratives of people becoming disgusting to other people, the construction focuses on the ruined relationship. The smelly person is always smelly to a specific audience, not smelly in general. The audience repelled by the stinky person is likely to respond violently.[59] The stinky person is morally repugnant as a result of doing something treacherous. Wicked acts are stinky and shameful to the righteous (Prov 13:8). The offended party may, like the vintner in Isaiah 5:1–7, respond with anger and aggression. Only the example in Exodus 5:21 redundantly amplifies *stinky* with *our odor*, and only this example marks the disgusted party with *in the eyes of*.[60] The Exodus example captures attention both for the rarity of its construction and for its anomalous explicit juxtaposition of vision and smell. These features draw attention to the blend of physical and moral disgust that might otherwise pass unnoticed as a Hebrew idiom. The writer wanted the audience to recognize the disgust inherent in this episode because of its thematic connection to the thread of disgust through the exodus narrative.[61]

Disgust appears prominently in the plagues on Egypt.[62] The Egyptians find the Hebrews disgusting and oppress them. YHWH responds with several repugnant plagues. YHWH specifically identifies the justice of the plague of the firstborn by noting the parallel between the mistreatment of YHWH's firstborn Israel and the firstborn of the Egyptians (Exod 4:21–23). The narrative similarly presents Pharaoh's disgust at the Hebrews as justification for the repulsive plagues.

The first two plagues involve a disgusting smell identified by the same verb used to describe the stinkiness of the Hebrews in the eyes of Pharaoh (5:21). In the first plague, YHWH turns the water of the Nile into blood. Blood is disgusting in itself, so the Egyptians cannot drink water from the Nile.[63] The situation gets worse: "The fish in the Nile died and the Nile itself stank" (Exod 7:21). Fish cannot survive in a river of blood. The smell drives the people away from the undrinkable Nile to dig holes to find water. Bad odors elicit disgust, especially when they signal the presence of repulsive substances like decay or excrement. Rotten fish have a particularly pungent and unpleasant stench. The impurity of blood in biblical law indicates its likely role in eliciting disgust, and this plague renders Egypt ritually impure.[64] The second plague leaves the land filled with frogs. This disgusting swarming creature (7:28) goes up from the Nile to cover the land (8:2) and enter houses. The frogs exceed all limits and appear in ovens and kneading bowls, which amplifies disgust by association with food.[65] Disgust does not end when the plague ends: "The frogs died off in the houses, the courtyards, and the fields. Heaps of them were piled up and the land stank" (Exod 8:9b–10). The smell is so strong and omnipresent that the land itself stinks.[66] The stench of rotting frogs afflicts the people even after the end of the plague after the frogs have been cleaned up into piles. In Psalm 78:45, the frogs destroy the Egyptians, magnifying the damage of the plague. In Psalm 105:30, the land swarms with frogs, magnifying the disgusting nature of the plague. The Hebrews disgust the Egyptians in Exodus 1:12 because of their prodigious animal-like fecundity. The same verb of swarming here draws attention to the excessive fecundity of the frogs, which enhances the disgust reaction elicited by the smell of their rotting flesh.[67] The Egyptians were repelled by the Hebrews, so YHWH sends them something truly repulsive.

The first two plagues feature water-based creatures whose deaths create a disgusting stench. The second two plagues involve disgusting swarming insects. The lice are everywhere: "All the dust of the earth turned into lice throughout the land of Egypt."[68] The lice were on humans and animals, and the magicians could not replicate this power and declare that the plague of lice are "the finger of God" (Exod 8:13–15). The Hebrew term rendered *lice* profiles a biting insect.[69] Lice occur with maggots and worms in the context of human decomposition (Sir 10:11), suggesting that these small insects elicited disgust among the ancient Israelites due to their association with rotting flesh. The creatures are otherwise absent from Hebrew literature. The next plague of flies afflicts only the Egyptians, while the Hebrews are free of them: "Thick swarms of flies entered the house of Pharaoh and the houses of his servants. Throughout Egypt the land was devastated on account of the swarms of flies"[70] (Exod 8:20). The flies ruin the land. The specific insect and the ruin it causes remain elusive. The term may profile a category of swarming insects.[71] This swarm may consist of flies, which triggered disgust in the ancient Near East.[72] Ecclesiastes says "Dead flies make a stench pour forth from the perfumer's oil" (Eccl 9:18).[73]

The fifth and sixth plagues involve disgust related to illness. First, "a very severe pestilence" kills the Egyptian livestock but not the livestock of the Hebrews. The text highlights the economic disaster of the extermination of the Egyptian livestock. Pestilence triggers disgust, and rotting animal carcasses make the land impure (Lev 11:39–40).[74] The text need not dwell on the specific symptoms or decaying carcasses to elicit revulsion. The word *pestilence* occurs in conjunction with disgusting (e.g., Deut 28:21; 1 Kgs 8:37; Amos 4:10) or terrifying things (Jer 14:12; 21:9; 27:8, 13; 29:18). The next plague of boils on humans profiles the disgusting nature of the sickness. When Moses casts soot from a kiln into the sky, it became fine dust over "the whole land of Egypt" (Exod 9:9) and "caused festering boils on human being and beast alike" (9:10). The text employs two words for boils, one unique and one profiling disgusting skin deformities elsewhere.[75] Job suffers severe boils all over his body (Job 2:7), and the same affliction appears in Deuteronomy 28:35 as a punishment for disobeying the law. The "boils of the Egyptians" may be a reference to this Exodus plague (Deut 28:35).[76] Leviticus 13:18–23 mentions boils, but the focus is on other skin irregularities that may prove infectious. Infectious diseases like smallpox, chickenpox, or measles cause skin boils. Hezekiah's near-fatal illness (2 Kgs 20:1 // Isa 38:1) included boils that Isaiah healed with figs (2 Kgs 20:7 // Isa 38:21). Skin boils elicited disgust in themselves and as potential signs of serious infectious illness. The boils on Job are large and from the soles of his feet to the top of his head (Job 2:7), magnifying the disgust he evokes in others.[77]

After the boils, the plagues of hail and locusts both devastate the Egyptian economy, with the locusts finishing off whatever the hail did not destroy. Locusts may have inspired disgust, although these insects were consumed as food (Lev 11:12). The text focuses on the surprising severity of the locust plague that destroys the plants that survived the hail. The locusts fill up the homes of the Egyptians (Exod 10:6), recollecting the disgusting presence of the frogs in cooking utensils. Like the hail, it may provoke fear more than disgust, although their sheer numbers may elicit disgust as with the other insects and frogs.[78] The excessive fecundity of locusts affords metaphorical uses that construe invading enemy soldiers as numerous, destructive, and disgusting (Judg 6:5; 7:12; Jer 46:23).

The plagues of hail, darkness, and death of the firstborn inspire fear rather than disgust. These three plagues resemble the phenomena that accompany divine theophanies and the day of YHWH. Joel associates locusts with the day of YHWH (Joel 1:4). The plagues on Egypt, however, involve multiple disgust elicitors rather than more directly fearsome phenomena found in Isaiah 13. The exodus narrative might have involved multiple storm events (hail, wind, lightning) and earthquakes, but instead draws on blood, rotting animals, insects, pestilence, and festering boils. The narrator notes the stench of the rotting fish and frogs, using a word that profiles the disgust that the Hebrews trigger in Pharaoh (Exod 5:21). YHWH afflicts the Egyptians with multiple disgusting plagues, but no amount of disgust motivates Pharaoh to vomit the Hebrews out of the land. Only the death of the firstborn achieves this result.

God sends disgusting plagues on Israel's enemies again in 1 Samuel 5. The Philistines defeat Israel in battle and capture the ark of the covenant. The statue of Dagan falls before the ark (1 Sam 5:3–4). Every city that hosts the ark suffers from a plague. The narrative foreshadows this result when the Philistines recall the plagues on the Egyptians before the battle (1 Sam 4:8–9). The term often rendered *tumors* reflects a Hebrew term of uncertain meaning. It is related to swelling, and has been understood as tumors or boils.[79] The same word profiles the five golden images that the Philistines return to Israel with the ark after they cry out for mercy (5:12) and seek the advice of priests (6:2). Five golden mice also accompany the ark, but the text does not clarify what mice have to do with the plague. The precise meaning of key words remains opaque, as with the Exodus plagues. The suffering of the Philistines comes through clearly, and the plague evokes disgust. The narrator might have presented the Philistines afflicted by darkness, earthquake, drought, infertility, or other fear-inducing events. The story involves a disgusting bodily ailment that can be fatal and somehow involves mice.

The escape from Egypt does not end the theme of disgust in Exodus. The Israelites receive the gift of manna in the desert. They gather it in the morning after the dew evaporates and discover it as fine flakes like frost (16:14) that taste like wafers with honey (16:31). Moses orders them not to keep any over until the following morning. "But they did not listen to Moses, and some kept a part of it over until morning and it became wormy and stank" (16:20). The term *stank* is the same word for disgusting smells in Exodus 5:21; 7:18, 21; 8:10. In advance of the sabbath, they gather twice as much and keep the extra by boiling or baking it for the sabbath day when none appears on the ground (Exod 16:25–26). With this preparation, the manna is not wormy (16:24).[80] The disgusting corruption of the manna serves as punishment for disobedience. Manna emerges again as something unwelcome as food in Numbers 11:6. The people become greedy for meat, remember the range of foods they ate in Egypt, and lament that they now have nothing except the manna. The context depicts manna as something tiresome because their diet lacks variety, but it is not specifically disgusting. The text describes the appearance and taste of manna in terms that appear desirable, but the murmuring people want something more.

## Conclusion

Disgust arises directly from nature. It can be extended to the social world as moral disgust at repulsive behaviors. The Hebrew language captures the duality of disgust by blending physical and moral disgust in an idiom describing morally repugnant behavior as making one stinky. The Egyptians and Philistines behave in disgusting ways toward the Israelites (Exod 1:13–14; 1 Sam 4:9), so YHWH sends disgusting plagues on them. Moral disgust may elicit or intensify anger. Characters who realize that they have made themselves morally disgusting to others fear violent attack. The divine vintner angrily attacks the vineyard for yielding sour disgusting grapes. This parable presents moral disgust under the analogy of physical disgust. The text invites the hearers into YHWH's experience of disgust and anger so that they can have a new perspective on themselves as vines that have produced repugnant fruit. If the vine had produced no fruit or merely adequate fruit, YHWH's anger might be reduced to disappointment. The contrast between the hoped-for excellent fruit and the disgusting sour fruit triggers anger. These texts blend physical and moral disgust, obfuscating the fuzzy boundary between nature and culture.

# 4

## PRIDE AND SHAME

SELF-CONSCIOUS EMOTIONS REQUIRE self-awareness and mental representations of the self.[1] These emotions include pride, shame, guilt, and embarrassment.[2] Self-conscious emotions help us achieve status and avoid rejection. They provide a barometer that indicates our reputation in the community. Self-conscious emotions emerge relatively late in development compared to anger, fear, grief, and joy. These emotions can be seen in the first nine months, but self-conscious emotions do not emerge until three to four years of age. A sense of self-consciousness develops at this time.[3] Around nine months, babies understand others as intentional agents with goals, knowledge, and attention. They become able to participate as partners in relationships and acquire language. Around four years of age, they evaluate themselves in terms of how others see them and regulate their behavior according to social norms. They feel pride and shame. Pride and shame vary across cultures. Some cultures eschew public displays of pride, while others highly value it.[4] Pride involves a sense of personal responsibility for socially desirable outcomes. Authentic pride and hubristic pride differ in their sources and outcomes.[5] We are authentically proud when we attribute our positive actions to our effort and control. For example, we believe we passed a test because we studied for it. We are hubristically proud when we attribute our success to our intrinsic excellence. For example, we believe we passed the test because we are highly intelligent.[6] Cultures that avoid displays of pride may be concerned about the negative social effects of hubristic pride. Other cultures may value authentic pride because of its pro-social effects. The hubristic person believes in their intrinsic excellence and may therefore demand or expect special treatment from the group even when they have done nothing to deserve it. The authentically proud person may expect rewards for specific accomplishments understood as a result of intentional effort rather than inherent superiority. Biblical literature reflects both kinds of pride.[7]

Pride and shame appear in a contrastive relationship in Hebrew. Hebrew identifies pride as up and shame as down.[8] Hebrew words for pride also mean high or elevated.[9] A proud person has high breath/spirit (Prov 16:18), and a humble person has low breath/spirit (Prov 29:23).[10] Speakers in many languages use similar conceptual blends, combining up and down with a range of domains, including emotion. Emotional up/down is not limited to pride/shame, but encompasses positive and negative experiences and circumstances more generally. The widespread use of up/down across languages provides an example of an image schema.[11] Image schemas arise from our embodied experience of the world. We create meaningful spatial schemas that underlie conceptual content and give it meaning. The verticality schema builds on our perception of the action of gravity, the structure of the environment, and our own upright posture. Many factors may have motivated Hebrew speakers to use up/down to understand pride/shame.[12] Our posture is tall and erect when we are proud, but shame makes us shrink.[13] People describe shame as making them want to disappear. Pride and shame involve the self.[14] The self may be high-achieving, possess great wealth, wisdom, virtue, and high social status. A proud self has all these assets and qualities, but their lack or loss is shameful. Job contrasts his proud past with his present shame, which emerges in how others respond to him in relation to his wealth and happiness as opposed to poverty and misery (Job 29–30). As we come to understand that other people have bodies and minds like ours, we develop a sense of self that encompasses our environment and community. We develop a sense of pride and shame that serve as emotional barometers of our social environment and personal status. Our interior sense of self and self-conscious emotion derive from our exterior world.[15]

## Pride Demands Humiliation
### *Isaiah 14*

The "taunt-song" (Isa 14:4) against the king of Babylon never names the tyrannical king and even forbids that his name be used (14:20). The Assyrian king Sargon II provides the best fit since his corpse was not recovered from the battlefield (Isa 14:19).[16] The main features of the king fit any Mesopotamian imperial ruler. These kings routinely engaged in building activities with trees from Lebanon, ruled harshly over a vast territory, and destroyed cities. In its final form and context the passage applies this critique of empire to kings generally. The text reflects Mesopotamian realities and connects the poem to Babylon, but the theme of pride fits well with any powerful ruler. The poem critiques hubristic pride as the root of sinful behavior. The text makes extensive use of nonhuman creation to depict the pride of the king and his dramatic humiliation.

The opening lines of the poem (vv. 4–6) emphasize the wickedness of the king to make his death cause for celebration. He is immediately identified as an oppressor like the Egyptian overseers (Exod 3:7; 5:6, 10, 13, 14; cf. Job 3:18; 39:7; Isa 3:12; 9:3). The next line identifies the king as a despot.[17] The text blends the symbol of the king's authority (rod) with a symbol of wickedness (14:5). A staff profiles a scepter as a symbol of authority, but it can also be a weapon (2 Sam 23:21; Isa 11:14) like "the rod of the wicked" (Isa 9:3; 10:5, 24, 26; 30:32) in parallel with "the staff of tyrants" (14:6). The king is a tyrant who "struck the peoples in wrath with relentless blows" (14:6), showing the constancy and brutality of his violence. A shepherd also has a rod but does not wield it in anger against sheep. A good king, like a shepherd, guides and protects the flock (Gen 49:24; 2 Sam 5:2; Pss 23:1; 80:1–2; Isa 40:10–11; 63:11; Mic 2:12–13; Jer 23:1–4), but this king rules in wrath and limitless persecution (14:6). The king of Babylon richly deserves what happens to him next.

Creation rejoices over the dead king: "The whole earth rests peacefully, song breaks forth" (14:7). The speech of the trees suggests that all creation is in view, not only human inhabitants of the earth.[18] The tree imagery informs the sense of *cut down* in 14:12 (cf. Isa 10:33). The tall cedars stand on a height to which the woodcutters must come up. The king seeks height, power, and pride but is cut down. The cedars and cypresses are here victims of imperial pride, but they elsewhere represent pride that needs to be humbled. Assyrian kings boasted of their lumber activities in the mountainous forests of Lebanon, and Isaiah 37:24 (//2 Kgs 19:23) reflects knowledge of this Assyrian boast.[19] Isaiah 10 makes Assyria into a cedar tree cut down by YHWH. Cedars of Lebanon represent human pride in Isaiah 2:11–13 (cf. Amos 2:9; Zech 11:2).[20] The great old-growth forests of Lebanon appear as dark wilderness places in ancient literature that heroes and kings dared to enter and tame.[21] The forests contained once-great quantities of enormous trees that could only be harvested for timber by an imperial power. The trees were too big and remote to be cut down without significant resources and organization to mobilize the work. The great trees would not be worth the effort without large building projects requiring long and thick beams that could only be extracted from old-growth trees. Mesopotamian kings boasted of their access to this construction material used in their palaces and temples. The glory of Solomon likewise depends on his access to cedar supplied by Hiram of Tyre. Solomon's palace and the temple in Jerusalem consumed copious amounts of cedar for their construction. Solomon builds the House of the Forest, a monumental structure included in the temple complex that may have been an armory (1 Kgs 7:2; 10:17, 21; Isa 22:8). The biblical text focuses on its grand scale, cedar building material, and identity as a forest. It consisted of cedar pillars in three rows connected by cedar beams. Solomon uses real cedar to build an artificial forest. The nineteen mentions of cedar in Solomon's reign culminate in the observation: "The king made silver as common in Jerusalem as stones, and cedars as numerous as the sycamores of the Shephalah." (1 Kgs 10:27) The biblical account of Solomon's building activity emphasizes the extraordinary volume of precious cedar used. The biblical account accords with ancient Near Eastern royal inscriptions in which kings boast of their access to cedar and their elaborate building projects. The cedars of Lebanon signify pride. Kings boast of their conquest of these mighty trees as a means of amplifying their power and glory. Kings increase their own pride by reducing the cedar to a resource for their own building projects. In this taunt-song, the cedars of Lebanon and the cypresses appear as victims to be pitied rather than persecutors to be humbled. They symbolize pride indirectly by characterizing the violent arrogance of the king who sends woodcutters up the mountains of Lebanon to cut great trees for his building projects. The woodcutter coming up against the trees depicts the violent attack that the trees fear. But with the king laid low, this upward striving has ended and the trees rejoice. The whole earth also has rest from the violent attack of the king (Isa 14:20).

The king journeys to Sheol (Isa 14:9–11). Sheol is below, under the earth, far from God, and the lowest place a human can go.[22] The text personifies Sheol.[23] Sheol makes the shades of dead kings rise from their thrones to greet the great king of Babylon.[24] Their speech to the new arrival encapsulates the humiliation of the king: "You too have become weak like us, you are just like us!" (14:10) The shades reflect with amazement on the humiliation of the king of Babylon. The king has grown weak or sick like the other shades. This weakness corresponds to a downward movement and passage from life to death. The king's pride/height is brought down to Sheol: "Down to Sheol your pride is brought, the sound of your harps. Maggots are the couch beneath you, worms are your blanket" (14:11).[25] The song draws on high and low elements of creation to communicate pride and shame. The downward motion to Sheol construes pride as up and shame as down. The image of the king's corpse sandwiched between worms and maggots blends the image of a comfortable bed and covering with rot and decay. The worms and maggots consume the dead flesh of the king. These disgusting creatures draw attention to the repulsive decomposition of the king's corpse. Maggots infest rotten food (Exod 16:24), clothe Job's disgusting body (Job 7:5), and appear with the decay of death (Job 17:14; 21:26; 25:6).[26] Worms appear with decayed corpses also in Isaiah 66:24 and rotten food in Exodus 16:20. Worms can illustrate the smallness and humiliation of humans in Psalm 22:7 and Job 25:6. The speech of the shades compounds the depth of the king's fall by drawing attention to the putrefaction of his corpse.

The speaker of the taunt-song likewise reflects amazement at the downfall of the king: "How you have fallen from the heavens, O Morning Star, son of the dawn, how you have been cut down to the earth, lying on your back."[27] (Isa 14:12) The poem identifies the downward motion as a fall from heaven. The term *heavens* profiles the highest place in the cosmos, translated as *heaven(s)* or *sky* depending on context. The many terms pointing to celestial realities emphasize the height from which the king has fallen. *Morning Star son of the dawn* profiles the planet Venus, which appears brilliantly in the sky before and after dawn part of the year but fades as the sun rises and overwhelms its luminance.[28] This astral phenomenon provides inspiration for a Canaanite myth in which a minor deity seeks to ascend to the throne of the gods only to fail and descend to the underworld. Isaiah 14 and the Ugaritic version of this story reflect the same myth using some of the same language for six key points: (1) going up, (2) on Mount Zaphon, (3) sitting, (4) on a throne, (5) then descending, and (6) to the underworld.[29]

The poem presents a speech of the king that he spoke *in his heart*. This private speech interprets the king's behavior as a consequence of his internal mental life.[30] His violence and cruelty arise from his hubris. Creation serves to express his arrogance: "I will ascend the heavens; above the stars of God, I will set up my throne. I will sit on the mount of assembly, on the heights of Zaphon. I will ascend above the tops of the clouds. I will be like the Most High" (Isa 14:13–14).[31] The poet places these words in the heart of the king to interpret the king's behavior as a result of his interior life. The king believes in his own divinity and treats other people with contempt, destroying cities and burdening creation with his violence. His speech clarifies his upward striving in ways that clearly mark it as hubristic. All the high places mentioned in this speech have long-standing associations with the divine. Heaven is the dwelling of God. Multiple cultures associate stars with deities. *The stars of God* profile the highest stars. The gods met in council on the Mount of Assembly identified with Mount Zaphon. Ugaritic texts identify Mount Zaphon as the home of Baal and Anat. The mountain peak itself is often above the clouds, which are themselves heights associated with deities. The final line of the king's speech summarizes the significance of the references to high places: "I will be like the Most High."[32] In sum, the king of Babylon strives to be god-like in his power and glory. His hubris explains his humiliation.

The upward ambition of the king is shattered in Isaiah 14:15–21. Instead of rising to the highest places, he will be brought down to Sheol, the depths of the pit (14:15), the foundations of the pit (14:19). The poem contrasts the highest imaginable place with the lowest imaginable to emphasize the extreme contrast between the king's hubris and the reality of his lowness. Sheol and the pit are the same subterranean abode of the dead. The depths of the pit emphasize the farthest possible reaches of Sheol, its lowest part or foundations, the opposite of the farthest reaches or heights of Zaphon (14:13).[33] For a second time, the poem narrates the king's arrival in Sheol (14:16–17). The great distance between the king's pride and humiliation encoded in creation evokes wonder from the shades who stare at him and consider what they see: "Is this the man who made the earth tremble, who shook kingdoms, who made the world a wilderness, razed its cities, and gave captives no release?" The shades recall the extraordinary power and violence of the king's rule. He transforms the world and makes the earth and its kingdoms shake in ways reminiscent of yhwh's activities in Isaiah 13:9, 12, 13. His god-like power has faded, and his grand ambitions to ascend to heaven have ended with his descent into Sheol. The state of his body mirrors the humiliation of his spirit. The text blends his corpse with a miscarriage that is cast forth from the grave like a misbegotten fetus from the womb.[34] His corpse is called loathsome or abominable, emphasizing the disgusting quality of the king's corpse. He is clothed with the slain (14:19) reminiscent of his bed of maggots and covering of worms (14:11). His royal luxuries of bedding and clothing have become rot and decay. His shame and humiliation appear in the mistreatment of his trampled corpse. His body is underfoot and his spirit at the bottom of Sheol. This ignominious end fits his crime. He ruined his land and slaughtered his people (14:20). He is seed of evil (14:20), indicating his inherent and irredeemable wickedness. His sons must die lest they continue the destructive work of their father.

The poem in Isaiah 14:4–21 conceptualizes pride as up and shame as down. The poem draws on the highest and lowest parts of creation to illustrate the pride and humiliation of the king of Babylon. Gravity assists his fall and ultimate degradation and decay. Creation is more than a setting in which events happen. It makes the narrative coherent and emotionally evocative. Organisms also contribute to the story. The cedars of Lebanon amplify the pride of the king and the joy and relief that accompanies his death. The worms and maggots draw attention to the disgusting decay of the king's corpse.

## The Depths of Shame
### *Psalm 69*

The Psalter includes ninety-seven occurrences of shame vocabulary. Ten psalms use more than two words. Psalm 69 has the highest concentration of shame vocabulary of any psalm and Psalms 69–71 form a collection of shame psalms at the end of Book II of the Psalter.[35] This mini collection connects to surrounding psalms with its concern for the poor.[36]

The individual speaker of Psalm 69 complains of suffering and rejection as a result of an unspecified public commitment to the temple and

YHWH that place him in opposition to the majority: "because zeal for your house has consumed me, I am scorned by those who scorn you" (69:9–10).[37] His pious fasting and sackcloth lead to shame. "You know my reproach, my shame, my disgrace" (69:20). Although he claims to have no comforters in verse 20, the language in verse 7 indicates that a community of like-minded people suffer with him. The speaker separates himself from his companions to focus on his specific individual suffering. He has a leadership position, which explains why people at the gates complain about him and drunkards sing songs about him (69:13). The shame of the speaker derives from his pious public persona. He acknowledges unspecified faults and guilt (69:6), but he does not deserve to be disgraced for his good behavior. This contrast indicates a distinction between shame and guilt.[38] Guilt arises for specific violations of normative behavior that cause harm, create anxiety over the threat to relationship, and motivate people to repair the harm done through apology, confession, or reparation. The person feeling guilt sees the harmful act as volitional, and the consequent behavior is pro-social and reparative. Shame involves a global negative evaluation of the whole self as a bad person due to behaviors seen as uncontrollable. Shame may involve depression and hopelessness or defensiveness and anger. Instead of seeking to repair harm, the shamed person seeks to avoid others and disappear, becoming passive and seeking to avoid the evaluation of others.[39] The speaker of Psalm 69 knows his guilt, but his unspecified faults do not make him ashamed. The threat of shame comes from people at the gate (69:13) or public opinion. He experiences shame as an external sanction on his behavior, but he is not inwardly ashamed of his devotion to YHWH's house.[40] His guilt has no connection to his zeal for the temple. He feels no shame but experiences the act of shaming from others. This shaming involves serious risks. Shaming seeks to enforce social norms by threatening reputation and social bonds. Shaming affords a means of punishment that does not involve the costs of trial and litigation, imprisonment, fine, or execution.[41] It can still be highly effective because the shamed person suffers ruptured relationships and isolation (69:5, 9, 21). This shame need not be an internalized subjective emotion, although it can be. Some texts associate shame and blushing, strongly indicating a subjective feeling (Ps 34:6; Isa 1:29; 54:4). The inability to blush when engaged in shameful behavior reflects unrepentant wickedness (Jer 3:3; 6:15; 8:12). The speaker of Psalm 69 is not ashamed of his devotion to YHWH's house, so does not blush or repent. He does, however, experience painful shaming from his community.

The speaker of Psalm 69 closely ties his experience of shaming to the sensation of sinking into water and mud, both in his opening description of his suffering (69:2–5) and in his petition for rescue (69:14–19). In the opening lament, the speaker's body serves as a measuring rod for how far he has sunk into shame. The water has reached his neck, threatening his life (69:2). The introduction paints a picture of drowning to express a sense of helplessness and distress arising from the threats to his social life. The next lines (69:3) describe his sinking into the mire of the deep. *Sinking* profiles a downward movement that is not specific to drowning (Job 38:6; Ps 9:16; Prov 8:25; Jer 36:8, 22), although it can depict drowning (Exod 15:4). The term for *mire* appears only here and Psalm 40:3 where it profiles muck or mud in which a person may become stuck. The mire is at the bottom of a body of water, threatening drowning. In Psalm 69:3, the body of water is the depths, the deepest reaches of the sea (Ps 68:23; Jon 2:4; Mic 7:19), indicating a major threat.[42] In these muddy depths, there is no sure place to stand. The term *foothold* occurs only here. It is related to standing and emphasizes the dangerous position of the speaker in deep water with a muddy bottom. He can find no solidity beneath his feet to resist the downward pull of gravity. The speaker in Psalm 40:3 celebrates that God pulls him up from the mire and "and sets my feet upon rock and steadies my steps." The speaker of Psalm 69 begs for similar help (69:14–19). The flood of water images continues. The term *depths* is rare (Ps 130:1; Isa 51:10; Ezek 37:34). It profiles the deep parts of the sea similar to the proceeding *deep* (69:3). It appears with *water* in all its occurrences except Psalm 130:1 where it may be assumed. The speaker has entered the depths of the water so that the water contains him. Underworld waters overflow him. The verb *flooding* applies to excess water and only metaphorically of other subjects such as an army (Dan 11:10, 40) or a warhorse exploding into battle (Jer 8:8). This flood of images expresses "the suppliant's pain and distress, his abandonment, and his betrayal."[43]

The speaker returns to the image of drowning in the petition in Psalm 69:15–16 and uses the same vocabulary. The petition seeks rescue from the *mud* (69:15), using a term that recalls the *mire* from 69:2. The speaker who complained of sinking pleads "Do not let me sink." (69:15) The petition repeats the rare word *depths* (69:3, 15) while asking God for rescue from it and from those who hate him. The petition also conjoins the verb *overwhelm* and the noun *flood* that appeared together in verse 3. The petition escalates the image in each line: "Do not let the flood waters overwhelm me / nor the deep swallow me / nor the pit close its mouth over me." (69:16). At first, he asks that the waters not rise above his head. Then the threat of flood becomes the deep reaches of the sea where there can be no hope of a foothold. The verb *swallow* hints at predation, which becomes explicit in the mouth of the pit closing over him. Sheol appears like a ravenous beast and the psalmist as helpless prey (Isa 5:14; Hab 2:5; Prov 1:12).

"The psalmist is drowning in shame."[44] The speaker exploits the element of water to depict a sense of helplessness resulting from the threat to his social existence posed by the enemies who shame him. Near the end of the prayer, the psalmist says, "your salvation O God lifts me up" (69:30).[45] The image of lifting communicates protection (Pss 20:2; 59:2; 91:14; 107:41), a fitting image following the repeated sinking. The psalmist likewise complains that "insult has broken my heart" (69:21), indicating the serious psychological harm caused by the shaming his enemies direct at him.[46] He does not feel shame for his devotion to the temple, but he experiences the shaming as a major threat to his existence. Shaming is easy for a community to do but hard for an individual to bear.[47] He can find no comforters, only tormentors who give him poison for food and vinegar to drink (69:21–22). He is in pain (69:30). His pain derives from the shaming efforts of his enemies. He does not complain of physical pain, and he is not literally in danger of drowning, but the power and danger of shaming pose a serious threat to life.

Sinking in mud under water depicts the dangers of shaming in Psalm 71. The elderly speaker (71:9, 18) recalls past acts of divine salvation as lifting him up: "Whatever bitter afflictions you sent me, you would turn and revive me. From the watery depths of the earth once more raise me up. Restore my honor, turn and comfort me, that I may praise you with the lyre" (71:20–22). The expression *restore my honor* is literally *make large my greatness* (Ps 71:22). It captures the sensation of pride in contrast to shame. Shame and shaming motivate retreat and hiding, but pride wants to be seen. The speakers in Psalms 69 and 71 draw on the muddy pit image to depict helplessness and the downward motion of shame and humiliation. They do not seek the depths as a means of escape or hiding. Both speakers resist the efforts of others to shame them as they ask YHWH for vindication against their enemies. Indeed, the speaker of Psalm 71 asks YHWH to shame his enemies (71:13). The brief psalm between Psalm 69 and 71 consists almost entirely of a prayer that YHWH may shame the enemies of the speaker (Ps 70:3–4) with language identical to Psalm 40:15–16.

Shame is extremely dangerous. Biblical writers treat shame as a matter of life and death. Psalm 119:16 presents living and not being put to shame as parallel requests. Psalm 31:18 asks that the wicked be put to shame and descend into Sheol. Shame appears frequently in the psalms either as a fate to be avoided or something to be imposed on the wicked. Many psalms present shame as more than just another element of suffering but a focal point of pain (e.g., Pss 22:7–9; 25:2–3, 20b; 35:4, 26; 40:15–16; 42:11; 44:8b, 10, 14–17; 71:1, 13, 24; 89:42, 46, 51–52; 129:5; 132:8). Shame makes life not worth living anymore.[48] The power and pain of shame can operate independently of whether the target feels ashamed. People may experience dramatic consequences from widespread attacks on their character and reputation. The social death imposed by shaming can lead to serious harm, including loss of livelihood, relationships, and health.[49] Others seek to shame the speakers of Psalms 69 and 71 and thereby threaten their well-being and social existence. They panic as gravity draws the speakers down into the pit of shame, whether they feel subjectively ashamed or not.

The downward thrust of shame appears in some texts that present the shamed person as trampled underfoot into the dust or mud. Isaiah 25:10–12 presents the devastation of Moab through a personification of the nation as one individual. Moab will be trampled like straw in mud, submerged in the muck, spreading his arms and struggling to keep his head above the mire. The text explicitly connects this image to Moab's pride brought low: "his highness will be lowered" (25:11) where the term for *highness* can be rendered as *pride*, and *lowered* as *humiliated*.[50] The passage concludes by depicting YHWH razing the high-walled fortress and "bringing it low, leveling it to the ground, to the very dust" (Isa 25:12). The passage describes the fall of the pride of Moab in ways that resemble the shaming experience of the psalmists with its threat of drowning to represent the dangers of shame. The natural elements of straw, mire, ground, and dust depict the humiliation of Moab's pride. Some passages use downward motion to the ground to indicate shame without reference to drowning. The descent into Sheol illustrates the shame of the king of Babylon in Isaiah 14. Daughter Babylon also experiences a fall from pride into shame associated with downward movement. Isaiah 47:1 calls on her to "come down, sit in the dust, sit on the ground, dethroned." Her loss of status leaves her naked and ashamed (47:2), sitting in the dust.

Hebrew writers profile humiliation with trampling into mud. Isaiah presents Assyria as an instrument of YHWH's punishment of Israel and commands Assyria: "trample them like the mud of the street" (Isa 10:6). Cyrus "shall trample the rulers down like mud, like a potter treading clay" (Isa 41:25). Psalm 7:6 explicitly connects this image to shame or dishonor when the speaker says that if he is guilty of mistreating others, then "let my enemy pursue and overtake my soul, trample my life to the ground, and lay my honor in the dust." The term for *honor* can profile the glory of God or the reputation and honor of people (Gen 45:15; 1 Sam 2:8; Prov 15:33; Isa 62:2), sometimes associated with wealth (Gen 31:1; 1 Kgs 3:13; Isa 61:6). The psalmist invites disgrace upon himself if he is guilty.[51] He stakes his honor on his innocence, welcoming shame if he is guilty. Micah looks forward to when his enemy city is covered in shame, employing a clothing metaphor (Mic 7:10).[52] Her shame manifests as downward movement: "My eyes shall see her downfall. Now she will be trampled underfoot like mud in the streets" (Mic 7:10). The description of military defeat in Psalm 44:10–17 draws heavily on shame vocabulary. The speaker provides a vivid concluding image of the people's shame involving the natural world: "For our soul has melted into the dust, and our belly clings to the earth" (Ps 44:26). Zophar speaks of the wicked man whose pride goes up to heaven and his head to the clouds (Job 20:6), "yet he perishes forever like dung he uses for fuel." (20:7) His bones lie in the dust (20:11). Zophar elicits disgust in connection with shame in his mention of dung. He speaks of a man's pride going up to heaven only to end up as bones in the dust, evoking the up-down movement of pride and shame described in Isaiah 14.

The vertical contrast of pride and shame structures Isaiah 2. The elevation of Zion imagined in 2:1–4 represents its superiority and centrality as a place to which the nations come to receive the law of YHWH. The increased height of the mountain represents its elevated status in the world and manifests the power of YHWH. The remainder of the chapter develops the contrast of high and low. Isaiah 2:5 opens a new section that focuses on the sins of Israel and the punishment of YHWH. The passage indicts Israel for various sins, such as divination, foreign alliances, idolatry, and self-reliance reflected in wealth and military power. The text introduces their punishment on the Day of YHWH: "all shall be abased and each one brought low" (v. 9). People enter into the crevices and hide in the dust and caves (2:10, 19, 20) to escape YHWH's wrath and punishment. All that is proud and arrogant will be lowered so that only YHWH will be exalted (2:11–12). Creation serves to mark out the high and low places. The dust, crevices, and holes in the earth mark the low places that the people will seek out on that day. YHWH will have a day "against all the cedars of Lebanon and against all the oaks of Bashan, against all the lofty mountains and all the high hills against every lofty tower and every fortified wall, against all the ships of Tarshish and all stately vessels." (Isa 2:13–16) The targets of YHWH include natural and artificial objects that represent pride. The cedars of Lebanon and oaks of Bashan acquire their height partly through the trees themselves and partly through the mountains on which they grow. Both Lebanon and Bashan are heights. These trees serve as emblems of pride. The adjectives *lofty* and *high* emphasize the height of the hills and mountains. The trees, mountains, and hills all share a vertical structure. The majestic trees and mountains must be reduced because they impinge on YHWH's unique power. Towers and fortification walls also have "heads" (tops) that intentionally tower above humans to overawe them and discourage attack. YHWH will level them. The ships of Tarshish and stately ships tower above the waves with their masts.[53] They represent the capacity of humans to engineer transportation across the sea in vessels that appear stately and graceful. On this day of YHWH, people will realize that their idols are worthless and cast them to the moles and bats that dwell in holes and caves, perhaps the same subterranean hideouts the humans seek as they are overawed by YHWH. Moles and bats may evoke disgust but appear here for their subterranean dwellings.[54] The whole passage, with its multiplication of words and images for up and down, concludes with a summary of its meaning: "As for you, stop worrying about mortals, in whose nostrils is but a breath; for of what worth are they?" (Isa 2:22) The rhetorical question assumes that humans have no basis for pride. The text draws attention to the basic animality of humans who breathe through their noses like animals.[55] Other passages associate human breath with the divine gift of life (Gen 2:7; 7:22; Job 33:4) and with understanding (Job 32:8).[56] The present context presents humans as low and without divine understanding. Breath here has a more negative salience, emphasizing that humans have no special value that they should pride themselves in their ships, fortified cities, or lumber from the mountains of Lebanon. The breath of humans draws attention to their fragility and creatureliness. An element of disgust enters into the presentation of human breathing as animal-like rather than distinctively human or associated with the divine. Isaiah 2 emphasizes more the shame and humiliation people will experience on the day of YHWH, while Isaiah 13 focuses more on fear. Humans experience fear and shame in the presence of this divine manifestation (2:19).[57]

The sun and moon will be abased like the mountains and trees. Isaiah 24–27 universalizes the proceeding oracles against the nations (Isaiah 13–23). The whole world suffers YHWH's punishment on that day (24:21; 2:11, 17). The passage collapses distinctions between humans and their environment. The earth suffers in 24:19–20, the inhabitants of heaven and earth in 24:21–22, and the sun and moon in 24:23. All creation appears humiliated in the presence of YHWH. The earth, construed as a drunkard, will fall and not rise. The heavenly host and human kings will be gathered into a pit. The lowering of these entities corresponds to their shame and parallels the shame vocabulary used to describe the sun and moon. The sun and moon experience shame as YHWH's reign from Mount Zion shines forth. On the day of YHWH, "the moon will blush and the sun be ashamed, for YHWH of hosts will reign on Mount Zion and in Jerusalem, glorious in the sight of the elders" (24:23). The sun normally precedes the moon in lines of poetry, except when the text uses these unusual words for the moon and sun (Isa 30:26; Song 6:10). The speaker profiles the moon with a term used for the full moon specifically that means "white one."[58] The term for the sun profiles the light or heat of the sun (Ps 19:7).[59] Song of Songs 6:10 uses both terms in the poetic comparison of the beauty of the woman to the beauty of moon (the white one) and sun (the hot one).[60] Both terms reappear also in Isaiah 30:26. The use of a term for whiteness seems an appropriate way to profile the moon in the expression "the moon will blush."[61] The construction captures the whiteness of the full moon becoming dimmed. The full moon is radiant and glorious, and a suitable comparison to a woman's beauty, but this celestial luminary will suffer shame manifested as reduced light. Similarly, the sun, the hot/bright one, will be ashamed. The language construes the darkening of the luminaries as a consequence of shame. The shame of the sun and moon reflects YHWH's punishment of the hosts of heaven and earth. The celestial lights suffer YHWH's wrath, manifesting the punishment of the heavenly host.

## Conclusion

Creation shaped how Hebrews conceptualized pride and shame. Gravity pulls things down to earth, or below the surface of the earth if there is no foothold (Ps 69:3). Hebrew maps emotion onto this vertical dimension. Pride is high and up, and shame is down. Upward motion represents striving for pride and power, and downward movement reflects loss of power and status that may or may not include feeling ashamed. Creation can represent these emotions through association with height or depth. The natural world thereby becomes more than an inert setting for events. Elements of the natural world profile emotions thematic to the text. Isaiah 14 does not say that the king of Babylon is shamed because his downward motions communicate it more vividly. The author uses creation to show emotion rather than tell about it. The psalmist speaks of the shaming that his enemies direct at him, as a threat to life analogous to drowning. Even though he is not ashamed of his zeal for God's house, he suffers from the taunts of others and the social isolation and enmity they create (69:8–13). Creation can communicate the emotions of humans but also experiences emotion itself. Tall trees and mountains will be made low, and the sun and moon will be ashamed. The vertical mapping of emotion involves image schema developed from experiences of the physical environment. Creation embeds deeply in the mind, shaping how we think about how we feel.

# 5

## JOY AND AWE

POSITIVE EMOTIONS GIVE rise to cooperation. Survival involves taking advantage of opportunities and resources as well as avoiding dangers.[1] Positive emotions like joy and awe have two main adaptive benefits. First, they encourage cooperative behaviors, creative thinking, problem-solving, meaning-making, and resilience.[2] Positive emotions broaden the scope of attention and shape an approach to the environment that aids survival and adaptation beyond immediate rewards. Most positive emotions build community by engendering a sense of safety and trust that facilitates cooperation. Psalm 122, for example, begins with individual joy that quickly becomes communal joy expressing love for Jerusalem. Second, positive emotions can have a calming or "undoing" function by reducing sympathetic nervous system arousal (i.e., elevated heart rate and respiration, etc.) associated with negative emotions like fear. The person can rest and restore energy for future challenges.[3] Isaiah 40, for example, begins with language designed to elicit joy and pull the audience out of sorrow and despair. In this way, positive emotions build recovery and resilience.[4]

## Isaiah 55

Isaiah 40–55 seeks to undo negative emotions deriving from the destruction of Jerusalem and the exile by inducing joy. Isaiah 55 concludes and recapitulates this section of the book by blending YHWH's word with precipitation. Like YHWH's word "from the heavens the rain and snow come down and do not return there till they have watered the earth making it fertile and fruitful, giving seed to the one who sows and bread to the one who eats." (Isa 55:10) YHWH's word elsewhere resembles rain and dew (Deut 31:2). The water images infuse YHWH's word with joy at the power of water to make land fertile. Like precipitation, YHWH's word comes from heaven and creates an effect on earth that benefits people. The Israelites had a rudimentary understanding of the water cycle.[5] The rain-word blend has positive implications. It involves a gentle fructifying rain, not a violent storm or flood. The diaspora audience lives in a world shaped by a previous word from YHWH that obliterated their nation and left them desolate. Now, YHWH has a new word that calls for new songs (Isa 42:9–10). The new word falls on the desolate audience like rain on arid ground. The transformation of the community corresponds to a transformation of the environment. Because of literal rain, the cypress and myrtle trees will replace the thornbushes and nettles (Isa 55:13). Israel will be restored to its land and Zion will be reconstructed. YHWH's word comes to fruition like the rain. The rain does not return to heaven until it has accomplished its purpose. This purpose may take time. Rainfall can cause grasses to spring up quickly, but it takes time for trees to grow and arid land to be transformed. Farmers must cooperate in the project of making land arable. The blend accentuates the power of YHWH's word and the need for humans to accept and cooperate in YHWH's plan. This section of Isaiah repeatedly evokes joy and awe to reverse negative emotions and motivate the audience to open themselves to a new future. Isaiah 1–39 often describes drought and desiccation as a result of divine punishment. Isaiah 40–55 reverses arid wilderness back to arable land, drawing on water to elicit joy.

Restoration texts in Isaiah use water and its effects to evoke joy. Hebrew and English have multiple expressions that profile various aspects of joy. First, joyful experiences may be exciting, intense, and involving high energy or they may be serene, calm, and involving a sense of harmony and unity. Biblical literature includes descriptions of excited joy (Exod 15:10) and serene domestic scenes (Psalm 133). Second, joy may be individual or affiliative depending on whether a person experiences it individually or a group experiences it collectively.[6] Biblical texts express joy in thanksgiving psalms, both individual (Pss 30; 40) and communal (Pss 67; 124). Third, joy may be anticipatory or consummatory. Anticipatory joy emerges when the fulfillment of desire seems near and consummatory when the desire or goal is realized. Thanksgiving psalms express experiences of consummatory joy. Prophetic texts describe the consummatory joy of people in the future in order to evoke anticipatory joy in the present audience. The three dimensions of joy (excited/serene, individual/community, anticipatory/consummatory) orient one to the descriptions of joy in biblical texts.[7]

Water can elicit joy, calm, and creativity, or fear and stress. The many meanings of water can be seen in its use as a source domain in a wide variety of blends. Within Isaiah, water can represent life and life-giving abundance (12:3; 32:2; 48:18; 55:10; 58:11), danger (4:6; 17:12–13; 25:4; 32:2; 57:20), or enemy attack and divine judgment (8:7; 28:2, 17; 30:28, 30). Water affords joy when it represents life or the prospect of fruitful fields. The arid environment of Israel motivated a significant cultural concern with arid and watered landscapes.[8] The prophetic motif of drying vegetation recruits the emotional impacts of drought to elicit grief. The blooming desert motif reverses the drying motif. It reverses grief with joy. Isaiah 28–35 includes four restoration texts that parallel the reconstruction of Israel with the repair of creation (29:17–21; 30:18–26; 32:9–20; 35:1–10).[9] These passages share a vision of coming peace and joy and the absence of pain and sorrow.

The vision of redemption in the first restoration text in Isaiah 29:17–24 begins with ecological transformation. Lebanon, known for its forest, will become farmland, and farmland will be regarded as scrubland. The dark forests of Lebanon could be construed as places to avoid and useless for growing food.[10] It will become arable land, and the scrubland, that is widespread in the arid environs of Israel, will become suitable for farming.[11] This ecological transformation parallels changes in the human domain. YHWH heals people, restores justice (29:19), and ends shame (29:22).[12] The second restoration text in Isaiah 30:18–26 announces the restoration of Zion. The people who wait for YHWH will be happy (30:18).[13] The people will dispose of their idols and listen to the word of YHWH. YHWH will send rain for the sown seed, and the land will produce ample food for livestock and humans (30:23–24). Streams will flow from every hill (30:25), and the light of the moon will be like the sun, and the sun will be seven times brighter. The darkness or brightness of the heavenly luminaries offers a barometer of emotion and justice. The passage depicts a joyful development, and the text communicates joy directly through the specific images of light, water, fertility, and justice without any emotion words. The contrast with prior (i.e., present) misery, manifested as weeping (30:19), adversity, affliction (30:20), and injuries (30:26), heightens the anticipatory joy by contrast. The third restoration text in Isaiah 32:9–20 uses vocabulary for confidence and peace, painting a picture of comfort and safety inducing a quiet joy. The wilderness will become a fruitful farm and the farmland as common as thickets (32:15; cf. 29:17). Justice will dwell in these renewed lands and produce peace, calm, and safety forever (32:17–18).[14] These serene images recur in the description of the people living in peaceful country, within secure dwellings and restful places (32:18). They will be happy (32:20) sowing crops by streams with their livestock wandering freely. This idyllic picture engenders a future calm joy. The transformation of nature is closely connected to justice and human happiness. The fourth text (Isaiah 35) describes the restoration of Israel and its natural environment by means of water transforming the Arabah into fertile land. The Arabah likely profiles a large arid region encompassing the Great Rift Valley from Galilee to the Dead Sea ("the sea of Arabah" in Deut 4:49; Josh 3:16; 12:3; 2 Kgs 14:25) and beyond to the Gulf of Aqaba.[15] The passage envisions an ecological transformation of this large arid region, encompassing substantial parts of Israel and Judah. This arid landscape will become like Lebanon, Carmel, and Sharon, each exceptionally fruitful farmlands with more rainfall than Judah. The blooming desert induces joy in humans, and the flowers express the joy of the land itself. The Arabah will bloom like the crocus.[16] The transformation of the desert accompanies transformations in the human realm where the blind will see, the deaf hear, the lame leap, and the mute sing for joy. In keeping with these descriptions of exuberantly joyful activities, the water will "burst forth" (35:6) in the wilderness, indicating the suddenness of the transformation.[17] The passage includes multiple terms for joy, focused especially on energetic joy.[18] The purpose of this joy appears explicitly stated in 35:3–4: to "strengthen hands that are feeble" and give courage to the fearful.

The second major section of Isaiah also includes several images of the restoration of Israel, which is the main topic of chapters 40–55. Some of these visions of a bright future involve the motif of the blooming desert (41:17–20; 43:18–20; 44:2–4; 48:17–21). First, the focus of Isaiah 41:17–20 is YHWH's care for the poor and needy. They are thirsty, so YHWH will bring water to the wilderness. A variety of tree species will thrive in the watered land. The passage has an emotional and attention-grabbing quality but eschews emotional vocabulary in favor of verbs of knowing ("that all may see, and know, observe, and understand that the hand of YHWH has done this" in v. 20). This knowledge of YHWH's action engenders joy and gratitude. Second, the newness of God's (re-)creation appears explicitly in 43:18–20 where a new thing "springs forth," using a verb also used of plants that sprout. Wild animals will honor YHWH for making a river in the desert. Third, in Isaiah 44:2–4, the water in the arid land produces plants that blend with the restoration of Israel. As YHWH "pours out" waters on the dry land, it produces plants. The text blends the plants with people, and YHWH "pours out" the spirit on the Israelites' descendants. The language construes these descendants as seeds who sprout like trees adjacent to streams.[19] The arid land made fertile can now support a large population, and Jacob's seed will sprout. The text blends descendants with trees, which are more substantive and durable than the grass and flowers that blend with humans when the frailty and brevity of human life is in view. This text focuses on the power of positive emotion to alleviate fear (44:2). The new thing that will sprout in the transformed desert should move the audience beyond past terror and present fear so that they may broaden their perspective of future possibilities and build for the future accordingly. Fourth, in Isa 48:17–21, the speaker presents the imminent return from exile as a second exodus.[20] This passage focuses specifically on YHWH's provision of water from rock in a dry land. The returning exiles must cross a great distance where water is scarce, but YHWH will provide for them. The past experience of water from the rock (Exod 17:6; Num 20:11) should encourage present confidence in God's guidance, fostering positive emotions that reverse prior misery, prepare for a brighter future, and enhance cooperation and trust. Their peace will be like a river, their vindication like the unceasing waves of the sea, and their descendants like the sand of the sea. These nature blends present the perpetual happiness of a large population.

Isaiah 55:10–13 recapitulates these restoration texts in Isaiah 28–35 and 40–55 and their use of water to evoke joy. Like the prior restoration texts, Isaiah 55:10–13 includes water, fertility, joy, and landscape transformation. The Israelites preferred well-watered landscapes to the dry desert areas of the wilderness and lived in some anxiety about the prospect of drought.[21] Isaiah 55:10 highlights the effect of precipitation on humans. Water makes the land fruitful so that the sower has seed and the eater has food. The watered land provides fruit for harvest, which affords an opportunity for joyful celebration (Isa 9:2; 16:9–10).

The people do not celebrate their restoration alone. The reestablishment of their social community coincides with a restoration of the ecology, and creation itself rejoices with them. Nature sings joyfully (42:11; 44:23; 49:13; 52:12) and the trees clap their hands (55:12).[22] Outside chapters 40–55, these emotion terms appear with nature only in 14:8 and 35:2.[23] This section of Isaiah, then, shows an unusually high frequency of personified nature involving high-energy joyous emotion. Three passages in Isaiah 40–55 that construe the natural world as rejoicing (44:23; 49:13; 55:12–23) contribute to a larger pattern of personified nature (42:10–12; 44:27; 45:8; 51:3; 52:9). Isaiah 55:12 concludes this section of the book and recapitulates the joy of creation:

> *Yes, in joy you shall go forth,*
> *in peace you shall be brought home;*
> *mountains and hills shall break out in song before you,*
> *all trees of the field shall clap their hands.*

These passages address nature as a human-like audience. It construes these elements of nature as singing and clapping hands. The earth, mountains, hills, forest, and trees are all called to rejoice in solidarity with Israel over YHWH's restoration of the community. Outside these contexts of joy, additional personification appears for these same parts of nature (e.g., heaven and earth in 1:2; wilderness in 35:1), as well as the sea (23:4), Sheol (14:9; 26:19; 28:15), and the sun and moon (24:23). Judeans personified larger cosmic structures (heaven, earth, sea, Sheol), massive geographic features (large land areas, mountains, hills), and trees.[24]

The image of trees clapping their hands appears particularly striking.[25] The Isaiah text employs personification, using the knowledge domain most familiar to us (ourselves) to help make something else more accessible and understandable.[26] The plant-people blend occurs within an Israelite culture that understood creation as an integrated whole encompassing the natural and social order.[27] Human violations of the social order cause ecological catastrophes (Isa 24:1–6, 18–23; Jer 4:22–28; Hos 4:1–3). Conversely, YHWH as creator can reestablish the proper order of creation, understood as nature *and* culture (Ps 85:11–13; Hos 2:23–25). The author of Isaiah

55:12 composed the text within this conceptualization of creation. The text assumes that humans and the natural world are bound up together in a singular order of divine creation and that trees may share in human joy or dry out in response to human sin. In other words, the trees in Isaiah 55:12 rejoice because there is no separation between the idea of trees flourishing and bearing fruit and the idea of trees enjoying this fruitfulness due to God's restoration of Israel. In a worldview that connects human conduct and the drying and wetting of land, a tree is healthy and fruitful because the people surrounding it construct a just social order. Correspondingly, this just society enjoys peace and prosperity through the fertility of the tree and the wider ecology. If the people become arrogant and abusive, then the land will dry up, the tree will wither, and the community will grieve. The restoration texts maintain a close connection between ecological and social transformation.

Isaiah 55:8–13 uses creation to evoke joy by focusing on water, fertility, harvest, and the rejoicing of nature. Each of these four topics separately elicits joy, and this concluding passage recapitulates these themes.[28] The speaker seeks to reverse negative emotions and encourage people to change their ways, trusting in YHWH's forgiveness and power to restore the broken community. The passage inspires awe in order to disrupt the conventional thinking of the audience and open them to new possibilities. Awe involves vastness and the need for accommodation. "Vastness refers to anything that is experienced as being much larger than the self, or the self's ordinary level of experience or frame of reference."[29] Vastness may involve physical size, power, or complexity. YHWH's plans in Isaiah 55:9–11 encompass enormous scope, irresistible power, and unfathomable complexity. They are as high above human plans as the heavens are high above the earth. Vastness elicits a need for accommodation or a way of assimilating the experience of vastness into knowledge structures. The sense of vastness overwhelms typical means of making sense of experience.[30] The experience of awe consequently reduces the sense of self and leads to greater orientation to transcendent realities.[31] The speech of YHWH presents human plans as low and unworthy compared to YHWH's plans. The audience may embrace YHWH's plans if they can be overawed and opened up to radical new possibilities (Isa 42:9; 43:19; 48:6). Creation provides a common trigger for awe.[32] Sweeping views of natural scenery provide the prototypical awe scenario because so many awe experiences involve creation.[33] Awe may have originated as a response to nature that later became generalized to the social order where pomp and power likewise inspire awe.[34] Biblical writers seek to elicit awe in order to challenge accepted ways of thinking and redirect attention to transcendent realities or novel ways of perceiving and evaluating familiar things.[35] Awe emerges in biblical passages involving the vastness of creation and the creator.[36]

Isaiah 55:9 makes the audience feel small by construing YHWH's plans as high above human plans, like heaven is high above the earth. The blend of YHWH's word and precipitation presents YHWH's plans as completely reliable and desirable. Human plans often fail, but YHWH's plans never do. Humans plan wickedness and harm (Gen 6:5; Isa 59:7; 65:2; Jer 4:14; 6:19; Prov 6:18), but YHWH plans redemption and justice (Isa 55:7). The contrast between the grand and powerful plans of YHWH and the modest and fragile plans of mortals (Ps 94:7; Prov 19:21) instills awe. Other passages in Isaiah 40–55 use the vastness of creation and the power of the creator to elicit awe as part of the larger goal of comforting the people and opening their minds to a new future. Isaiah 42:5 describes YHWH as the one "who created the heavens and stretched them out, who spread out the earth and its produce, who gives breath to its people and spirit to those who walk on it." This evocation of awe at YHWH as creator introduces YHWH's speech that describes the divine plan to redeem Israel and opens the audience to "the new things I now declare" (42:9). YHWH's creative power (Isa 44:24) instills confidence that YHWH can rebuild Jerusalem and Judah (44:26). YHWH overawes opposition to the divine plan by invoking YHWH's power as creator (45:9–12) in a passage that includes language of YHWH's uniqueness.[37] YHWH points to creation (51:13, 16) to instill awe in the audience of humans in order to encourage them to stop being afraid (51:13) and trust in YHWH's plan. These and other awe-inspiring references to creation build on the beginning of Isaiah 40–55, which opens with a call to comfort the people followed by concentrated efforts to create a sense of vastness in the audience. Isaiah 40:12–14 closely resembles Job 38 with its rhetorical questions that point to YHWH as the creator of an ordered and awesome cosmos:

*Who has measured with his palm the waters,*
*marked off the heavens with a span,*
*held in his fingers the dust of the earth,*
*weighed the mountains in scales,*
*and the hills in a balance?*

*Who has directed the spirit of YHWH,*
*or instructed him as his counselor?*

*Whom did he consult to gain knowledge?*
*Who taught him the path of judgment,*
*or showed him the way of understanding?*

The questions place the hearer in the familiar position of measuring and building a human-scale structure or weighing items in a scale but presents YHWH in these familiar situations with impossibly large objects. The text construes mountains, that seem enormous to humans, as small items in the hands of YHWH. The mountain provides a point of comparison that establishes the enormity of YHWH compared to humans. Subsequent questions draw attention to the fact that YHWH has no counselor and has learned from no one. The prophet plainly states what the audience should understand from these questions: "before him all the nations are as naught, as nothing and void he counts them." (40:17) The great nations that have afflicted Israel with exile may seem extraordinarily powerful. Their awe-inspiring power makes their idols seem worth worshipping. This appearance is deceitful. In reality, YHWH sits enthroned above the vault of the earth, looking down on its inhabitants like grasshoppers (cf. Num 13:33). Idols fail (Isa 46:5–7), and YHWH brings the mighty kings to nothing (Isa 40:24). Nothingness is hard to comprehend. The human-plant blend quickly offers a more accessible image: they flourish for a moment like plants before YHWH wilts them and the wind carries them away like straw (40:24). The statements that follow the rhetorical questions clarify their meaning and purpose. The prophet confronts the audience with their own smallness in comparison to the vastness of creation and the still greater vastness of YHWH in order to evoke awe. Awe helps accomplish the comfort promised at the start of the chapter.

# Transcendent Creator
## *Job 38–41*

The speeches of God at the end of Job draw heavily on creation to elicit awe. The speeches respond to Job.[38] As a traumatized and embittered man, Job needs comfort and healing, but his friends blame him for his suffering. He devalues creation (Job 3) and God's governance of the cosmos due to his inward focus on his misery.[39] YHWH captures Job's attention through the storm and directs his mind to consider the created world in its mysteriously majestic structure. YHWH reminds Job that YHWH maintains order in creation. YHWH seeks to inspire awe in Job in order to overcome his suffering and consequent exaggeration of negative aspects of the world.[40] In this respect, the speeches of YHWH in Job resemble the divine speeches in Isaiah 40–55. In both, YHWH seeks to comfort the afflicted by inspiring awe through creation. The beginning of YHWH's speech in Job 38 sets the tone for the whole discourse:

> *Then YHWH answered Job out of the storm and said:*
> *Who is this who darkens counsel with words of ignorance?*
> *Gird up your loins now like a man!*
> *I will question you and you tell me the answers!*
> *Where were you when I founded the earth?*
> *Tell me if you have understanding.*
> *Who determined its size? Surely you know!*
> *Who stretched out the measuring line for it?*
> *Into what were its pedestals sunk,*
> *and who laid its cornerstone,*
> *While the morning stars sang together*
> *and all the sons of God shouted for joy?*

A storm accompanies the appearance of YHWH (as in Zech 9:14; Ezek 1:4).[41] Job assumes that even if he could achieve his wish of meeting God (13:3; 23:4; 31:35), God would overwhelm him with a storm, multiply his wounds, and fill him with grief (9:17–18). The actual confrontation with God unfolds differently from his expectation. God, here called YHWH, *answers* Job.[42] When people seek an *answer* from YHWH, they are innocent, in need, or under attack, and they expect that God's answer will be vindication or rescue. The narrative frame clarifies Job's innocence, so YHWH's answer may be expected to deliver Job.[43] YHWH's opening question "Who is this?" (38:2) is not dismissive or hostile. The question *who* with demonstrative *this* "is not used to seek information, but to express awe at someone already known."[44] YHWH knows who Job is, just as the Psalmist knows who YHWH is when asking "Who is this king of Glory?" (Ps 24:8; cf. Isa 63:1; Jer 47:5; 49:19; 50:44).[45] YHWH appears to stand in awe of his favorite servant whom YHWH singled out for special attention in Job 1:8: "Have you noticed my servant Job? There is no one on earth like him." The question draws attention to Job. YHWH does not condemn Job but addresses him as the dignified man that Job understands himself to be (3:3, 23) and invites him to gird his loins.[46] This imperative verb is softened with a Hebrew particle rendered as *now*.[47] Job must gird his loins, or pay full attention. The introduction to YHWH's speech indicates a care and concern for Job evident in the remainder of the discourse.

YHWH's speech takes the form of rhetorical questions. Not all questions seek information. Exclamatory questions like "Why did I not die at birth?" (3:11) express anger, grief, and protest. Rhetorical questions seek to transform. YHWH's rhetorical questions consist of queries that Job can answer and some that he cannot answer.[48] Job knows he was not present when YHWH founded the earth, although he does not know where he was. Most of the questions are easy to answer because Job need only acknowledge that he has not walked on the bottom of the sea (38:16) or that YHWH is the one who has laid out a channel for the thunderstorm (38:25). YHWH sometimes breaks the question form to draw attention to Job's knowledge. These breaks cluster around mentions of the earth (38:4, 5, 18, 21) that draw a comparison between the vastness of the earth and the smallness of Job. The questions do not humiliate Job any more than the similar questions in Isaiah 40:12–14; 41:2–4, 26 humiliate the Israelite audience. The questions remind the audience of their human limitations and creatureliness. The questions and the accompanying statements draw the contrast between the grandeur of the universe and the smallness of humans.

The questions elicit awe. The questions focus on Job, who appears repeatedly in the second-person verbs and pronouns that pepper chapters

38–42. If formulated as statements, the questions of YHWH would read like a hymn of self-praise, potentially selfish and boastful.[49] As questions, however, they focus on Job and call his attention to the majestic order of creation. This move by YHWH serves as a response to Job's speech in chapter 3 and thereby to the larger problem of Job's suffering. In chapter 3, Job wishes to undo creation because it is so chaotic it does not deserve to exist.[50] YHWH leads Job to see creation differently. The questions emphasize the order of creation and point to the creator. The question is not "What are the dimensions of the earth?" but "Who measured the earth?" Job cannot answer the first but can answer the second. The first question leads nowhere, but the second leads to YHWH as the answer.[51] These rhetorical questions draw Job's attention away from his fixation on his own pain and directs it toward awe-inspiring aspects of creation. Awe and other positive emotions aid in reversing trauma and grief and establishing new life.[52] Awe disrupts prior knowledge and leads to curiosity and new meaning-making, which aids recovery.[53] Job's trauma and grief derive from the painful contrast between his former worldview and his experience of innocent suffering. His friends repeat the view that creation is ethically ordered and blame Job for his suffering. Job makes sense of innocent suffering by understanding creation and the creator in extremely negative ways. The chaotic and evil world does not deserve to exist (Job 3).[54] YHWH seeks to shatter Job's negative constructions and lead him toward a new appraisal of the cosmos. Creation is not all chaos or all order but a dynamic mix beyond his understanding. Awe can lead Job to a new appreciation of creation and his place within it. Awe, joy, and gratitude build resilience and open suffering people to future hope.[55] YHWH's questions seek to induce awe to make Job feel small and shatter his worldview so that he can endure and overcome his suffering.

Job's lament in chapter 3 makes repeated references to birth that reflect his desire to have never lived. He laments that knees received him and breasts nursed him (3:12). YHWH makes considerable use of procreation imagery to draw attention to YHWH's parent-like care for creation. Job's desire to have died at birth rejects the gift of life and despises the love of his mother. Job's lament expands from his personal misery to a condemnation of all creation and therefore the Creator (3:20–23). Job misreads reality through the lens of his pain. The cosmos has strict limits on chaos, and YHWH shows constant care for creation. Divine love infuses the order of creation. It is not the cruel or indifferent chaos that Job imagines.

YHWH elaborates on the opening question about the earth (Job 38:4–7). The details point toward awe as a goal of the rhetorical questions. The first question draws attention to Job's absence from the dawn of creation (Job 38:4). Three of the next four questions draw attention to YHWH as the one who did the work of creating the earth and sinking foundations into the void (38:5–6). The questions include specifics that point to the enormous size of the earth, a size determined by YHWH who has the power to build something so vast. The immensity of the earth provides a spatial reference that makes Job small, just as the moment of creation provides a temporal reference that makes him small. The last question adds the information that the morning stars sang and the gods shouted for joy as the earth was founded.[56] These superhuman entities respond with joy to the wonder and magnificence of YHWH's creation, which implies that Job needs to reorient his own perspective.

The next section turns to the sea, presented at the moment of its birth (Job 38:8–12). Job speaks of the sea in ways that allude to the myth of YHWH's conflict with watery chaos in Job 7:12; 9:8; 26:12. In YHWH's questions, however, the sea appears as an infant whom God delivers as midwife and wraps in swaddling clothes of clouds and thick darkness. YHWH sets limits for the sea as a parent sets limits for a child. There is no great conflict or battle, only YHWH both restraining and sustaining the child-like sea.[57] Human imagination presents the sea as vast, chaotic, and dangerous, yet it is small like an infant in comparison to YHWH. The step-wise comparison instills a sense of vastness by showing the relative sizes of Job, the sea, and YHWH. The birth image upends Job's existing knowledge about creation involving violence and chaos in favor of a more tender image.

The next section encompasses questions about the revolution of the sun from dawn to the netherworld (Job 38:12–21). The rising sun discourages the wicked who prefer to act in darkness (Job 24:15; Prov 7:9). YHWH asks if Job has ever grabbed hold of the ends of the earth and shaken the wicked from it. The embodied image invites Job to blend the vastness of the earth with a small board or table that he might hold and shake. The blend reduces the earth to human scale only to show the vast scale of YHWH. Job can extend his arms only a negligible distance relative to the expanse of the earth. Additional embodied images help Job see his smallness in comparison to the cosmos, and the smallness of the cosmos in comparison to YHWH. The dawn changes the earth like dye alters a garment or a seal impresses the clay (38:14). These everyday objects present the scale of YHWH relative to the earth. Walking on the bottom of the sea provides another embodied image that presents Job's limitation compared to YHWH (38:16). These images lead to the summarizing question, "Have you comprehended the breadth of the earth?" (38:18) The prior questions have led Job to become aware of how vast the earth must be and how small he is within it. The passage concludes with two expressions about the limitations of Job's knowledge (38:18b, 21), indicating that his growing experience of awe unravels his prior knowledge.

The questions about the physical cosmos conclude with attention to the constellations and weather (Job 38:22–38). The questions again point to parent–offspring imagery that imply YHWH's care for creation (38:28–29). YHWH brings rain on unpopulated wilderness and makes the desert bloom. YHWH can understand and control prodigious meteorological phenomena because YHWH is father of the rain and mother of the ice (38:28–29). Job sees precipitation as chaotic oscillation between destructive drought and devastating flood (Job 12:15). YHWH presents its power of fertility, gifted even to remote uninhabited wilderness (38:26–27). Moreover, the rainstorm and lightning have conduits and paths made by YHWH, indicating the ordered structure of creation (38:25). The jugs of heaven that pour the water that holds the earth together provides another image that uses a familiar everyday experience to present the enormity of YHWH (38:37–38). Job must imagine the analogue between jugs of water familiar to him on earth to those much larger jugs in heaven that YHWH can handle. The constellations of heaven have evoked wonder in many stargazers, and the vastness of the night sky makes people feel small. Psalm 19 evokes this wonder and awe of the luminaries to point to YHWH's glory and correlates the regular patterns of the heavens with the ordered law of YHWH. The ordinances of heaven (Job 38:33) guide earthly events in ways that Job cannot comprehend. He cannot make the stars move through the sky as the seasons change because he is small and powerless. YHWH questions Job to give him an experience of vastness that instills awe. Awe, in turn, can comfort Job as it comforts the audience of Isaiah 40–55.

The second half of the first divine speech (Job 38:39–39:30) brings Job's attention to the animals, especially wild animals. The opening questions bring the young of the lion and raven into focus to profile the parent–offspring relationship in these animals (38:39–41). The adult lioness and raven must seek food in order to feed their young. Job considers lions to be dangerous wild predators to be hunted down and killed. He sees himself as a lion hunted by God (19:16; cf. 16:9). YHWH, however, offers a different perspective on lions as vulnerable creatures that need to feed their young and implies that YHWH provides for them (cf. Ps 104). YHWH undermines Job's argument that YHWH is hunting him like a lion by indicating that YHWH hunts *for* lions.[58] Similarly, young ravens cry out (38:41) for food as Job cries out (19:7) for justice (19:7). Job did not believe that God would hear his cry, yet YHWH responds to Job as he responds to ravens.[59] The questions decenter Job from focusing on his own pain and letting that pain color his perceptions. The questions about the mountain goats and deer likewise focus on reproduction.[60] These wild creatures avoid humans who have no role or oversight of their procreation, yet they manage to thrive and grow up in wilderness areas without human help (39:4). The secrets of their survival are known to YHWH alone because the world is too vast and the mysteries of life too hidden for Job to grasp.

The contrast between wild and domestic animals emerges forcefully in the questions about the onager (wild donkey) and aurochs (wild ox). The first question imagines that the onager began in domestic servitude and became free.[61] The onager laughs at the noise of the city and knows no driver because it roams freely in the mountains (39:6–8). Its laughter highlights the joy the creature experiences in its freedom. Humans live in social contexts that they cannot fully escape much as they may long for the freedom enjoyed by desert creatures. YHWH draws on human yearning for freedom to present the awesome power of the onager that can thrive in arid regions far from human society.[62] The several rhetorical questions about using the aurochs as a domesticated animal assume that the great strength of this creature cannot be tamed and set to human purposes.[63] The auroch resists human servitude, but the text offers no hint of a violent confrontation of wills. Instead, YHWH asks if the aurochs would consent to serve Job (39:9).[64] As for Job, would he trust the aurochs to work for him (39:10–11)?[65] The awesome strength of the animal and its temperament keep it separated from domestic life.

The ostrich (39:13–18) lays eggs on the ground, cannot fly, but flaps its wings to turn and stop when running at speeds (45mph) that exceed a galloping horse (30mph).[66] Ostriches lay eggs in the sand to keep them warm and guard them, but ancient observers interpreted this behavior as carelessness. In yet another reference to parenthood, the ostrich is deemed cruel and lacking wisdom and understanding because of her poor parenting behavior. She has no fear and laughs at the horse and rider who hunt her. Her laughter signals joy in freedom from the normal cares of parenting and fear of predators. Her escape from the horse segues into questions about the only domesticated animal in the passage. The horse needs to be broken for domestic use and specially trained for use in war.[67] The passage focuses on the strength and courage of the cavalry horse. It laughs at fear. The text captures the fear and awe the warhorse inspires by highlighting its strength, thunderous snort, and capacity to inspire terror while feeling no fear, even in the thick of battle. This majestic animal rejoices in its power (39:21). The hawk and eagle have the power of flight and can see prey at extraordinary distances. As with the lion, raven, and ostrich, the questions include the young of the eagle who drink blood where the slain are found. This final animal image ends on a note of disgust at wondrous birds consuming blood. Job would be repelled and unwilling to feed the blood of corpses to birds, but YHWH's parental concern for animals extends to this service. YHWH's generous care includes bringing water to wasteland and blood to scavengers.

The series of creatures culminates in the speeches about Behemoth and Leviathan. YHWH continues questioning Job in a second speech (40:1–41:26). The speech begins by comparing Job directly to divinity ("Have you an arm like that of God's? Can you thunder with a voice like his?") to highlight his impotence. YHWH invites Job to "look at Behemoth, whom I made along with you" (40:15). This mythic monster represents cosmic evil and chaos. It resembles a hippopotamus, which is the most dangerous animal in the world.[68] The description emphasizes the size and strength of Behemoth, whom only YHWH can safely approach. The text devotes more space to Leviathan, the other mythic monster that resembles a crocodile. He cannot be tamed (40:25–29), and his description involves fire and smoke (41:11–13). He is well-armored and laughs at weapons that cannot hurt him (41:18–21) and fearlessly rules over all beasts (41:26). The speeches of YHWH culminate with the mythic monsters who can evoke awe that exceeds real-word animals. Like the onager, ostrich, and horse, Leviathan laughs at fear (41:21, cf. 39:7, 18, 22). Laughter appears repeatedly with these animals to signal their joy.

YHWH's questions point to the vastness of creation and the smallness of Job, or any human. Job cannot come to an easy accommodation with this experience of immensity. YHWH keeps piling on new questions and switching topics to maintain an unsettling sense of minuteness in Job. Even when Job can answer the rhetorical questions, the questions reveal how tiny and powerless he is compared to YHWH, the cosmos, and the animals that live in it. The experience of awe disrupts Job's concepts, specifically the highly negative view of creator and creation he has developed from his experience of suffering. Job's response to YHWH's speeches indicates that an experience of awe has changed his perspective on himself and moved him to repent of his prior devaluation of creation. Job's answer to YHWH's first speech perfectly captures the experience of awe: "Look, I am small. How can I answer you? I put my hand upon my mouth" (40:4).[69] Job does not say "I have sinned" as his friends would wish, or "I am wrong" as Elihu may wish, or even "I am terrified" as Job himself imagined he would be in this moment (9:34; 13:21).[70] Job expresses his surprise (Hebrew particle *look!*) and sense of insignificance in the face of YHWH's presentation of the majesty of creation. A sense of smallness aptly describes the experience of awe or the encounter with vastness.[71] Job expresses surprise and awe. His resolve not to speak further reflects the dissolution of his former knowledge structures. He has misunderstood the nature of the cosmos and of YHWH, informed too narrowly by his pain and prior knowledge. He mistakenly imagined that he could speak with authority due to his wisdom and experience, but his knowledge has crumbled in the face of his encounter with YHWH. He determines to be silent because he has no answer to YHWH in this state of awe-inspired dumbness.[72] Job's response to the first speech prepares the way for his retraction after YHWH's second speech. Job begins by acknowledging, "I know that you can do all things and that no purpose of yours can be hindered." (42:2) This acknowledgment resembles YHWH's claim in Isaiah 55:10 that YHWH's plans are as high above human plans as the heaven above the earth. YHWH's word returns to YHWH only after accomplishing its purpose.[73] Job recalls and quotes YHWH's opening question from 38:2 ("who is this who obscures counsel with ignorance?") and then answers "I have spoken but did not understand; things too wonderful for me, that I did not know" (42:3). Job acknowledges the awe he now feels toward things too wonderful (or too awesome) for him to understand.[74] His awe reduces his sense of self and shatters his conceptualizations. He admits that he does not know the things he previously thought he could speak about authoritatively (12:2; 13:1–2; 23:2–6). Job next quotes YHWH's prior address to Job from 38:3 ("Listen now and I will speak; I will question you and you will tell me the answers") and replies "By hearsay I had heard of you, but now my eye has seen you." Job had yearned to see YHWH in 19:25–27, and now his wish is fulfilled. His prior knowledge about God was grounded in hearsay and rational inferences from the nature of creation, but now he has had a direct encounter with YHWH. He concludes, "Therefore I retract and change my mind being but dust and ashes."[75] Job's reaction manifests his awe. He has a change of heart instigated by his encounter with YHWH. He does not repent of any sin (he has not sinned), but he senses his smallness, impotence, and ignorance and regrets that he confidently spoke about things too wonderful for him to understand. He may also say that he accepts the consolation that YHWH offers in the form of awe, and therefore ceases his mourning and lamenting to open himself to a new life and restoration.[76]

## Conclusion

Joy and awe drive out fear and grief. Experiences of trauma and loss leave people isolated in their pain and sadness, disconnected from others and from the shared beliefs that once held them in a community. Job's shattered faith in the justice of God shatters his relationship with his friends. The fault lies with the friends who defend God rather than comfort Job. Negative emotions following painful experience can lead to hopelessness. Job expresses how his pain leads to anger at the injustice of creation and the creator. Isaiah 40–55 addresses an audience of exiles whose particular feelings can only be inferred from the speaker. Like Job, they appear to be discouraged by past trauma and ongoing misery, without hope for a better future. Both books seek to elicit joy and awe to reverse the negative emotions and create an opening for hope and motivation to build a better future. Both books draw on creation to elicit these emotions. Isaiah depicts the transformation of creation parallel to the restoration of Israel, with particular focus on water in dry places. Job 38–42 depends on the vastness of creation and the power of wild animals and mythic monsters to evoke awe. Creation provides a fruitful source of awe and wonder.

# CONCLUSION

PLACES SHAPE EMOTION. Every reference to place in Scripture has some emotional resonance. Creation and emotion do not form two separable topics that partially overlap like a Venn diagram. Emotion permeates all creation. No discussion of creation can be complete without attention to its emotional resonances. Likewise, no discussion of emotion can be complete without attention to the environment in which the embodied organism experiences emotion and behaves accordingly. This book discusses only ten emotions and a limited selection of passages touching on various aspects of creation. Much more work may be done on each emotion and its relation to creation (or on creation and its emotional resonance).

Emotions do not come to us in pure form. The prior chapters do not analyze all the emotions that appear in a given passage because the complex results would obscure the view of each specific emotion. I have intended instead to offer insight into each individual emotion so that the reader may analyze any passage for these emotional elements. Even in the previous chapters, the passages do not neatly divide between the two emotions discussed. In chapter 1, Mother Zion emerges as a focal point of both love and grief. Grief can only grow where there is love. The grief that arises from drought reflects the love of place and hope of harvest threatened by desiccation. In chapter 2, the day of YHWH involves surprise and fear. Hebrew can profile both emotions with one word. Creation provides regular patterns that elicit surprise and terror when violated. The ordered patterns of nature contrast with human disorder and evoke surprise and amazement at human folly. In chapter 3, the divine vintner flies into a disgust-fueled rage at the vineyard. The sour grapes present a blocked goal that elicits anger, but also a disgusting result that enhances the rage. Physical and moral disgust blend in the vineyard parable and Exodus. Pharaoh finds the Hebrews disgusting. YHWH retaliates against Pharaoh for his disgust by sending disgusting plagues on Egypt. Moral disgust blends with anger. Biblical characters worry that they will suffer the angry violence of others whom they have disgusted by their treacherous behavior. Pride and shame pair and contrast like up and down in chapter 4. Pride carries the risk of humiliation (Prov 16:8). Shame can be an emotion but often appears in Psalms as an external sanction that others seek to impose on someone who refuses to feel ashamed. Even in these cases, the person experiencing shaming suffers emotional pain that feels like drowning. Shaming can be ruinous for those targeted by the community. Creation blends with pride and shame in Isaiah 14. The text represents the king's hubris through his upward striving to the highest places in creation. His punishment appears in his downward movement to the deepest reaches of Sheol. In chapter 5, awe appears with joy. Isaiah 40–55 uses creation to make the audience feel small and open them to the joy of Jerusalem's impending restoration. Several texts correlate water with joy overcoming the prior aridness of grief. Similarly, yhwh draws Job out of his pain and misery by using creation to trigger awe. yhwh's description of creation includes several mentions of joy. The stars rejoiced when yhwh laid the foundations of the earth (Job 38:7). The onager, ostrich, horse and Behemoth laugh, reflecting the joy they experience in being wondrously made and wild. Joy mixes with awe.

The above pairings of emotions oversimplify the reality of human experience as refracted through the texts. The emotions discussed above may be imagined as emotional building blocks. Emotional experiences are complex, but they can be analyzed into simpler components. The work of this book has been to elucidate some emotions that commonly appear in biblical texts. One can engage in more complex analysis armed with a working knowledge of these elements. For example, awe may evoke joy or fear. The day of yhwh uses creation to evoke surprise and fear, but awe also emerges in these passages. Isaiah 13 includes several elements that make the audience feel small. The assembling army is vast and comes from far away, even "the ends of the heavens." (13:5) The expansive army will destroy the entire land (13:5). They will be merciless and cruel. In the face of this overwhelming threat, people will lose courage and become weak. The cosmic catastrophes accentuate the divine power of the army and the hopelessness and futility of resistance. People will become like hunted animals, trying and failing to escape the slaughter. They can neither run nor purchase their way to safety. The greatest city in the world will become a ruin inhabited by wild animals and only a remnant of humanity will survive. Other descriptions of the day of YHWH likewise overwhelm the audience to make them feel small, mixing awe with surprise and fear. Isaiah 13 might spark joy for an audience safe in Judea that understands the destruction as limited to Babylon. The awesome destruction of the great civilization might evoke joy instead of fear. Fear is for the enemy. The fall of the king of Babylon in Isaiah 14 is an awesome and joyful vision. The fall from the highest heaven to the lowest pit makes the audience (and the king) seem small and creation seem vast. Correspondingly, the seemingly awesome power of the king becomes small compared to what YHWH does. This extraordinary fall from pride evokes awe and wonder at the vastness of creation and joy at the humiliation of the arrogant king.

Disgust punctuates a range of texts. Other emotions like fear (Isa 13), joy (Isa 40–55), or awe (Job 38–41) sustain longer passages. YHWH concludes the first speech to Job with the disgusting image of baby birds drinking blood. The speech that primarily elicits awe ends on a note of disgust, which accentuates that awe. YHWH so loves the world that YHWH gives the blood of corpses for baby birds to drink. The image contrasts YHWH's care for creation with Job's view of YHWH's cruelty and indifference. Job has a serious illness with disgusting boils, and his repulsive physical condition emerges periodically in the dialogues in parallel with his changed social condition. He is disgusting to others, but YHWH speaks to him out of the whirlwind contrary to Job's expectation. Job has fallen from pride to shame, but YHWH still cares for him while others shun him and his friends blame him. Disgust enhances the shame and humiliation of the king of Babylon in Isaiah 14. The text repeatedly draws attention to his rotting corpse. It is sandwiched between worms and maggots and buried under corpses. The king appears more shamed and humiliated by becoming an object of revulsion and disgust. The psalmist's enemies in Psalm 69 cruelly offer him poison and vinegar as food and drink, enhancing their shaming by teasing him with disgusting food. The gesture presents these enemies as morally disgusting. They deserve the punishment that the psalmist wishes on them. Disgust appears in many passages previously analyzed with a focus on other emotions. Various emotions combine to achieve complex effects.

Biblical texts reflect complex emotional experiences that shape their wider context and purpose. Emotion is not an ornament added to a discourse after the fact but the reason for speaking in the first place. If we read without attention to emotion, then we fail to engage the experience and conceptual understanding of the authors. The meanings and intentions of the authors can never be fully known, but the texts have no meaning without them. Emotional resonances with nature shape how the texts summon emotion because creation is emotionally charged.

# NOTES

## Introduction

1 Growing research on human emotion and the impacts of nature on human minds and bodies can correlate with ancient textual evidence. "Humans crave and need access to the outdoors and to nature and suffer in its absence, yet few of us appreciate how fundamental that need is." Sarah Williams Goldhagen, *Welcome to Your World* (HarperCollins, 2017), 19. Louv draws on evidence that time spent in nature alleviates a range of physical and mental health problems and argues that many of these problems derive in part from lack of access to nature. See Richard Louv, *Last Child in the Woods: Saving Our Children From Nature-Deficit Disorder* (Chapel Hill, NC: Algonquin Books, 2008). Similarly, Gary Paul Nabhan and Stephen Trimble, *The Geography of Childhood: Why Children Need Wild Places* (Boston, MA: Beacon, 1994). For an accessible summary of evidence that nature impacts well-being, see Florence Williams, *The Nature Fix: Why Nature Makes Us Happier, Healthier, and More Creative* (New York, NY: Norton, 2017). Most of the evidence on the benefits of being in nature focuses on industrialized populations, and more diverse and comparative research is needed. See Carlos Andres Gallegos-Riofrío et al., "Chronic Deficiency of Diversity and Pluralism in Research on Nature's Mental Health Effects: A Planetary Health Problem," *Current Research in Environmental Sustainability* 4 (2022) 1–11. The most influential account of how nature heals is Attention Restoration Theory, which holds that natural environments offer opportunities for people to relax and restore their capacity to pay effortful attention. Depletion of this capacity results in a range of symptoms that resemble stress (irritability, etc). See Rachel Kaplan and Stephen Kaplan, *The Experience of Nature: A Psychological Perspective* (Cambridge: Cambridge University Press, 1989); Stephen Kaplan, "The Restorative Benefits of Nature: Toward an Integrative Framework," *Journal of Environmental Psychology* 15 (1995) 169–82; Stephen Kaplan and Marc G. Berman, "Directed Attention as a Common Resource for Executive Functioning and Self-Regulation,"

*Perspect Psychol Sci* 5 (2010) 43–57. Stress Reduction Theory offers an alternative theory, although some see it encompassed within attention restoration theory. See Roger S. Ulrich, "Aesthetic and Affective Response to Natural Environment," in *Behavior and the Natural Environment* (Springer, 1983), 85–125; Roger S. Ulrich, "Biophilia, Biophobia, and Natural Landscapes," *The Biophilia Hypothesis* 7 (1993) 73–137. On these and other theories and research, see Agnes E. Van den Berg and Hank Staats, "Environmental Psychology," in *Oxford Textbook of Nature and Public Health*, ed. Matilda van den Bosch and William Bird (Oxford: Oxford University Press, 2018), 51–56; Mardie Townsend et al., "Herapeutic Landscapes, Restorative Environments, Place Attachment, and Well-Being," in *Oxford Textbook of Nature and Public Health*, ed. Matilda van den Bosch and William Bird (Oxford: Oxford University Press, 2018), 57–62; Caroline Hägerhäll et al., "Biological Mechanisms and Neurophysiological Responses to Sensory Input From Nature," in *Oxford Textbook of Nature and Public Health*, ed. Matilda van den Bosch and William Bird (Oxford: Oxford University Press, 2018), 79–88; Ann Sloan Devlin, "Concepts, Theories and Research Approaches," in *Environmental Psychology and Human Well-Being: Effects of Built and Natural Settings*, ed. Ann Sloan Devlin (London: Academic Press, 2018), 1–28.

2  Many studies in psychology rely on priming, or providing information to a subject to see how it impacts their response to a later stimulus. Priming may involve subtle environmental adjustments, staged social interactions, or exposure to discourse. Isaac Alderman, *The Animal At Unease With Itself: Death Anxiety and the Animal-Human Boundary in Genesis 2–3* (Lanham, MD: Lexington Books/Fortress Academic, 2020), 30–33. On the influence of place on the mind, see scholarship in environmental psychology, ecological psychology, architecture and design, medicine, and public health. For example, Linda Steg and Judith J. M. de Groot, *Environmental Psychology: An Introduction* (2nd ed.; Hoboken, NJ: Wiley, 2019); Ann Sloan Devlin, *Environmental Psychology and Human Well-Being* (Academic Press, 2018); Matilda van den Bosch and William Bird, *Oxford Textbook of Nature and Public Health* (Oxford: Oxford University Press, 2018); Thomas J. Lombardo, *The Reciprocity of Perceiver and Environment: The Evolution of James J. Gibson's Ecological Psychology* (London: Routledge, 1987); Goldhagen, *Welcome to Your World*; Stephen R. Kellert, *Nature By Design: The Practice of Biophilic Design* (New Haven, CT: Yale University Press, 2018); Toru Ishikawa, *Human Spatial Cognition and Experience: Mind*

*in the World, World in the Mind* (London: Routledge, 2021). Research on embodied cognition, or study of the ways the body shapes thinking, corrected prior assumptions that the mind was an abstract and disembodied entity. Since minds are embodied, they are also situated in places, and places impact cognition. On embodied cognition, see Mark Johnson, *The Body in the Mind: The Bodily Basis of Meaning, Imagination, and Reason* (Chicago, IL: University of Chicago Press, 1987), widely regarded as a classic in the field. See also Xu Wen and Canzhong Jiang, "Embodiment," in *The Routledge Handbook of Cognitive Linguistics*, ed. Xu Wen and John R. Taylor (New York, NY: Routledge, 2021), 145–60; Benjamin Bergen, "Embodiment," in *Cognitive Linguistics: Foundations of Language*, ed. Ewa Dąbrowska and Dagmar Divjak (Berlin: Walter de Gruyter, 2019), 11–35; Raymond W. Gibbs, "Embodiment," in *The Cambridge Handbook of Cognitive Linguistics*, ed. Barbara Dancygier (Cambridge: Cambridge University Press, 2017), 449–62; Zoltán Kövecses, *Where Metaphors Come From: Reconsidering Context in Metaphor* (Oxford: Oxford University Press, 2015); Tim Rohrer, "Embodiment and Experientialism," in *The Oxford Handbook of Cognitive Linguistics*, ed. Dirk Geeraerts and Hubert Cuyckens (Oxford: Oxford University Press, 2007), 25–47; Mark Johnson, *Embodied Mind, Meaning, and Reason* (Chicago, IL: University of Chicago Press, 2017).

3 Edward O. Wilson, *Biophilia* (Cambridge, MA: Harvard University Press, 1984), 83–100; Stephen R. Kellert, *Birthright: People and Nature in the Modern World* (New Haven: Yale University Press, 2012), 111–14; Alderman, *The Animal At Unease With Itself: Death Anxiety and the Animal-Human Boundary in Genesis 2–3.* Both snakes and fear of snakes are products of evolutionary processes. The widespread fear of snakes has been a much-studied example of inherited fear. Biological evolution and learning often align since both depend on the environment, making it difficult to disentangle the two. See Nobuyuki Kawai, *The Fear of Snakes: Evolutionary and Psychobiological Perspectives on Our Innate Fear* (Singapore: Springer, 2019); T. N. Headland and H. W. Greene, "Hunter-Gatherers and Other Primates as Prey, Predators, and Competitors of Snakes," *Proceedings of the National Academy of Sciences* 108 (2011) E1470–4; S. Hoehl et al., "Itsy Bitsy Spider . . . : Infants React with Increased Arousal to Spiders and Snakes," *Frontiers of Psychology* 8 (2017) 1710; C. C. Luck, R. R. Patterson, and O. V. Lipp, "'Prepared' Fear or Socio-Cultural learning? Fear Conditioned to Guns, Snakes, and Spiders is Eliminated by Instructed Extinction in

a Within-Participant Differential Fear Conditioning Paradigm," *Psychophysiology* 57 (2020) e13516; S. C. Soares et al., "Exogenous Attention to Fear: Differential Behavioral and Neural Responses to Snakes and Spiders," *Neuropsychologia* 99 (2017) 139–47; Arne Öhman and Susan Mineka, "Fears, Phobias, and Preparedness: Toward an Evolved Module of Fear and Fear Learning," *Psychological Review* 108 (2001) 483–522; Arne Öhman and Susan Mineka, "The Malicious Serpent: Snakes as a Prototypical Stimulus for an Evolved Module of Fear," *Current Directions in Psychological Science* 12 (2003) 5–9.

4 Richard J. Clifford, "The Hebrew Scriptures and the Theology of Creation," *Theological Studies* 46 (1985) 507–23. Biblical literature tells the story of Israel's history by beginning with creation.

5 See Cornelis Houtman, *Der Himmel Im Alten Testament: Israels Weltbild Und Weltanschauung* (Leiden: Brill, 1993), esp. pp. 26–49 with the data for all the occurrences of the word pair. On the verb "to profile" to indicate the meaning of a word, see note 29.

6 Aristotle famously called humans social-political animals and recognized that the city arises from human nature. Aristotle, *Politics*, 1253a: ὁ ἄνθροπος φύσει πολιτικὸν ζῷον ("the human by nature is a social/political animal"). The human brain evolved to become experience-expectant, meaning that its full development requires human community and culture. In this sense, nature and culture interact with one another, making the "nature vs. nurture debate" antiquated. Engagement with relevant science can improve humanities scholarship. For example, David Carr correlates scientific research on human memory with manuscript evidence to develop the concept of memory variants and offer well-grounded insight into ancient scribal practice with implications for text, source, and redaction criticism. See David M. Carr, *The Formation of the Hebrew Bible: A New Reconstruction* (Oxford: Oxford University Press, 2011).

7 Robert Murray, *The Cosmic Covenant: Biblical Themes of Justice, Peace and the Integrity of Creation* (London: Sheed and Ward, 1992); John Barton, "Ethics in Isaiah of Jerusalem," *Journal of Theological Studies* 32 (1981), 1–18. See also Clifford, "Hebrew Scriptures"; Richard J. Clifford and John Joseph Collins, *Creation in the Biblical Traditions* (Washington, DC: Catholic Biblical Association of America, 1992); Richard J. Clifford, *Creation Accounts in the Ancient Near East and in the Bible* (Washington, DC: Catholic Biblical Association of America, 1994); Ronald Simkins, *Yahweh's Activity in History and Nature in the Book of Joel* (Lewiston, NY: Edwin Mellen, 1991); Ronald Simkins,

*Creator and Creation: Nature in the Worldview of Ancient Israel* (Peabody, MA: Hendrickson, 1994); Bernhard W. Anderson, *From Creation to New Creation* (Minneapolis: Fortress, 1994).

8 Prior research on biblical creation represents a rich stream of tradition that places creation at the center of biblical theology. Biophilia completes this picture by joining creation and anthropology. The term *biophilia* was coined to profile human emotional engagements with nature. Biophilia emerges in emotional responses to nature directly and as mediated through digital, artistic, and literary representations. The concept has stimulated considerable research in multiple fields (environmental psychology, architecture and design, medicine, public health). Many hope that human biophilia can be recruited to motivate more environmentally sustainable behaviors, an area explored by conservation psychology. Similarly, the biblical subfields of environmental ethics and ecological hermeneutics are motivated by biophilia. Stephen R. Kellert, *The Biophilia Hypothesis* (Washington, DC: Island Press, 1995); Stephen R. Kellert, *Kinship to Mastery: Biophilia in Human Evolution and Development* (Washington, DC: Island Press, 1997); Kellert, *Nature By Design*; Ulrich, "Biophilia, Biophobia, and Natural Landscapes"; Edward O Wilson, "Biophilia and the Conservation Ethic," in *Evolutionary Perspectives on Environmental Problems* (Routledge, 2017), 263–72; Kaplan and Berman, "Directed Attention"; Kaplan, "Restorative Benefits of Nature"; Ulrich, "Aesthetic and Affective Response to Natural Environment."

9 Randolph R. Cornelius, *The Science of Emotion: Research and Tradition in the Psychology of Emotion* (Upper Saddle River, NJ: Prentice Hall, 1996), 3. The integrative role of emotion has motivated the "affective turn" across disciplines. Previous to this shift, many scholars considered affect and cognition distinct and believed that affect had a dysfunctional impact on thinking. There was some truth to this perspective. Humans have two modes of thinking that underlie many discussions about emotion and thinking. Type 1 thinking is fast, intuitive, and emotional but also prone to errors. Type 2 thinking is slow, but logical and explicit so that its steps can be traced and errors detected and corrected. We generally operate with the fast Type 1 thinking unless something forces us to shift to more careful Type 2 reasoning. The view that emotion is dangerous to thought, therefore, has some truth to it. This perspective, however, underestimates the positive values of our dominant mode of thinking. More recent work has clarified that affect interpenetrates with cognition so deeply that the distinction

between the two becomes hard to delineate, as both types of thinking involve emotion. See Daniel Kahneman, *Thinking, Fast and Slow* (New York, NY: Farrar, Straus and Giroux, 2011); S. Ian Robertson, *Human Thinking: The Basics* (London: Routledge, 2021). Much work pursued under the umbrella of "affect theory" in the humanities derives from poststructuralist theory independent of affective science. The present work pursues the alternative understanding of affect theory that is grounded in scientific research. For an overview of these two approaches as applied to literature see Patrick Colm Hogan and Bradley J. Irish, "Introduction: Literary Feelings: Understanding Emotions," in *The Routledge Companion to Literature and Emotion*, ed. Patrick Colm Hogan, Bradley J. Irish, and Lalita Pandit Hogan (London: Routledge, 2022), 1–11. For approaches to emotion in biblical scholarship, see F. Scott Spencer, *Mixed Feelings and Vexed Passions* (Atlanta, GA: Society of Biblical Literature, 2017). The volume encompasses a range of approaches with introductions by the editors that orient the reader to various approaches and the importance of emotion in biblical scholarship. For approaches more narrowly confined to affect theory in the poststructuralist tradition, see Fiona C. Black and Jennifer L. Koosed, eds. *Reading With Feeling: Affect Theory and the Bible* (Atlanta, GA: Society of Biblical Literature, 2019).

10   During my next visit to a bookstore, I purchased Ted Levin, *America's Snake: The Rise and Fall of the Timber Rattlesnake* (Chicago, IL: University of Chicago Press, 2016).

11   Elizabeth Johnston and Leah Olson, *The Feeling Brain: The Biology and Psychology of Emotions* (New York, NY: Norton, 2015), 308.

12   Ralph Adolphs and David J. Anderson, *The Neuroscience of Emotion: A New Synthesis* (Princeton, NJ: Princeton University Press, 2018), 18–23. Haidt proposes a rider and elephant metaphor to understand how emotion (the elephant) drives human behavior and reason (the rider) mostly goes along for the ride (in his metaphor, reason is a rider, not a driver). See Jonathan Haidt, *The Righteous Mind: Why Good People Are Divided By Politics and Religion* (New York, NY: Vintage, 2013). Elaine Fox, *Emotion Science: Cognitive and Neuroscientific Approaches to Understanding Human Emotions* (London: Palgrave Macmillan, 2008), 16–17, 23–25. The distinction between surprise and startle illustrates the difference between emotion and reflex. The startle reflex cannot be extinguished. You start at a popping balloon even if you know it is about to happen. Surprise, however, depends on the unexpected. Surprise captures and focuses attention, leading to a wide

variety of possible emotions and behaviors. The startle reflex is an auto-nomic reaction with a fixed action pattern (closed eyes and jaw, brows drawn). Paul Ekman, *Emotions Revealed: Recognizing Faces and Feelings to Improve Communication and Emotional Life* (Rev. ed.; New York, NY: Holt, 2007), 151. Emotions can be distinguished from moods, which are longer-term predispositions to stronger emotions (the irri-table person is easily triggered to anger). Feelings are the subjective experience of the emotional state. Adolphs and Anderson, *Neuroscience of Emotion*, 49–53, 71–73; Fox, *Emotion Science*, 16–17, 25–29. Affect may be used as a synonym for emotion. I avoid the term *affect* in order to avoid confusion with affect theory, as normally understood within biblical studies, as opposed to its use in affective sciences. The present analysis engages the relevant sciences rather than the poststructuralist theory. On the distinction, see Hogan and Irish, "Introduction," 3. Like Hogan and Irish (2–3), I understand emotion as a motivational system. Some motives are more prototypically emotional than oth-ers (e.g., fear vs. thirst). The more prototypically emotional motives involve moods and feelings as defined above. Emotion shapes other systems (physiology, attention, cognition) in service of the motivation.

13  Disagreements about the meaning of emotion appear at the root of several differences between people who substantively agree. For exam-ple, after years of distinguished research on fear in rats, Joseph LeDoux declared that we should not speak of emotions in animals because emo-tions involve feelings that require consciousness. David J. Anderson disagrees (and I agree with Anderson). He recounts this conversation with LeDeux: "'If you tell people that flies have emotions,' he has said to me, 'they will think you mean that flies have feelings'–which is not what I mean. I would counter that if you tell people that one cannot use the word 'emotion' when talking about animal behavior and brain mechanisms, people may think you mean that these animals are just little robots—which is not what LeDeux means." David Anderson, *The Nature of the Beast: How Emotions Guide Us* (New York, NY: Basic Books, 2022), 40–41. LeDoux and Anderson share substantial agree-ment about emotion but use the term in different ways. For LeDoux's excellent research presented to a wide audience, see Joseph LeDoux, *The Emotional Brain: The Mysterious Underpinnings of Emotional Life* (New York, NY: Simon and Schuster, 1996); Joseph LeDoux, *Synaptic Self: How Our Brains Become Who We Are* (New York, NY: Penguin, 2003); Joseph LeDoux, *Anxious: Using the Brain to Understand and Treat Fear and Anxiety* (New York, NY: Penguin, 2016). LeDoux has

recently pursued the question of consciousness as the next develop-
ment of his thinking about emotion as feeling in Joseph LeDoux, *The
Deep History of Ourselves: The Four-Billion-year Story of How We Got
Conscious Brains* (New York, NY: Penguin, 2019).

14  Some emotion researchers in the biblical field deny the validity of emotion as a concept applied to ancient peoples. Their objections to the
category of emotion appear to me grounded in a misreading of what
modern English-speaking people mean by emotion. They argue that
emotion is more than subjective experience, which strikes me as common sense and is the view of the most affective scientists. They do not
engage the extensive discussion of emotion emerging from affective
science. Phillip Michael Lasater, "'The Emotions' in Biblical Anthropology? A Genealogy and Case Study with ירא," *Harvard Theological
Review* 110 (2017) 520–40; Gary A. Anderson, *A Time to Mourn, a
Time to Dance: The Expression of Grief and Joy in Israelite Religion* (Penn
State University Press, 1991); Françoise Mirguet, "What is an 'Emotion' in the Hebrew Bible?: An Experience that Exceeds Most Contemporary Concepts," *Biblical Interpretation* (2016) 442–65; Françoise
Mirguet, "The Study of Emotions in Early Jewish Texts: Review and
Perspectives," *Journal for the Study of Judaism* 50 (2019) 557–603;
David A. Lambert, "Refreshing Philology: James Barr, Supersessionism, and the State of Biblical Words," *Biblical Interpretation* 24 (2016)
332–56. Sometimes these writers (especially Lambert) appear to deny
that ancient peoples experienced consciousness and a sense of interi-
ority in ways reminiscent of the (in)famous thesis of Julian Jaynes, *The
Origin of Consciousness in the Breakdown of the Bicameral Mind* (Boston: Houghton Mifflin, 1976), although none cite this work. Sometimes they critique a dualistic modern thinking that is foreign to the
biblical material. Modern thinking is not as dualist as they claim, and
biblical conceptualizations are more dualist than they acknowledge. A
basic mind–body distinction may be a human universal, although conceptualization of emotion varies. On this fascinating line of research,
see Kara Weisman et al., "Similarities and Differences in Concepts of
Mental Life among Adults and Children in Five Cultures," *Nature Human
Behaviour* 5 (2021) 1358–68. This cross-cultural finding may be grounded
in how we perceive our bodies and our minds. Bodies and minds are
not separate in reality, but we perceive them with different systems
in the brain. "Just as colors and numbers are experienced as radically
different because they depend on dissociated systems in the brain, our
mind and body are forever cleaved from one another." Matthew D.

Lieberman, *Social: Why Our Brains Are Wired to Connect* (New York, NY: Crown, 2013), 186. A school of scholarship known as "the history of emotions" suffers from lack of engagement with affective science and general psychology but influences other humanities fields. See, for example, Richard Firth-Godbehere, *A Human History of Emotion: How the Way We Feel Built the World We Know* (New York, NY: Little, Brown Spark, 2021); Thomas M. Dixon, *Weeping Britannia: Portrait of a Nation in Tears* (Oxford University Press, USA, 2015).

15  On mentalization (as this skill is called), theory of mind, and the importance of "mind reading," see Peter Fonagy, Gyorgy Gergely, and Elliot L. Jurist, *Affect Regulation, Mentalization, and the Development of the Self* (New York, NY: Other Press, 2004); Fredric N. Busch, *Mentalization: Theoretical Considerations, Research Findings, and Clinical Implications* (Routledge, 2011); Janet Wilde Astington and Jodie A. Baird, *Why Language Matters for Theory of Mind* (Oxford: Oxford University Press, 2005); Helen Tager-Flusberg and Michael Lombardo, *Understanding Other Minds: Perspectives From Developmental Social Neuroscience* (3rd ed.; Oxford: Oxford University Press, 2013); Simon Baron-Cohen, *Mindblindness: An Essay on Autism and Theory of Mind* (Cambridge: MIT Press, 1997). Our ability to "read minds" enables us to learn language and acquire culture, making mentalization a fundamental aspect of our nature. See Lieberman, *Social*; Namhee Lee et al., *The Interactional Instinct: The Evolution and Acquisition of Language* (Oxford: Oxford University Press, 2009); Anna Dina L. Joaquin and John H. Schumann, *Exploring the Interactional Instinct* (Oxford: Oxford University Press, 2013). Cognitive biases, however, inhibit the accuracy of our mindreading. See Nicholas Epley, *Mindwise: Why We Misunderstand What Others Think, Believe, Feel, and Want* (New York, NY: Vintage, 2015).

16  Mirguet rightly understands emotion words in Hebrew as encompassing behaviors but mistakenly claims that the modern English concept of emotion does not. Mirguet, "What is an 'Emotion'?"

17  Wierzbicka seeks to overcome cultural specificity and diversity by developing (or discovering) a "Natural Semantic Metalanguage," which claims to be culturally independent. The present study does not assume this idiosyncratic approach. Anna Wierzbicka, *Emotions Across Languages and Cultures: Diversity and Universals* (Cambridge: Cambridge University Press, 1999).

18  Tiffany Watt Smith, *The Book of Human Emotions* (New York, NY: Little, Brown and Co., 2016), 20.

19   Smith, *Book of Human Emotions*, 21.

20   All the major theories of emotion in affective science have value for humanities research. Affective science in general does not appear often in biblical scholarship. In literary studies, those who draw in the sciences limit themselves to constructivist theories. Critiques of basic emotions theory attack caricatures or "straw men" that bear little resemblance to the work of basic emotions theorists or the views of any serious researcher. For example, they typically overlook how basic emotions include ample room for cultural construction in addition to species-wide commonality. On basic emotions, see Paul Ekman, *Darwin and Facial Expression: A Century of Research in Review* (Cambridge, MA: Malor Books, 2006); Ekman, *Emotions Revealed*; Jaak Panksepp and Lucy Biven, *The Archaeology of Mind: Neuroevolutionary Origins of Human Emotions* (New York, NY: Norton, 2012). On constructivist theories, see Lisa Feldman Barrett, *How Emotions Are Made: The Secret Life of the Brain* (Boston: Houghton Mifflin Harcourt, 2017); Lisa Feldman Barrett and James A. Russell, *The Psychological Construction of Emotion* (New York, NY: Guilford, 2014). On the resistance of humanities scholars to large swaths of emotion science, see Hogan and Irish, "Introduction." They state that humanist scholars resist any hint of universalism due to misuses of universalist claims in racist and sexist discourse. This reaction fails to observe how exaggerated claims of difference between cultures is also implicated in racist discourse. A study of multiple cultures found a correlation between racist attitudes and skepticism about evolution. The authors suggest that evolutionary belief may expand in-group identity and/or increase empathy for out-groups as fellow humans. See Syriopoulos Syropoulos et al., "Bigotry and the Human-Animal Divide: (Dis)belief in Human Evolution and Bigoted Attitudes across Different Cultures," *Journal of Personality and Social Psychology* (2022) 1–29.

21   Three aspects of language emerge as especially important for mentalization. First, spoken languages are full of sentential complements, or constructions that prototypically use a psychological verb expressing a proposition or attitude, such as "I know that you have many cattle" (Deut 3:19). Second, children regularly participate in interactions in which they encounter the fact that different people have different perspectives on the same situations and they must often negotiate these differences in conversations. Perspective-shifting discourse reinforces that other people are mental agents and offers means of discovering and representing this fact. Third, reflective discourse represents

a further development in which linguistic interactions incude comments on these diverse perspectives, thus encompassing thoughts about thoughts, or perspectives on perpectives, such as "Now I know that you fear ʏʜᴡʜ" (Gen 22:12). Children's individual interactions with caregivers become internalized as a generalized cultural or collective other. In this way, reflective language draws children into culture and community, with culturally supported means of representing the mental states of others in language so that they can better navigate relationships and regulate emotions. Michael Tomasello and Hannes Rakoczy, "What Makes Human Cognition Unique? From Individual to Shared to Collective Intentionality," *Intellectica* 46–47 (2007) 25–48, esp 136–38; Michael Tomasello, *Constructing a Language: A Usage-Based Theory of Language Acquisition* (Cambridge, MA: Harvard University Press, 2003), 249–53.

22 When our brains are not engaged in any specific goal-oriented task, then the brain's default network becomes active. The work of this "resting" network appears to be oriented to social life, suggesting that human brains evolved to think about the social world. See Lieberman, *Social*, 15–23. Similarly, Tomasello argues persuasively that human language depends on shared intentionality, which evolved to support cooperative activities. Michael Tomasello, *Origins of Human Communication* (Cambridge, MA: MIT Press, 2010). Humans have internal mental states and seek to understand the mental states of others in order to navigate relationships. Consequently, languages have expressions that profile these internal states.

23 Tomasello, *Origins of Human Communication,* 342.

24 Cognitive linguists explain language in ways that cohere with other disciplines studying the human mind. For a popular and accessible introduction to cognitive linguistics, see Vyvyan Evans, *The Language Myth: Why Language is Not an Instinct* (Cambridge: Cambridge University Press, 2014); Vyvyan Evans, *The Crucible of Language: How Language and Mind Create Meaning* (Cambridge: Cambridge University Press, 2015). For more advanced and detailed discussions, see Vyvyan Evans, *Cognitive Linguistics: A Complete Guide* (Edinburgh: Edinburgh Universty Press, 2019); William Croft and D. Alan Cruse, *Cognitive Linguistics* (Cambridge: Cambridge University Press, 2004); John R. Taylor, *Linguistic Categorization* (3rd ed.; New York, NY: Oxford University Press, 2003). Several publishers have produced helpful handbooks: Dirk Geeraerts and Hubert Cuyckens, *The Oxford Handbook of Cognitive Linguistics* (Oxford: Oxford University Press, 2007); Barbara

Dancygier, *The Cambridge Handbook of Cognitive Linguistics* (Cambridge: Cambridge University Press, 2017); Xu Wen and John R. Taylor, eds. *The Routledge Handbook of Cognitive Linguistics* (New York, NY: Routledge, 2021); Jeannette Littlemore and John R. Taylor, *The Bloomsbury Companion to Cognitive Linguistics* (London: Bloomsbury, 2014); Ewa Dąbrowska and Dagmar Divjak, *Cognitive Linguistics: A Survey of Linguistic Subfields* (Berlin: Walter de Gruyter, 2019); Ewa Dąbrowska and Dagmar Divjak, *Cognitive Linguistics: Foundations of Language* (Berlin: Walter de Gruyter, 2019); Ewa Dąbrowska and Dagmar Divjak, *Cognitive Linguistics: Key Topics* (Berlin: Walter de Gruyter, 2019). For an introduction aimed at biblical scholars, see Ellen Van Wolde, *Reframing Biblical Studies: When Language and Text Meet Culture, Cognition, and Context* (Winona Lake, IN: Eisenbrauns, 2009).

25    For an overview of the research on the human tendency to share emotional experiences and the consequences of this sharing, see Bernard Rimé, "Emotion Elicits the Social Sharing of Emotion: Theory and Empirical Review," *Emotion Review* 1 (2009) 60–85. For more depth, see Bernard Rimé, *Le Partage Social Des Émotions* (Paris: Presses Universitaires de FrancePUF, 2009); Bernard Rimé, "Mental Rumination, Social Sharing, and the Recovery From Emotional Exposure," in *Emotion, Disclosure, and Health*, ed. James Pennebaker (Washington, DC: American Psychological Association, 1995); Bernard Rimé and Véronique Christophe, "How Individual Emotional Episodes Feed Collective Memory," in *Collective Memory of Political Events*, ed. James Pennebaker, Dario Paez, and Bernard Rimé (Mahwah, NJ: Lawrence Earlbaum, 1997), 131–46; Bernard Rimé, Susanna Corsini, and Gwénola Herbette, "Emotion, Verbal Expression, and the Social Sharing of Emotion," in *The Verbal Communication of Emotions: Interdisciplinary Perspectives*, ed. Susan R. Fussel (Mahwah, NJ: Lawrence Erlbaum, 2002), 185–208; Bernard Rimé, Gwénola Herbette, and Susanna Corsini, "The Social Sharing of Emotion: Illusory and Real Benefits of Talking About Emotional Experiences," in *Emotional Expression and Health: Advances in Theory, Assessment, and Clinical Applications*, ed. Ivan Nyklíček, Lydia Temoshok, and Ad Vingerhoets (New York, NY: Brunner-Routledge, 2004), 29–42; Bernard Rimé, "Interpersonal Emotion Regulation," in *Handbook of Emotion Regulation, First Edition*, ed. James J. Gross (New York, NY: Guilford, 2007), 466–85; Bernard Rimé et al., "The Social Sharing of Emotions in Interpersonal and in Collective Situations: Common Psychosocial Consequences," in *Emotion Regulation and Well-being*, ed. Ivan Nyklíček, Ad

Vingerhoets, and Marcel Zeelenberg (New York, NY: Springer, 2011), 147–63.

26  The prior five sentences paraphrased from Tomasello, *Origins of Human Communication*, 310–11. Construction grammar describes the conventional nature of syntax.

27  For example, cultures associate different body parts with emotion. English, Dutch, and Persian have been identified as head/heart-centering languages, Basque, Indonesian, and Malay as abdomen-centering, and Chinese as heart-centering. These diverse ways of mapping emotion on the body draw attention to diverse aspects of the embodied emotional experience. Wen and Jiang, "Embodiment," here 149–50. On the importance of culture in human development, see Eric B. Shiraev and Davids A. Levy, *Cross-Cultural Psychology: Critical Thinking and Contemporary Applications* (5th ed.; London: Routledge, 2013); Barbara Rugoff, *The Cultural Nature of Human Development* (Oxford: Oxford University Press, 2003); Mary Helen Immordino-Yang, "Embodied Brains, Social Minds: Towards a Cultural Neuroscience of Social Emotion," in *The Oxford Handbook of Cultural Neuroscience*, ed. Joan Y. Chiao et al. (Oxford: Oxford University Press, 2016), 129–42.

28  James Barr published his justly famous critique of the biblical theology movement before cognitive linguistics emerged. His focus on semantics, however, matched the semantic interests of early cognitive linguists who became disenchanted with the failures and limitations of Chomsky's theory. As a result, Barr's work has stood the test of time well. He argued against the tight relationship between thought and language that the biblical theologians assumed. Nuanced discussions of this issue are rare and often invoke the Sapir–Whorf hypothesis in ways that obfuscate the issue since people understand this hypothesis in widely divergent ways. For a level-headed summary, see Evans, *Crucible of Language*, 192–228. James Barr, *The Semantics of Biblical Language* (Eugene, OR: Wipf and Stock, 2004). On lexical semantics, see Zeki Hamawand, *Semantics: A Cognitive Account of Linguistic Meaning* (Sheffield: Equinox, 2016).

29  The term *profile* in this context means to highlight or draw attention to something. On this understanding of language and meaning, see Hamawand, *Semantics*; Ronald W. Langacker, *Cognitive Grammar: A Basic Introduction* (Oxford: Oxford University Press, 2008); Evans, *Cognitive Linguistics: A Complete Guide*, 351–564. The meaning of words involves a profile and a base. The base is the concept or knowledge domain involved and the profile is the part or aspects of

the concept that the word points toward. For example, the English word *anger* is the prototypical term for a general concept of anger. The word *rage* does not profile a different concept, but the intense aspect of anger. The word *irritation* profiles less intense anger. Many words with multiple meanings derive their various meanings from changes in the base. The word *bank* can profile a financial institution or the side of a river. The context clarifies which base is in view and shapes the meaning of the word accordingly.

30 Biblical scholars still sometimes mistake word studies for studies of concepts. See Barr, *Semantics*; Alan E. Kurschner, "James Barr on the 'Illegitimate Totality Transfer' Word-Concept Fallacy," in *James Barr Assessed: Evaluating His Legacy over the Last Sixty Years*, ed. Stanley E. Porter (Leiden: Brill, 2021), 70–114. They correspondingly assume that the absence of a word signals the absence of a concept. Construction grammar clarifies that words are not the unit of meaning. See Joan Bybee, *Frequency of Use and the Organization of Language* (Oxford: Oxford University Press, 2006); Joan Bybee, *Language, Usage and Cognition* (Cambridge: Cambridge University Press, 2010); Adele E. Goldberg, *Constructions At Work: The Nature of Generalization in Language* (Oxford: Oxford University Press, USA, 2006); Adele E. Goldberg, *Explain Me This: Creativity, Competition, and the Partial Productivity of Constructions* (Princeton, NJ: Princeton University Press, 2019).

31 This work embraces the cognitive commitment characteristic of cognitive linguistics. These linguists strive to describe general principles of language in terms consistent with "what is known about the human mind and brain for other disciplines." Evans, *Cognitive Linguistics: A Complete Guide*, 25. My research delves into psychology and affective science because I seek to describe biblical literature in ways coherent with what scientific disciplines have learned about the human mind. Theories isolated from these fields miss opportunities to avoid errors and strengthen insights. This strategy has been highly effective for cognitive linguistics. For bibliography introducing cognitive linguistics, see note 24.

32 Biblical study is corpus linguistic study. The corpus is small and unrepresentative of the language, which complicates the work. On corpus linguistics Anne O'Keeffe and Michael McCarthy, *The Routledge Handbook of Corpus Linguistics* (2nd ed.; London: Routledge, 2022); Magali Paquot and Stefan Th. Gried, *A Practical Handbook of Corpus Linguistics* (Cham: Springer Nature Switzerland, 2020).

33 Mari Joerstad, *The Hebrew Bible and Environmental Ethics: Humans, Nonhumans, and the Living Landscape* (Cambridge: Cambridge University Press, 2019), 123, suggests that the frequency of personification indicates the possibility that the Israelites were animists. The overall data indicate the rarity of personification of ארץ *land*. Construal is our capacity to represent the same situation on multiple ways (e.g., "I made mistakes" or "Mistakes were made"). Any linguistic utterance construes a situation in one of many possible ways. See Langacker, *Cognitive Grammar*, 55–89.

34 Expressions that appear frequently with a given sense (e.g., land as a place) become entrenched in the mind through frequent use, and their frequency enables the mind to process them more rapidly. Language describing a human speaking elicits no surprise. A talking sea is rare and surprising (Isa 23:4; Job 28:14), so it draws more attention. See Hans-Jörd Schmid, "Entrenchment, Salience, and Basic Levels," in *The Oxford Handbook of Cognitive Linguistics*, ed. Dirk Geeraerts and Hubert Cuyckens (Oxford: Oxford University Press, 2007), 117–38; Dagmar Divjak and Catherine L. Caldwell-Harris, "Frequency and Entrenchment," in *Cognitive Linguistics: Foundations of Language*, ed. Ewa Dąbrowska and Dagmar Divjak (Berlin: Walter de Gruyter, 2019), 61–86.

35 In terms of human working memory, the corpus is large, allowing attentional biases to operate. The corpus of ancient Hebrew is tiny, however, compared to ancient Greek, Latin, or the corpora of modern languages used for linguistic research. The ideal corpus is representative of the language as a whole, which biblical Hebrew certainly is not. The scope and biases of the biblical corpus facilitate errors. Joerstad, for example, focuses only on texts that construe nature in human-like ways to the exclusion of the much larger set of texts in which it does not. She refers to the frequency of passages personifying nature as evidence for her animist argument without realizing how selective her reading must be to find these passages common rather than rare. Joerstad, *Hebrew Bible and Environmental Ethics*.

36 To access the spreadsheet, see cua.academica.edu/DavidBosworth or researchgate.net/profile/David-Bosworth.

# Chapter 1

1 Aldo Leopold remarks on the wisdom of not visiting the places we have loved in the past: "Despite several opportunties to do so, I have

never returned to the White Mountain. I prefer not to see what tourists, roads, sawmills, and logging railroads have done for it, or to it." Aldo Leopold, *A Sand County Almanac With Essays on Conservation From Round River* (New York, NY: Ballantine Books, 1984), 137. Similarly, he remarks, "It is the part of wisdom never to revisit a wilderness, for the more golden the lily, the more certain that someone has gilded it. To return not only spoils a trip, but tarnishes a memory." (p. 150)

2 This emotion has been termed solastalgia, defined as "the pain or distress caused by the ongoing loss of solace and the sense of desolation connected to the present state of one's home territory. It is the existential and lived experience of negative environmental change, manifest as an attack on one's sense of place." Glenn A. Albrecht, *Earth Emotions: New Words for a New World* (Ithaca, NY: Cornell University Press, 2019), 38. He also calls it "the homesickness you have when you are still at home." The term solastalgia returned 182,000 results in a Google search in June 2022. I first encountered the term in this description of environmental degradation due to resource extraction: "People living in mining areas in Appalachia and beyond often grieve the loss of home as they would the loss of a dear friend, a condition some are calling *solastalgia*." Catholic Committee of Appalachia, *The Telling Takes Us Home: Taking Our Place in the Stories That Shape Us: A People's Pastoral From the Catholic Committee of Appalachia* (Spencer, WV: Catholic Committee of Appalachia, 2015), 14. Albrecht has coined many neologisms based on Greek and Latin roots that seem unlikely to be used outside a small circle of scholars and activists. He provides a needed glossary of his jargon. Albrecht, *Earth Emotions*, 199–201.

3 Victor Counted and Fraser Watts, "Place Attachment in the Bible: The Role of Attachment to Sacred Places in Religious Life," *Journal of Psychology and Theology* 45 (2017) 218–32.

4 Most commentators agree that Isaiah 49:1 introduces a new transition from 40:1–48:21, but the theme of comfort (נחם) continues through 55:13. For discussion of the division, the separate emphases of Isaiah 40:1–48:21 and 49:1–55:13, see Gary V. Smith, *Isaiah 40–66* (Nashville, TN: B&H Publishing Group, 2009), 336–40, 357–60; John Goldingay and David Payne, *Isaiah 40–55 Vol 2* (London: Bloomsbury, 2006), 152–53.

5 Place attachment is an outgrowth of attachment theory, which describes interpersonal relationships, especially parent–child relationships. On place attachment specifically, see Leila Scannell and Robert Gifford, "Defining Place Attachment: A Tripartite Organizing Framework,"

*Journal of Environmental Psychology* 30 (2010) 1–10; Leila Scannell and Robert Gifford, "Comparing the Theories of Interpersonal and Place Attachment," in *Place Attachment: Advances in Theory, Methods and Application*, ed. Lynne Manzo and Patrick Devine-Wright (London: Routledge, 2013), 23–36; Leila Scannell et al., "Parallels Between Interpersonal and Place Attachment: An Update," in *Place Attachment: Advances in Theory, Methods and Applications*, ed. Lynne Manzo and Patrick Devine-Wright (London: Routledge, 2021), 45–60; Maria Lewicka, "Place Attachment: How Far Have We Come in the Last 40 Years?," *Journal of Environmental Psychology* 31 (2011) 207–30; Linda Steg and Judith I. M. de Groot, eds. *Place Attachment* (Hoboken, NJ: Wiley, 2019); Nikolay Mihaylov and Douglas D. Perkins, "Community Place Attachment and Its Role in Social Capital Development," in *Place Attachment: Advances in Theory, Methods and Application*, ed. Lynne Manzo and Patrick Devine-Wright (London: Routledge, 2013), 61–74; Nikolay Mihaylov, Douglas D. Perkins, and Richard C. Stedman, "Community Responses to Environmental Threat: Place Cognition, Attachment, and Social Action," in *Place Attcahment: Advances in Theory, Methods and Applications*, ed. Lynne Manzo and Patrick Devine-Wright (London: Routledge, 2021), 161–76. On the more general attachment theory, see Robert Karen, *Becoming Attached: First Relationships and How They Shape Our Capacity to Love* (Oxford: Oxford University Press, 1998); Jude Cassidy and Phillip R. Shaver, *Handbook of Attachment* (3rd ed.; New York, NY: Guilford, 2016); Mario Mikulincer and Phillip R. Shaver, *Attachment in Adulthood: Structure, Dynamics, and Change* (New York, NY: Guilford, 2010); Mario Mikulincer and Phillip R. Shaver, "Adult Attachment and Emotion Regulation," in *Handbook of Attachment*, ed. Jude Cassidy and Phillip R. Shaver (New York, NY: Guilford, 2016), 507–33; Ross A. Thompson, Jeffry A. Simpson, and Lisa J. Berlin, eds. *Attachment: The Fundamental Questions* (New York, NY: Guilford, 2021). For a previous attempt to introduce place attachment into biblical studies, see Counted and Watts, "Place Attachment in the Bible."

6  Randolph T. Hester, "Do Not Detach! Instructions From and for Community Design," in *Place Attachment: Advances in Theory, Methods and Application*, ed. Lynne Manzo and Patrick Devine-Wright (London: Routledge, 2013), 191–206, here 191; Randolph T. Hester, "Reattach! Practicing Endemic Design," in *Place Attachment: Advances in Theory, Methods and Applications*, ed. Lynne C. Manzo and Patrick Devine-Wright (London: Routledge, 2021), 208–25. Hester restates

and elaborates: "Attachment to place exerts the most positive influence of any force on the design of community. When values and meanings embedded in place are awakened, they remind people of their common identity and shared fate. People become more empathetic toward others, more aware of their dependence on local ecosystems, and how the form of their community enriches or diminishes their lives."

7  Much research on place attachment focuses on survey data, but Di Massio et al. argue for greater attention to discourse analysis. Andrés Di Masso, John Dixon, and Kevin Durrheim, "Place Attachment as Discursive Practice," in *Place Attachment: Advances in Theory, Methods and Application*, ed. Lynne Manzo and Patrick Devine-Wright (London: Routledge, 2013), 75–86; Andrés Di Masso, John Dixon, and Kevin Durrheim, "Place Attachment as Discursive Practice: The Role of Language, Affect, Space, Power, and Materiality in Person-Place Bonds," in *Place Attachment: Advances in Theory, Methods and Applications*, ed. Lynne C. Manzo and Patrick Devine-Wright (London: Routledge, 2021), 77–92. Hart argues that discourse analysis and cognitive linguistics need each other because discourse analysis draws out the social dimension of language assumed by cognitive linguistics and cognitive linguistics describes the connection between language and social practice that discourse analysis assumes but does not show. See Christopher Hart and Dominik Lukeš, *Cognitive Linguistics in Critical Discourse Analysis* (Newcastle upon Tyne: Cambridge Scholars Publishing, 2009); Christopher Hart, "Discourse," in *Cognitive Linguistics: A Survey of Linguistic Subfields*, ed. Ewa Dąbrowska and Dagmar Divjak (Berlin: Walter de Gruyter, 2019), 81–107.

8  On mental spaces, see Gilles Fauconnier, *Mappings in Thought and Language* (Cambridge: Cambridge University Press, 1997). On domains, see Ronald W. Langacker, *Cognitive Grammar: A Basic Introduction* (Oxford: Oxford University Press, 2008), 44–54. Mental spaces and domains represent nonequivalent ways of speaking about conceptual structure. A domain encompasses a body of knowledge about a topic that is relatively stable and coherent, encompassing everything a person knows about the topic. A mental space construes this conceptual structure in a more dynamic way, often partitioning the body of knowledge into autonomous units. A mental space may draw elements from a domain stored in long-term memory into working memory for "online" processing. Conventionalized blends like Mother-Zion may be described as an overarching set of correspondences found in various texts in terms of correspondences between these domains, or as specific

instantiations of the metaphor in particular passages that might be better described in terms of mental spaces. Since the present discussion involves analysis of specific passages and wider discussion of the personification of Zion across a range of texts, the terms *mental space* and *domain* will be used with these different nuances.

9 By convention, capitalized words indicate that the word refers to the mental concept of domain of knowledge, not only the word. I will not use this convention, but represent blends with hyphenation like Mother-Zion as opposed to ZION IS A MOTHER.

10 For a detailed argument that YHWH is here the mother of Zion, not the husband of Zion, see Hanne Løland, *Silent or Salient Gender? The Interpretation of Gendered God-Language in the Hebrew Bible, Exemplified in Isaiah 42, 46, and 49* (Tübingen: Mohr Seibeck, 2008), 161–92.

11 This and other metaphors may be understood through the lens of conceptual blending theory. Metaphor is not merely a linguistic surface-level ornament, but deeply embedded in the structure of cognition. In conceptual blending as applied to metaphor, the source domain (MOTHER) and target domain (ZION) both constitute mental spaces called input spaces. When a person "runs the blend," the two input spaces project into a blended space that gives rise to a new conceptualization (MOTHER-ZION) that may include emergent structures not derived from either input. For example, the expression *That surgeon is a butcher* communicates that the surgeon is incompetent, but surgeons and butchers are both skilled professionals. Incompetence emerges from the blend, not from either input. See Gilles Fauconnier and Mark Turner, *The Way We Think* (New York, NY: Basic Books, 2008), 297–98. On conceptual blending theory, see Fauconnier and Turner, *Way We Think*; Todd Oakley and Esther Pascual, "Conceptual Blending Theory," in *The Cambridge Handbook of Cognitive Linguistics*, ed. Barbara Dancygier (Cambridge: Cambridge University Press, 2017), 423–48. Within conceptual metaphor theory, MOTHER is the source domain mapped onto the target domain CITY. On contemporary metaphor theory, see Zoltán Kövecses, *Metaphor: A Practical Introduction* (2nd ed.; Oxford: Oxford University Press, 2010); Zoltán Kövecses, *Where Metaphors Come From: Reconsidering Context in Metaphor* (Oxford: Oxford University Press, 2015); Jeroen Vandaele, "Cognitive Poetics and the Problem of Metaphor," in *The Routledge Handbook of Cognitive Linguistics*, ed. Xu Wen and John R. Taylor (New York, NY: Routledge, 2021), 450–83. The field began with the publication of the classic 1980 book George Lakoff and Mark Johnson, *Metaphors We*

*Live By* (Chicago, IL: University of Chicago Press, 2008). Much discussion of metaphor in biblical studies has focused on contemporary metaphor theory, but blending theory increasingly replaces it. For a review of literature, see Mason D. Lancaster, "Metaphor Research and the Hebrew Bible," *Currents in Biblical Research* 19 (2021) 235–85.

12  For example, baseballs may be used to model the solar system or an atom. Blending can go beyond the simple modeling of relative motion of the earth around the sun. If the earth were the size of a baseball, then the sun would be 26.5 feet in diameter and about 1,000 yards away. If a proton were the size of a baseball, then the first electron cloud would be about 12 miles away. Similar blends can reduce geologic time to human scale. If the earth were 24 hours old, originating at midnight, then dinosaurs emerged around 10:56pm and humans around 11:58:43pm. Oakley and Pascual, "Conceptual Blending Theory," esp. 426–27.

13  Zion, like any city, is a complex reality that is larger than human scale. A city remains at a fixed location, but its boundaries may be fuzzy or flexible. Its physical size and architectural features may mutate, perhaps dramatically, and its population constantly changes through birth, death, and migration. Despite its scale, internal complexity, and change over time, we conceptualize cities as fixed realities, and Zion remains a constant reality even as it undergoes several transformations from growing city, ruin, and restored city. A woman offers a more relatable and accessible entity. Women change over time and shift locations, but we construe people as "the same" individuals as we track them through time and space. Women and cities are also both social realities. A woman is embedded in a network of social relations, and cities likewise have relationships to the countryside and to other cities. Abel-Bethmaacah is a fortified city and "mother in Israel" in 2 Samuel 20:19.

14  Aristotle does not use parental imagery for the city but recognizes that the city, like a parent, is by nature prior to the individual (*Politics* 1253 a 25).

15  The expression "the children of your bereavement" (בני שכליך) profiles children who have died.

16  Length of residence correlates with place attachment, but it is not the cause. Maria Lewicka, "In Search of Roots: Memory as Enabler of Place Attachment," in *Place Attachment: Advances in Theory, Methods and Applications*, ed. Lynne C. Manzo and Patrick Devine-Wright (London: Routledge, 2013), 49–60.

17 Mindy Thompson Fullilove, "'The Frayed Knot': What Happens to Place Attachment in the Context of Serial Forced Displacement?," in *Place Attachment: Advances in Theory, Methods and Applications*, ed. Lynne C. Manzo and Patrick Devine-Wright (London: Routledge, 2013), 141–53, here 149.

18 Maggie Low, *Mother Zion in Deutero-Isaiah: A Metaphor for Zion Theology* (New York, NY: Peter Lang, 2013). She finds that Mother Zion is both city and community in many passages in Jeremiah, Lamentations, and Ezekiel.

19 Scannell and Gifford, "Comparing the Theories of Interpersonal and Place Attachment"; Scannell, "Parallels Between Interpersonal and Place Attachment: An Update"; Counted and Watts, "Place Attachment in the Bible," 119–20; Toru Ishikawa, *Human Spatial Cognition and Experience: Mind in the World, World in the Mind* (London: Routledge, 2021), 210–11.

20 Vandaele, "Cognitive Poetics and the Problem of Metaphor," here 470.

21 On maternal grief as the prototypical grief, see Ekaterina E. Kozlova, *Maternal Grief in the Hebrew Bible* (Oxford: Oxford University Press, 2017).

22 The German reads "begehter, verletzlicher, bedrohter Weiblichkeit." Othmar Keel, *Die Geschichte Jerusalems Und Die Entstehung Des Monotheismus* (Vandenhoeck & Ruprecht, 2007), 1.632. See also R. B. Salters, *Lamentations* (London: T&T Clark, 2010), 52. "an element of vulnerability and concern."

23 Marc Wischnowsky, *Tochter Zion: Aufname Und Überwindung Der Stadtklage in Den Prophetenschrift Des Alten Testament* (Neukirchen-Vluyn: Neukirchener Verlag, 2001); Brittany Kim, *"Lengthen Your Tent-Cords": The Metaphorical World of Israel's Household in the Book of Isaiah* (University Park, PA: Eisenbrauns, 2018), 51–78.

24 Johanna Stiebert, *Fathers and Daughters in the Hebrew Bible* (Oxford: Oxford University Press, 2013); Kimberly D. Russaw, *Daughters in the Hebrew Bible* (Lexington Books / Fortress: Fortress Academic, 2020).

25 Green notes that the motherhood of Zion makes Jerusalem the locus of life, joy, and comfort (or safe haven and secure base in attachment terms). See Stefan Green, "Zion as Mother in the Restored Relationship Between God and God's People: A Study of Isaiah 66:7–14a," (Sheffield: Sheffield Phoeniz, 2019), 266–97. On the personification of Zion, see Ulrich Berges, "Personifications and Prophetic Voices of Zion in Isaiah and Beyond," in *The Elusive Prophet: The Prophet as Historical Person, Literary Character and Annonymous Artist*, ed. Johannes

Cornelis De Moor (Leiden: Brill, 2001), 54–82; Mark J. Boda, Carol J. Dempsey, and LeAnn Snow Flesher, *Daughter Zion: Her Portrait, Her Response* (Atlanta, GA: Society of Biblical Literature, 2012); Christl M. Maier, *Daughter Zion, Mother Zion: Gender, Space, and the Sacred in Ancient Israel* (Minneapolis: Fortress, 2008). Most of this paragraph is paraphrased from David A. Bosworth, "Daughter Zion and Weeping in Lamentations 1–2," *Journal for the Study of the Old Testament* 38 (2013) 217–37, 224–26.

26 Katharina Galor and Hanswulf Bloedhorn, *The Archaeology of Jerusalem From the Origins to the Ottoman* (New Haven, CT: Yale University Press, 2013), 13.

27 The profile did shift more dramatically, however, in the first century CE, when the term evoked a separate location further west across the Tyropoean Valley, which is today called (New) Mount Zion. Inhabitants imagined that the city of David was located on this more dominant height with more acreage at its top to accommodate what they may have mistakenly imagined as a large urban space in David's time. This height was the focus of the city in subsequent ages. Only in the mid-nineteenth century did scholars begin to realize that this traditional identification of Mount Zion was mistaken. Galor and Bloedhorn, *Archeology of Jerusalem*, 5.

28 Galor and Bloedhorn, *Archeology of Jerusalem*, 18–26; Keel, *Die Geschichte Jerusalems Und Die Entstehung Des Monotheismus*, 1.45–47, 80–85, 122–25.

29 Mihaylov and Perkins, "Community Place Attachment and Its Role in Social Capital Development"; Scannell and Gifford, "Defining place attachment: A tripartite organizing framework," 5–7.

30 J. J. M. Roberts, "The Davidic Origin of the Zion Tradition," in *The Bible and the Ancient Near East: Collected Essays* (Winona Lake, IN: Eisenbrauns, 2002), 313–30; J. J. M. Roberts, "Zion in the Theology of the Davidic-Solomonic Empire," in *The Bible and the Ancient Near East: Collected Essays* (Winona Lake, IN: Eisenbrauns, 2002), 331–47; Frederik Poulsen, *Representing Zion: Judgment and Salvation in the Old Testament* (London: Taylor and Francis, 2014), 2–10; Lois K. Fuller Dow, *Images of Zion: Biblical Antecedents for the New Jerusalem* (Sheffield: Sheffield Phoenix, 2010), 76–107; Leslie J. Hoppe, *The Holy City: Jerusalem in the Theology of the Old Testament* (Collegeville, MN: Liturgical Press, 2000).

31 Magreet L. Steiner, "The Notion of Jerusalem as a Holy City," in *Reflection and Refraction: Studies in Biblical Historiography in Honor of A.*

*Graeme Auld*, ed. Robert Rezetko, Timothy Henry Lim, and W. Brian Aucker (Leiden: Brill, 2007), 447–58, esp. 451.

32  Steiner, "Notion of Jerusalem," 452–54.

33  Galor and Bloedhorn, *Archeology of Jerusalem*, 31–34; Adrian Curtis, *Oxford Bible Atlas* (4th ed.; Oxford: Oxford University Press, 2009), 143–44; Keel, *Die Geschichte Jerusalems Und Die Entstehung Des Monotheismus* 1.412–17; Avraham Faust, "Society and Culture in the Kingdom of Judah During the Eighth Century," in *Archaeology and History of Eighth-Century Judah*, ed. Zev I. Farber and Jacob L. Wright (Atlanta, GA: Society of Biblical Literature, 2018), 179–204; Ronny Reich and Eli Shukron, "The Urban Development of Jerusalem in the Late Eighth Century B.c.e.," in *Jerusalem in Bible and Archaeology: The First Temple Period*, ed. Andrew G. Vaughn and Ann E. Killebrew (Atlanta, GA: Society of Biblical Literature, 2003), 209–18.

34  Melody D. Knowles, *Centrality Practiced: Jerusalem in the Religious Practice of Yehud and Teh Diaspora in the Persian Period* (Atlanta, GA: Society of Biblical Literature, 2006).

35  Scannell and Gifford, "Defining Place Attachment: A Tripartite Organizing Framework," 2.

36  Sir Charles William Wilson, *Picturesque Palestine, Sinai, and Egypt* (London: J. S. Virtue, 1881).

37  For a summary of past scholarship in this topic with new contributions, see Eric J. Wagner, *The Mountain's Shadow* (Tübingen: Mohr Siebeck, forthcoming). On mountains, divinity, and personified Zion, see also, Julie Galambush, *Jerusalem in the Book of Ezekiel: The City as Yahweh's Wife* (Atlanta, GA: Society of Biblical Literature, 1992); Maier, *Daughter Zion, Motehr Zion*; Jon D. Levenson, *Sinai and Zion: An Entry Into the Jewish Bible* (New York, NY: Harper One, 1985).

38  This passage appears early in the book, and it may have been the opening oracle at some stage of its growth given the superscription in 2:1. There is no consensus about the date of this oracle. For an argument for Isaianic authorship, see Hans Wildberger, *Isaiah 1–12*, trans. Thomas H. Trapp (Minneapolis, MN: Fortress, 1990), 85–87. For a summary of the scholarly discussion, see H. G. M. Williamson, *Isaiah 1–5* (London: T & T Clark, 2006), 173–79. Although the motif of the nations coming to Jerusalem is common in post-exilic prophetic passages, the present passage stands out for the lack of imperialistic tone. Elsewhere, the nations come to Jerusalem as servants and experience humiliation and subordination. In Isaiah 2:2–4, they are happier for their pilgrimage to Zion. For an analysis of the passage in the context of the Psalms

of Zion, see John T. Willis, "Isaiah 2:2–5 and the Psalms of Zion," in *Writing and Reading the Scroll of Isaiah: Studies of an Interpretive Tradition, Volume One*, ed. Craig C. Broyles and Craig A. Evans (Leiden: Brill, 1997), 295–316.

39  Williamson, *Isaiah 1–5*, 168.

40  Michael J. Seufert, "A Walk They Remembered: Covenant Relationship as Journey in the Deuteronomistic History," *Biblical Interpretation* 25 (2017) 149–71.

41  On the land of Canaan as target of place attachment, see Counted and Watts, "Place Attachment in the Bible," 222–23.

42  Prior scholarship on the meaning of the verb אבל has suffered from a hyperfocus on the verb to the exclusion of the wider motif of drying vegetation. The ten occurrences of אבל strike many interpreters as ambiguous: the verb might profile drying or mourning. In my view, drying better fits these contexts, and this meaning emerges more clearly in the wider context of the prophetic motif of drying vegetation, which employs אבל and other verbs. On previous efforts to discern the meaning of אבל, see David J. A. Clines, "Was there an 'BL II 'Be Dry' in Classical Hebrew?," *Vetus Testamentum* 42 (1992) 1–10; Katherine Murphey Hayes, *The Earth Mourns: Prophetic Metaphor and Oral Aesthetic* (Leiden: Brill, 2002). The issue began with G. R. Driver, "Confused Hebrew Roots," in *Occident and Orient: Being Studies in Semitic Philology and Literature, Jewish History and Philosophy and Folklore in the Widest Sense, in Honour of Haham Dr. M. Gaster's 80th Birthday*, ed. Bruno Schindler and Arthur Marmorstein (London: Taylor's Foreign Press, 1936), 73–82. Clines's argument has persuaded John Barton, *Joel and Obadiah: A Commentary* (Louisville, KY: Westminster John Know, 2001), 53. Clines refuses to engage the specifics of any of the passages, but context shapes meaning. He wrongly states that speakers reduce polysemous meanings in words. He reflects no awareness of the wider context of a prophetic motif of drying. He dismisses both the Akkadian cognate *abālu to dry* and the Aramaic translations of אבל as חרב *to dry out*. Clines shaped the entry on אבל in CDH according to his poor arguments, so this lexicon does not even note "to dry" as a possible meaning of אבל. This meaning emerges in analysis of the texts within the context of the prophetic motif of drying.

43  The opening reference to the drought uses the word בצרות, perhaps a plural of intensity (William L. Holladay, *Jeremiah 1* (Philadelphia: Fortress, 1986)) or plural of extension (Robert P. Carroll, *Jeremiah: A*

*Commentary* (Philadelphia, PA: Westminster, 1986), 306). The singular appears in Jeremiah 17:8.

44 The term אמל appears, for example, in Isaiah 16:8 of dried plants, and emotionally exhausted people in Isaiah 19:8.

45 Recently, ecologists have found that wild donkeys in some arid regions dig holes to uncover water and that these water holes have long-term ecological impacts on other species. These holes are called ass holes (seriously!). See Erick Lundgren et al., "Equids Engineer Desert Water Availability," *Science* 372 (2021) 491–95. The opening of verse 4 connects the line to what follows (because of the ruined soil, the farmers cover their heads), not what precedes (the servants already have a reason to cover their heads). For a history of unnecessary emendations to the verse, see Holladay, *Jeremiah 1*, 318.

46 The term חתת in verse 4 generally refers to breaking of objects (Jer 50:2) or the fear and dismay of people (Jer 8:9), but applies to the land in this context, not the people. The term אדמה here refers to the land itself, not metonymically to the inhabitants and חתת applies to the damage that drought has caused to the soil.

47 Saul M. Olyan, *Biblical Mourning: Ritual and Social Dimensions* (Oxford; New York: Oxford University Press, 2004), 75.

48 The response to the desiccated land coheres with research on landscape preferences. A desire for water is one of the best documented preferences. Rachel Kaplan and Stephen Kaplan, *The Experience of Nature: A Psychological Perspective* (Cambridge: Cambridge University Press, 1989); Matthew P. White et al., "Blue Landscapes and Public Health," in *Oxford Textbook of Nature and Public Health*, ed. Matilda van den Bosch and William Bird (Oxford: Oxford University Press, 2018), 154–59.

49 Ronald Simkins, *Yahweh's Activity in History and Nature in the Book of Joel* (Lewiston, NY: Edwin Mellen, 1991), 137–38, 149–54; James L. Crenshaw, *Joel: A New Translation With Introduction and Commentary* (New York, NY: Doubleday, 1995), 90–94.

50 The opening אבלו is most likely an imperative ("mourn!" cf. LXX πενθεῖτε) in keeping with the multiple parallel imperatives later in the passage (vv. 11, 13, 14). See Simkins, *Yahweh's Activity* 132. He notes that repointing the verb to an imperative is more suitable for the genre of the text.

51 Reading with the LXX, which has ὅτι at the start of verse 10. MT reads only the כי at the head of verse 10b. Simkins argues that the second כי was added later as a result of dittography and the first כי subsequently

dropped from the text. Simkins, *Yahweh's Activity*, 132. Barton appreciates the sound logic of the emendation but rejects it as unnecessary and prefers the MT. Barton, *Joel and Obadiah*, 49–50.

52 If the MT accurately represents an original text with a perfect instead of imperative verb for the priests and no כי at the start of verse 10, then the meaning "to mourn" becomes possible. By this reading, the text describes the priests as mourning, the earth as ruined, and the land as אבל, which could be mourning or drying. The mourning argument would connect the verb back to its prior occurrence to argue that the priests and the land share a common emotional experience. The drying argument would focus within verse 10 and subsequent verses to connect the verb to the several verbs of drying in the passage. I prefer to follow Simkin's textual argument because the LXX imperative fits the genre and context and coheres with Jeremiah 14:1–7. A כי seems likely to have stood at the start of verse 10, although the terseness of Hebrew poetry allows syntactic markers to drop and even in the absence of the particle the sense that Simkins finds may still be read. See Simkins, *Yahweh's Activity*.

53 The author plays on the meanings of אבל (*dry up; mourn*) and the similar words for drying vegetation (הובישה) and shamed inhabitants (הבישו).

54 The verbs examined were: אבל (*to dry up*), יבש (*to dry up*), חרב (*to dry up*), נבל (*to wither*), אמל (*to wither*), נשת (*to dry up*), מלל (*to wither*).

55 Isaiah 15:5; 16:8–9; 19:5–9; 24:4–7; 27:10–11; 33:9; 42:15; Jeremiah 4:23–28; 8:13; 12:1–4, 7–13; 14:1–7; 23:9–12; 50:38; 51:36; Ezekiel 29:10; Hosea 4:1–3; Amos 1:2; 4:7; Joel 1:9–14; Nahum 1:4; Haggai 1:11; Zechariah 10:11.

56 Only in Isaiah 42:15 does drying vegetation appear as a positive development because it facilitates travel.

57 Isaiah 1:29–31; 28:1–6; 34:4; 40:6–8, 22–24; 64:5; Jeremiah 15:9; Zechariah 10:11; Psalms 1:3; 37:2; 58:8; 90:6; 102:12; 129:6; Job 8:12; 14:2; 15:30; 18:16; 24:24.

58 For comparison, annual rainfall is about 120 cm in New York City, 100 cm in Washington, DC, 100 cm in Seattle, 60 cm in San Francisco, and 58 cm in London.

59 Both these insects devour crops and rush as described by Joel 1, which also uses the verb *rush/attack* of locusts. The attacker may be Sennacherib. J. J. M. Roberts, *First Isaiah* (Minneapolis, MN: Fortress Press, 2015), 424–25, for a summary of prior proposals, mostly assuming a later date.

60 The passage paints a general picture of societal collapse following the broken covenant or violation of moral obligations to God. Thus Brevard S. Childs, *Isaiah* (Louisville, KY: Westminster John Knox Press, 2001), 247. Hans Wildberger, *Isaiah 28–39,* trans. Thomas H. Trapp (Minneapolis, MN: Fortress, 2002), 283–84. Others see the broken covenant more specifically as the treaty with Sennacherib. Thus Gary V. Smith, *Isaiah 1–39* (Nashville, TN: B&H Publishing Group, 2007), 555; Roberts, *First Isaiah,* 427;

61 Clines takes this context as evidence that the verb means *to mourn.* Clines, "Was there an 'BL II 'Be Dry' in Classical Hebrew?"

62 Kirsten Nielsen, *There is Hope for a Tree: The Tree as Metaphor in Isaiah* (Sheffield: JSPT Press, 1989), 126–28.

63 The ancient covenant is not any biblical covenant, but the universally understood norms of ethical behavior that also serve as the basis for the oracles against the nations. See Donald C. Polaski, *Authorizing an End: The Isaiah Apocalypse and Intertextuality* (Leiden; Boston: Brill, 2001); John Barton, "Ethics in Isaiah of Jerusalem," *Journal of Theological Studies* 32 (1981) 1–18.

64 The term for pollution is rare: חנף appears only here and in Jeremiah 3:1–2, 9; Psalm 106:38; Micah 4:11 txt; cf. Numbers 35:33. These texts connect this kind of pollution to the worst injustice: shedding innocent blood. Certain crimes are so heinous that all peoples may be expected to recognize their wrongness. This pollution reinforces the sense of the ancient covenant as fundamental ethical norms that all peoples know.

65 Modified from NABRE, which reads *mourn* for אבל.

66 Modified from NABRE, which reads *mourn* for אבל.

67 Alec Basson, "People are Plants: A Conceptual Metaphor in the Hebrew Bible," *Old Testament Essays* 19 (2006) 573–83; Patricia K. Tull, "Persistent Vegetative States: People as Plants and Plants as People in Isaiah," in *The Desert Will Bloom: Poetic Visions in Isaiah,* ed. A. Joseph Everson and Hyun Chul Paul Kim (Atlanta, GA: Society of Biblical Literature, 2009), 17–34; Nielsen, *There is Hope for a Tree*; Jennifer Metten Pantoja, *The Metaphor of the Divine as Planter of the People: Stinking Grapes or Pleasant Planting?* (Leiden: Brill, 2017); Benjamin M. Austin, *Plant Metaphors in the Old Greek of Isaiah* (Atlanta, GA: Society of Biblical Literature, 2019).

68 Psalms 1:3; 37:2; 58:8; 90:6; 102:12; 129:6; Job 8:12; 14:2; 15:30; 18:16; 24:24; Isaiah 1:30; 28:1, 4; 34:4; 40:7, 8, 24; 64:5.

69 Richard J. Clifford, *Psalms 73–150* (Nashville, TN: Abingdon, 2003), 96–102; Craig C. Broyles, *Psalms* (Peabody, MA: Hendrickson, 1999),

359–60. John Goldingay, *Psalms* (Grand Rapids, MI: Baker Academic, 2006), 3.21–35. Frank-Lothar Hossfeld et al., *Psalms 2: A Commentary on Psalms 51–100* (2005), 416–25.

70 The text of verse 7 is missing from LXX and the initial hand of 1QIsaᵃ, likely due to haplography.

71 John Goldingay and David Payne, *Isaiah 40–55 Vol 1* (London: Bloomsbury, 2006), 80.

72 The term here has sometimes been understood as "beauty" or "glory" on the basis of the LXX rendering δόξα, which itself may be motivated by the association with flowers here, the reference to God's glory in Isaiah 40:5, and the flower-beauty connection in Isaiah 28:1.

73 Goldingay and Payne, *Isaiah 40–55 Vol 1*; Jan Leunis Koole, *Isaiah: Isaiah 40–48* (Kampen: Pharos, 1997), 66.

74 Koole, *Isaiah 40–48*, 111.

75 Modified from NABRE. Reading 1QIsaᵇ (חציר גגת הנשדף לפני קדם). MT of Isaiah 1:27 and 1 Kings 19:26 both appear corrupt. See Roberts, *First Isaiah*, 464–65.

76 Reading 1QIsaᵃ קדים. MT reads קמה *standing grain*.

77 Modified from NABRE, which render *faints away* instead of *wilts*.

78 See the spreadsheet, which includes a list all the examples of drying vegetation with all the verbs used to identify these passages. Of the eight verbs of drying investigated, only three of them appear when drying vegetation is a source domain in a metaphor for mortality. Within Isaiah, נבל is by far the most common verb in metaphorical uses, occurring in seven of the eight examples (Isa 1:30; 28:1, 4; 34:4; 40:7, 8, 24; 64:5), paired with יבש twice (40:7, 8) and יבש occurs by itself once (40:24). The preferred verb in Psalms and Job is מלל, appearing in six of the eleven examples (Pss 37:2; 58:8; 90:6; Job 14:2; 18:16; 24:24). It occurs once with נבל (Ps 37:2) and twice with יבש (Ps 90:6; Job 18:16). The remaining examples in Psalms and Job appear with יבש only (Pss 102:12; 129:6; Job 8:12; 15:30). None of the metaphorical passages employ the verb אבל. The verbs חרב and נשת are also absent from these examples. The verb חרב describes the drying of water without reference to vegetation (Isa 19:5–6; 44:27; 50:2; 51:10), and נשת appears only once (Isa 19:5) to refer to water without vegetation in view. For emotion metaphors, the terms נבל and אמל occur most often, whereas יבש and מלל appear in context emphasizing mortality. God's power may also be manifest in the language of drying that makes no reference to plants. In these examples, the verb חרב describes the drying of water. In Isaiah 44:27 ʏʜᴡʜ dries up the

rivers, the deep, and the sea in ways that emphasize the power of God over the waters of chaos. Similarly, the king of Assyria boasts that he dried up the rivers of Egypt under his feet (Isa 37:25). These examples make no reference to plants but focus instead on a mythic meaning of water as chaos. The verb חרב can also mean to be in ruins (Qal) or make waste or lay in ruins (Hiphil), suggesting an association between dryness and wasteland.

# Chapter 2

1 The science of predicting the weather has become a multibillion dollar industry because the ability to predict weather removes surprise and enables people and institutions to prepare for weather events. See Elizabeth Austin, *Treading on Thin Air: Atmospheric Physics, Forensic Meteorology, and Climate Change: How Weather Shapes Our Everyday Lives* (New York: Pegasus, 2016), esp. 21–33.

2 Paul Ekman, *Emotions Revealed: Recognizing Faces and Feelings to Improve Communication and Emotional Life* (Rev. ed.; New York, NY: Holt, 2007), 164–68. Surprise provides an illustration of the difference between an emotion and a reflex. The startle reflex is even shorter than surprise, lasting one-quarter of a second at most and involves almost opposite expressions (eyes closed, brows down, jaw closed). Even if warned, the startle reflex cannot be eliminated, although it may be reduced. You start at a popping balloon even if you know it will pop. Knowing what will happen, however, extinguishes surprise since this emotion depends on the unexpected. Since surprise functions to capture and focus attention, it can lead to a wide variety of different emotions and behaviors, whereas the startle reflex is a simple self-protective response that does not necessarily involve a refocusing of attention and emotional response unless surprise quickly follows. Ekman, *Emotions Revealed*, 151; Brené Brown, *Atlas of the Heart: Mapping Meaningful Connection and the Language of Human Experience* (New York, NY: Random House, 2021), 66.

3 The expression (המראה הגדל) here profiles a surprising or remarkable sight, not something literally big but something impressive, that makes a big impression.

4 Note the many occurrences of כל that emphasize the universality of the events: Isaiah 13:5, 7 (twice), 15 (twice).

5 Modified from NABRE, which renders תמה as *aghast*. I will consistently represent this Hebrew verb with *astounded*.

6  Hebrew terms בהל and תמה appear in this passage. The prototypical Hebrew word for fear is ירא. Lasater provides statistics on words related to this root but does not investigate the couple of dozen or more Hebrew words that can profile fear. Phillip Michael Lasater, *Facets of Fear: The Fear of God in Exilic and Post-Exilic Contexts* (Tübingen: Mohr Siebeck, 2019). He argues that English and Hebrew conceptualizations of fear are very different, yet his evidence shows otherwise. In both, fear has affective and behavior dimensions and is not limited to social contexts (e.g., fear of briars and thorns in Isa 7:25). His work suffers from an overemphasis on a narrow set of lexemes and a corresponding assumption that concepts cannot be salient in passages where expected lexemes are missing. David is never said to be afraid in the cave in 1 Samuel 24, but audiences would likely assume fear given the danger of his situation, trapped in a cave by a superior force seeking to kill him. An early editor perceived fear in this context and therefore associated Psalm 142 with this episode. The psalm reflects fear, yet does not use any specific fear vocabulary. It speaks of distress, a weakened spirit, traps, persecutors, prison, and a sense of isolation as well as a lack of a safe place so that the speaker cries out to YHWH, employing a verb often used to profile the petitions of oppressed and frightened people. Lasater's work provides a good analysis of a lexical root, but not of the Hebrew concept of fear.

7  The Niphal of בהל profiles almost exclusively fear.

8  Modified from NABRE. On הנה as a mirative particle marking surprise, see Cynthia Miller-Naudé and C. H. J. van der Merwe, "הנה and Mirativity in Biblical Hebrew," *Hebrew Studies* 52 (2011) 53–81.

9  Modified from NABRE, which renders בהל with "thrown into confusion." I will consistently render the Hebrew verb as *terrified*.

10  The root ירא does not in itself profile surprise.

11  No Hebrew word precisely matches English *surprise*. The closest may be תמה, which profiles fear and surprise as described above. English translations render it *aghast* (NABRE, NRSV, ESV, CEB), a word profiling both fear and surprise. This sense appears also in Jeremiah 4:9 where it is parallel with שמם, which similarly profiles amazement in a negative sense (rendered *appalled*). The verb שער approximates the concept of surprise. The verb derives from the noun for hair, including body hair, and profiles the experience of goosebumps and by extension the strong emotion and surprise that triggers this physiological reaction. The root also refers to thunderstorms, perhaps because violent storms can elicit this hair-raising response.

12 Crozier W. Ray and Peter J. de Jong, eds. *The Psychological Significance of the Blush* (Cambridge: Cambridge University Press, 2012).

13 Claudia D. Bergmann, *Childbirth as a Metaphor for Crisis: Evidence From the Ancient Near East, the Hebrew Bible, and 1QH XI, 1–18* (Berlin: Walter de Gruyter, 2008), 219.

14 Research on Terror Management Theory supports the four major hypotheses of the theory. First, the mortality salience hypothesis claims that reminders of death increase our motivation to adhere to cultural worldviews. An early study found that judges who had been primed to think about their mortality set much higher bonds for accused people than those who were not so primed, showing that a simple reminder of mortality can have significant impacts on our behaviors and we may be unaware of the effect. Second, the death thought accessibility hypothesis holds that threatening or weakening cultural structures makes thoughts about personal mortality more accessible. Third, the anxiety buffer hypothesis holds that self-esteem reduces anxiety about death because it is an extension of the cultural structures that reduce death through accessibility and mitigate anxiety. On these three hypotheses, see Jeff Schimel, Joseph Hayes, and Michael Sharp, "A Consideration of Three Critical Hypotheses," in *Handbook of Terror Management Theory*, ed. Clay Routledge and Matthew Vess (London: Academic Press, 2019), 1–30. For an introduction to terror management theory for general readers, see Sheldon Solomon, Jeff Greenberg, and Tom Pyszczynski, *The Worm At the Core: On the Role of Death in Life* (London: Penguin, 2015). For a more detailed description of the state of the field, see the several essays in Clay Routledge and Matthew Vess, *Handbook of Terror Management Theory* (London: Academic Press, 2019). The main lines of the theory originated with Ernest Becker, *The Denial of Death* (New York, NY: Simon and Schuster, 1973).

15 Susanne Gillmayr-Bucher, "Metaphors of Space and Time: Imagining Stability in the Fourth Book of the Psalms," in *Networks of Metaphors in the Hebrew Bible*, ed. Danilo Verde and Antje Labahn (Leuven: Peeters, 2020), 215–32, describes how creation metaphors establish stability following the instability of Psalm 89 at the end of the third book of the Psalter.

16 Arne Öhman, "Fear and Anxiety: Overlaps and Dissociations," in *Handbook of Emotions*, ed. Michael Lewis, Jeannette M. Haviland-Jones, and Lisa Feldman Barrett (New York, NY: Guilford Press, 2008), 709–29, here 711.

17 The verb רעש reliably profiles a shaking earth over other subjects, but Ezekiel 38:20 makes humans and animals the subject of quaking. In Isaiah 13:13, YHWH shakes the heavens, clarifying divine agency. The LXX, however, reads a future passive verb form parallel to the next clause in which the earth is the subject of its own shaking. The verb געש profiles shaking earth only in 2 Samuel 22:8 // Psalm 18:8, and elsewhere describes surging water (Jer 5:22; 46:7, 8) and trembling or unstable people (Jer 25:16). The verb מוט profiles shaking or tottering more often of people than the earth. When it does describe the earth, the verb often appears with a negative adverb to indicate the stability of the earth (Ps 93:1; 96:10; 104:5; 125:1). In Isaiah 54:10, YHWH acknowledges that although the mountain and hills may move or be shaken, "my loyalty shall never move from you, nor my covenant of friendship be shaken."

18 Cooley argues that the ancient Israelites perceived the luminaries as personalities. See Jeffrey L. Cooley, *Poetic Astronomy in the Ancient Near East* (Winona Lake, IN: Eisenbrauns, 2013).

19 Eric Johnson, "A Phenomenological Investigation of Fear of the Dark," *Journal of Phenomenological Psychology* 19 (1988) 179–94; Krisztina Kopcsó and András Láng, "Uncontrolled Thoughts in the Dark? Effects of Lighting Conditions and Fear of the Dark on Thinking Processes," *Imagination, Cognition, Personality: Consciousness in Theory, Research and Clinical Practice* 39 (2019) 97–108; Joshua Levos and Tammy Lowery Zacchilli, "Nyctophobia: From Imagined to Realistic Fears of the Dark," *Psy Chi Journal of Psychological Research* 20 (2015) 102–10; Christian Grillon et al., "Darkness Facilitates the Acoustic Startle Reflex in Humans," *Biological Psychiatry* 42 (1997) 453–60.

20 Peter Joshua Atkins, "Mythology or Zoology?: A Study of the Impact of Translation History in Isaiah 13:21," *BibInt* 24 (2016) 48–59.

21 The Hebrew שכב means *to lie* and represents a euphemistic expression compared to שגל, which seems to have been a vulgar term for sex. See Emanuel Tov, *Textual Criticism of the Hebrew Bible* (3rd ed.; Minneapolis, MN: Fortress, 2012), 59–61. The scribes chose a word that normally implies consensual sex as opposed to an alternative way of speaking about rape (e.g., ענה in Deut 22:23–29; 2 Sam 13:14).

22 The term פז profiles refined gold, or gold of particular purity and desirability, and כתם is another poetic term for gold that elsewhere appears in construct with Ophir (Ps 45:10; Job 28:16), an uncertain location likely southern Arabia or points beyond associated with gold.

23 Miller-Naudé and van der Merwe, "הנה and Mirativity in Biblical Hebrew"; Paul Jouon and Tamitsu Muraoka, *A Grammar of Biblical Hebrew* (Rome: Gregorian Biblical BookShop, 2006), 162e.

24 NABRE does not translate these particles in 13:7 or 13:9. The particle does not translate well into English and translators vary in their practice. NRSV renders the particle *See* in both places, and CEB renders *Look*.

25 Francis I. Andersen and David Noel Freedman, *Amos: A New Translation With Introduction and Commentary* (New York, NY: Doubleday, 1989), 522. They persuasively argue that the passage involves two stories, not one story about an exceptionally unlucky man. Similarly James Luther Mays, *Amos: A Commentary* (Louisville, KY: Westminster John Knox Press, 1969), 105.

26 Marvin A. Sweeney, *The Twelve Prophets: Hosea, Joel, Amos, Obadiah, Jonah* (Collegeville, MN: Liturgical Press, 2000), 161.

27 The Hebrew root is שוב. See William L. Holladay, *The Root Šubh in the Old Testamernt With Particular Reference to Its Usage in Covenant Contexts* (Leiden: Brill, 1958).

28 Michael J. Seufert, "A Walk They Remembered: Covenant Relationship as Journey in the Deuteronomistic History," *Biblical Interpretation* 25 (2017) 149–71.

29 Modified from NABRE, which renders שטף with *dashes*.

30 Deborah O'Daniel Cantrell, *The Horsemen of Israel: Horses and Chariotry in Monarchic Israel (Ninth-Eighth Centuries B.c.e.)* (Winona Lake, IN: Eisenbrains, 2011), 12 emphasis original.

31 Cantrell, *Horsemen of Israel*, 14–18.

32 Nicole L. Tilford, *Sensing World, Sensing Wisdom: The Cognitive Foundation of Biblical Metaphors* (Atlanta, GA: Society of Biblical Literature Press, 2017); Michael Carasik, *Theologies of the Mind in Biblical Israel* (New York, NY: Peter Lang, 2006).

33 William L. Holladay, *Jeremiah 1* (Philadelphia: Fortress, 1986), 280; William McKane, *Jeremiah* (Edinburgh: T & T Clark, 1986), 1.184–85.

34 Modified from NABRE, which renders שמר here as *observe*.

35 Modified from NABRE, which renders מועד as *seasons*. The Hebrew word profiles an agreed-on time for a meeting or the meeting itself.

36 Holladay, *Jeremiah 1*, 281–83; McKane, *Jeremiah*, 1.186; H. L. Bosman, "Jeremiah 8:8: Why are Scribes Accused of Corrupting the Torah?," *Acta Theologica Supplementum* 26 (2018) 118–35.

37 The mirative particle הנה (*look!*) preceded by אכן appears only here. Both particles have a mirative force, indicating surprise, although אכן can be more generally emphatic (Gen 28:16; Isa 40:7) or contrasting (Ps 66:19).

38 H. G. M. Williamson, *Isaiah 1–5* (London: T & T Clark, 2006), 32. Williamson critiques those who read the passage as a covenant lawsuit on grounds that the genre is a product of scholarly imagination rather than textual evidence. He calls it "an abuse of form criticism." H. G. M. Williamson, "Isaiah 1 and the Covenant Lawsuit," in *Covenant as Context: Essays in Honor of E. W. Nicholson*, ed. Andrew David Hastings Mayes and Robert B. Salters (Oxford: Oxford University Press, 2003), 393–406, here 400. Scholars disagree about the genre itself, its application to Isaiah 1, and no one sees the genre fully realized in the passage anyway. Barton has located the ethical concern of Isaiah in a context larger than the Israelite legal tradition. See John Barton, "Ethics in Isaiah of Jerusalem," *Journal of Theological Studies* 32 (1981) 1–18. For prior discussion of the covenant lawsuit, see Herbert B. Huffmon, "The Covenant Lawsuit in the Prophets," *Journal of Biblical Literature* (1959) 285–95; Kirsten Nielsen, *Yahweh as Prosecutor and Judge: An Investigation of the Prophetic Lawsuit (Rîb-Pattern)* (Sheffield, 1981); Kirsten Nielsen, "Das Bild des Gerichts (*rib*-pattern) in Jes i–xii," *Vetus Testamentum* 29 (1979) 309–24; Hans Wildberger, *Isaiah 1–12*, trans. Thomas H. Trapp (Minneapolis, MN: Fortress, 1990), 9–11.

39 Modified from NABRE, which render בנים as *sons*.

40 In LXX, YHWH has begotten and raised children because LXX seems to have read ילדתי for MT גדלתי. The verb רמם (polel) profiles raising children only in conjunction with גדל (here and Isa 23:4), which is likely the original reading.

41 The metaphor of YHWH as father of Israel was well-known. The appearance of YHWH as father in Deuteronomy 32:5–6 seems especially relevant since several scholars argue that Isaiah 1:2–3 allude to these last words of Moses. Williamson, *Isaiah 1–5*, 31–32. Interpreters often posit a wisdom influence in Isaiah 1:2–3 because of its parent–child language, animal imagery, and use of cognitive verbs ידע and התבנן. Wildberger, *Isaiah 1–12*; J. William Whedbee, *Isaiah and Wisdom* (Nashville, TN: Abington, 1971); Joseph Jensen, *The Use of Tôrâ By Isaiah: His Debate With the Wisdom Tradition* (Washington, DC: Catholic Biblical Association, 1973); Hilary Marlow, *Biblical Prophets and Contemporary Environmental Ethics: Re-Reading Amos, Hosea, and First Isaiah* (Oxford: Oxford University Press, 2009). The strong distinction

once made between prophecy and wisdom has long been questioned and all three "wisdom" elements noted above can be found across biblical genres. Rather than positing an outsized "wisdom" influence on the whole canon, it seems simpler to suppose that the whole literary tradition drew on common cultural knowledge to create various genres of literature. Thus Williamson, *Isaiah 1–5*; Will Kynes, *An Obituary for "Wisdom Literature": The Birth, Death, and Intertextual Reintegration of a Biblical Corpus* (Oxford: Oxford University Press, 2019). Some emphasize the stupidity of the animals and imagine that the passage applies a contrast in intelligence, focusing on the cognitive senses of ידע and התבנן. See, for example, Michael Barrett, "The Danger of Heartless Religion: An Exposition of Isaiah 1:2–18," *Puritan Reformed Journal* 6 (2014) 5–15.

42 Kessler, however, argues that these verbs assume YHWH as mother in Isaiah 1:2. See Rainer Kessler, "'Söhne Habe Ich Grossgezogen Und Emporgebracht . . .': Gott Als Mutter in Jes 1,2," in *"Ihr Völker, klatscht in die Hände!" Festschrift für Erhard S. Gerstenberger zum 65. Geburtstag*, ed. Rainer Kessler et al. (Munich: Lit, 1997), 134–47.

43 Joshua Berman, "What does the Ox Know in Isa 1:3a," *Vetus Testamentum* 64 (2014) 382–88. See also Udo Rüterswörden, "Ochs Und Esel in Des 1,2–3," in *Die unwiderstehliche Wahrheit: Studien zur alttestamentlichen Prophetie, Festschrift für Arndt Meinhold*, ed. Rüdiger Lux (Leipzig: Evangelische Verlagsanstalt, 2006), 382–88.

44 Berman, "What does the Ox Know in Isa 1:3a."

45 Berman, "What does the Ox Know in Isa 1:3a."

46 Barton's description of something like "natural law" in Isaiah tends to focus on a divinely created order without much attention to the affective motivations for living in accordance with this order. Barton, "Ethics in Isaiah of Jerusalem."

47 Alphonso Groenewald, "Isaiah 1:2–3, Ethics and Wisdom. Isaiah 1:2–3 and the Song of Moses (Dt 32): Is Isaiah a Prophet like Moses?," *Hervormde Teologiese Studies* 67 (2011) 1–6, quote p. 3.

48 The lack of clear purpose or audience has long puzzled commentators who search for hidden meanings because of its location in a prophetic context. Marlow, *Biblical Prophets and Contemporary Environmental Ethics*, 211.

49 See Ugaritic *tlt*. John F. Healey, "Ancient Agriculture and the Old Testament (With Special Reference to Isaiah XXVIII 23–29)," in *Prophets, Worship, and Theodicy: Studies in Prophetism, Biblical Theology, and Structural and Rhetorical Analysis, and on the Place of Music in Worship:*

*Papers Read at the Joint British-Dutch Old Testament Conference held at Woudschoten, 1982* (Leiden: Brill, 1984), 108–19, here 111 and 114.

50  These obscure terms are שׂורה and נסמן, both omitted in LXX. NABRE omits any representation of שׂורה rendered here as *two-rowed barley*.

51  Healey, "Prophets, Worship, and Theodicy," 114–15.

52  Verse 28 includes many difficulties that may have motivated the interpretive rendering of LXX. The word לחם must here profile seeds suitable for making bread (cf. English "bread wheat"), not bread itself, and the verb יודק profiles an agricultural activity related to threshing (דושׁ). Healey, "Prophets, Worship, and Theodicy," 116.

53  Healey, "Prophets, Worship, and Theodicy," 116.

54  But note Psalm 94:12 places YHWH's discipline (Piel of יסר) in parallel with YHWH teaching law (Piel of למד and object noun תורה).

55  The positive dimension of divine instruction may motivate the LXX interpretation of יורנו as derived from רנן *to rejoice* (LXX: εὐφρανθήσῃ, *you will rejoice*). The verse emphasizes divine instruction, however, and only implies human joy.

56  Modified from NABRE, which renders עצה with *counsel*.

57  The introductory הוי *woe* in Isaiah 28:1; 29:1; 30:1; 31:1 and הן *see* in 32:1 structure Isaiah 28–33. The הוי in 29:14 and 33:1 introduce material subordinate to what precedes. These mirative particles distinguish these chapters from the surrounding material, which commentators have long recognized as a distinct section within Isaiah. Marvin Alan Sweeney, *Isaiah 1–39* (Grand Rapids, MI: Eerdmans, 1996), 353–54.

58  Allegorical readings emerged as early as the LXX. The LXX translates verse 29 on the limitation of threshing as a limitation to God's wrath. This transposition from MT threshing to LXX judgment has inspired some subsequent commentators to follow the LXX lead and see the poem as an allegory for God's judging and saving activities. Benjamin M. Austin, *Plant Metaphors in the Old Greek of Isaiah* (Atlanta, GA: Society of Biblical Literature, 2019), 192, renders the LXX "for I will not be angry with you forever, nor will the voice of my bitterness trample you" and notes that with this translation, "the entire section is an allegory for Israel." YHWH punishes but does not totally destroy Israel. Joseph Blenkinsopp, *Isaiah 1–39* (New Haven, CT: Yale University Press, 2000), 397, sees the parable as justifying YHWH's violent judgment on grounds that it has a limited duration. Similarly, Sweeney, *Isaiah 1–39*, 366; Brevard S. Childs, *Isaiah* (Louisville, KY: Westminster John Knox Press, 2001), 211; Gary V. Smith, *Isaiah 1–39* (Nashville, TN: B&H Publishing Group, 2007), 491. Some interpretations shift

the focus from YHWH's actions to the prophet's oracles. This reading assumes that Isaiah uses the parable to defend himself from the accusation that he keeps changing his message. For example, he portrays the Assyrians first as YHWH's instrument of punishment (Isa 10:5–15), then the object of YHWH's punishment (14:24–27), and YHWH as both protector of Jerusalem and its enemy. Thus Georg Fohrer, *Das Buch Jasaja: Kapitel 24–39* (Zürich: Zwingli, 1962), 67; J. J. M. Roberts, *First Isaiah* (Minneapolis, MN: Fortress Press, 2015), 56. Similarly, Bernhard Duhm, *Das Buch Jesaia* (Göttingen: Vandenhoeck and Ruprecht, 1922), 202–3; Hans Wildberger, *Isaiah 28–39*, trans. Thomas H. Trapp (Minneapolis, MN: Fortress, 2002), 56. Daniel J. Stulac, *History and Hope: The Agrarian Wisdom of Isaiah 28–35* (University Park, PA: Eisenbrauns, 2018), 72–77, contrasts the disciplined behavior of the farmer and the undisciplined conduct of the leaders of Judah depicted in Isaiah 28:1–11.

59  After a cursory analysis of Isaiah 28:23–29, Marlow relates it to Isaiah 1:2–3 due to the opening call for attention and the common thematic focus on the created order. Marlow does not delve into the agricultural specifics that constitute the focus of the passage or develop the architectural imagery of the oracle, so her effort to relate the passage to its context falls short. See Marlow, *Biblical Prophets and Contemporary Environmental Ethics*, 211–14.

60  Based on biblical descriptions of pre-predation creation, the passage has been seen as a deliberate depiction of an Edenic paradise. David H. Wenkel, "Wild Beasts in the Prophecy of Isaiah: The Loss of Dominion and Its Renewal through Israel as the New Humanity," *Journal of Theological Interpretation* (2011) 251–63. This reading is untenable, however, because the text makes no specific allusions to creation, holds no suggestion of humans returning to vegetarianism, and stands in continuity with texts depicting this-world blessings in the context of royal prophecy. See J. Van Ee Joshua, "Wolf and Lamb as Hyperbolic Blessing: Reassessing Creational Connections in Isaiah 11:6–8," *Journal of Biblical Literature* 137 (2018) 319–37; H. G. M. Williamson, *Isaiah 6–12* (London: Bloomsbury Publishing, 2018), 656–58.

61  On lions in the biblical world, see Brent A. Strawn, *What is Stronger Than a Lion? Leonine Image and Metaphor in the Hebrew Bible and Ancient Near East* (Göttingen: Vandenhoeck & Ruprecht, 2005).

62  Jacob Stromberg, *Isaiah After Exile: The Author of Third Isaiah as Reader and Redactor of the Book* (Oxford: Oxford University Press, 2011), 107; Williamson, *Isaiah 6–12*, 667.

63  R. Reed Lessing, "Yahweh Versus Marduk: Creation Theology in Isaiah 40–55," *Concordia Journal* 36 (2010) 234–44, quote 411.

64  Modified from NABRE, which renders כאחד as *together*.

65  Interpreters disagree about how to understand the snake here. The reference to eating dust seems to refer to the curse of the snake in Genesis 3:14. The serpent can no longer do harm. Some see this difference between Isaiah 11:8 and 65:25 as evidence that the snake remains a suspect and punished harmful creature that is not transformed like the other beasts. Gary V. Smith, *Isaiah 40–66* (Nashville, TN: B&H Publishing Group, 2009), 724; Joseph Blenkinsopp, *Isaiah 56–66* (New Haven, CT: Yale University Press, 2003), 290. Others do not see a great distinction made here between the wolf and the lion on the one hand and the snake on the other. John Goldingay and David Payne, *Isaiah 56–66* (London: Bloomsbury, 2014), 477.

# Chapter 3

1  Modified from NAB, which has *rotten grapes*. The root באש profiles stinking, but this noun form appears only in Isaiah 5:2, 4 where some kind of smelly disgusting grape must be in view. Hebrew disgust vocabulary includes הנן *to be fetid,* זור *to be loathsome* also hapax יקע (byform נקע) *to turn away in disgust,* קוט and קוץ *to feel disgust,* שקץ *to detest,* and שנה *to hate/detest.*

2  Hebrew has, by my count, almost thirty words that can profile anger. For the most important ones, see Deena E. Grant, *Divine Anger in the Hebrew Bible* (Washington, DC: Catholic Biblical Association, 2014), 21–39.

3  Michael Potegal and Gerhard Stemmler, "Cross-Disciplinary Views of Anger: Consensus and Controversy," in *International Handbook of Anger: Constituent and Concomitant Biological, Psychological, and Social Processes*, ed. Michael Potegal, Gerhard Stemmler, and Charles Spielberger (New York: Springer Science & Business Media, 2010), 3–8, here 3. Scholars also agree that anger expression is governed by context and cultural display rules learned in childhood.

4  Schweers has developed a means of identifying anger in texts that may not use anger vocabulary. For an application of the method to Psalms, see Katherine Schweers, "Uncovering Hidden Anger in the Psalms Using Psychological Models of Anger," *Biblical Theology Bulletin* (forthcoming).

5 The positive or negative valence of an emotion may refer to (1) whether the situation that triggered the emotion was pleasant or unpleasant, (2) whether the outcome of the emotion was adaptive or dysfunctional, (3) or whether the emotional experience involves pleasant or unpleasant feelings. Based on the first criterion, anger is a negative emotion. Although some theorists have described all anger as bad, anger leads to a wide range of consequences, good and bad. The second criterion, therefore, is not helpful. The third criterion is similarly ambiguous. Although most people report that the experience of anger is negative, anger commonly appears with positive sensations such as heightened attention, determination, enthusiasm, excitement, and sense of strength and pride. Consequently, many have noticed the peculiarity that anger is a negative emotion associated with an approach motivation. Eddie Harmon-Jones and Cindy Harmon-Jones, "Anger," in *Handbook of Emotions*, ed. Lisa Feldman Barrett, Michael Lewis, and Jeannette M. Haviland-Jones (New York, NY: Guilford, 2018), 774–91, here 777.

6 Harmon-Jones and Harmon-Jones, "Anger," 778.

7 Harmon-Jones and Harmon-Jones, "Anger," 778–79; Potegal and Stemmler, "Cross-Disciplinary Views of Anger: Consensus and Controversy."

8 Potegal and Stemmler, "Cross-Disciplinary Views of Anger: Consensus and Controversy."

9 Carey Ellen Walsh, *The Fruit of the Vine: Viticulture in Ancient Israel* (Winona Lake, IN: Eisenbrauns, 1996), 96.

10 Walsh, *Fruit of the Vine*, 123. This fable is modern, not ancient, but likely reflects ancient realities also reflected in Isaiah's mention of a hedge around the vineyard. Walsh notes several ways that ancient and modern vine cultivation resemble one another due to the constraints of grape vines (e.g., need for soil drainage). For the modern fable, see Thomas James, *Aesop's Fables* (London: John Murray, 1887), 112.

11 The term פורה in late texts may profile a treading floor that is unusually large (Isa 63:3; Hag 2:16). Of the two more common terms, גת profiles the activity that takes place in the press (i.e., treading grapes). The term יקב profiles more the result of the process, the bountiful liquid. For a simple treading floor, both גת and יקב are appropriate terms, but יקב was more suitable to describe more complex structures. Walsh, *Fruit of the Vine*, 163–64.

12 The choice of the word נטע *plant* rather than זרע *sow* reflects this reality of vine cultivation. Walsh, *Fruit of the Vine*, 100–106.

13  On the potential meanings of שׂרק, see Walsh, *Fruit of the Vine*, 106–110.

14  The term צעקה profiles a cry for help (Exod 5:8; 14:10; Num 20:16; Judg 10:12; Ps 34:18). The wordplay with צדקה *justice* highlights the surprising contrast (note הנה *look!* twice) between what YHWH expects and what YHWH receives. A similar wordplay contrasts expected מׁשׁפט *justice* and actual מׂשׂפח *bloodshed*. The unusual term מׂשׂפח has been understood as bloodshed in modern times based on an Arabic cognate. The ancient versions used generic terms for injustice based on the sense.

15  The verb באׁש *to stink* profiles smelling bad and being disgusting. In Job 31:40, the noun form באׁשה profiles a weed, likely one known for its bad smell (e.g., *Lolium temulentum*, whose blossoms exude an odor at night that attracts moths, or *Mercurialis annua*, known for its bad smell and toxicity). The noun באׁש occurs only in Isaiah 5:2, 4 for these sour grapes.

16  NRSV and NJPS translate *wild grapes*. NABRE and CEB translate *rotten grapes*. Fruit becomes rotten only when it is left too long, so this rendering suggests that the vintner is at fault for incompetence. NIV opts for *bad fruit*.

17  Unripe grapes (בסר, see Ezek 18:2) are also sour, but these grapes are ripe and should therefore be sweet. Walsh, *Fruit of the Vine*, 168–69.

18  Valerie Curtis, *Don't Look, Don't Touch, Don't Eat: The Science Behind Revulsion* (Chicago, IL: University of Chicago Press, 2013). For major works on disgust, see also Carolyn Korsmeyer, *Savoring Disgust: The Foul and the Fair in Aesthetics* (Oxford: Oxford University Press, 2011); Colin McGinn, *The Meaning of Disgust* (Oxford: Oxford University Press, 2011); Winfried Menninghaus, *Disgust: Theory and History of a Strong Sensation,* trans. Howard Eiland and Joal Golb (Albany, NY: SUNY Press, 2012); Susan Beth Miller, *Disgust: The Gatekeeper Emotion* (Hillsdale, NJ: Analytic Press, 2004); Bunmi O. Olatunji and Dean McKay, eds. *Disgust and Its Disorders: Theory, Assessment, and Treatment Implications* (Washington, DC: American Psychological Association, 2009).

19  Curtis, *Don't Look*, 21–35.

20  Thomas Kazen, *Emotions in Biblical Law: A Cognitive Science Approach* (Sheffield: Sheffield Phoenix Press, 2011), 71–94; Thomas Kazen, "Disgust in Body, Mind, and Language: The Case of Impurity in the Hebrew Bible," in *Mixed Feelings and Vexed Passions: Exploring*

*Emotions in Biblical Literature*, ed. F. Scott Spencer (Atlanta, GA: Society of Biblical Literature, 2017), 177–95.

21  On contact contagion, evident across cultures, see Kazen, *Emotions in Biblical Law*, 35–36, 73–81.

22  Curtis, *Don't Look*, 21–33.

23  Matthew R. Schlimm, *From Fratricide to Forgiveness: The Language and Ethics of Anger in Genesis* (Winona Lake, IN: Eidenbrauns, 2011), 58. Since Schlimm limits himself to explicit appearances of anger vocabulary, he finds many examples of social superiors becoming angry at inferiors. He notes that the absence of female anger may be a limitation of the corpus and that more stories might have yielded narratives of female anger. He overlooks places where female characters are angry but cannot express anger (Tamar, Abigail). He also acknowledges that the focus on interpersonal anger is also a limitation of the corpus. Isaiah 5:1–7 shows that the biblical corpus does have an example of human anger at a plant, but this example cannot be discovered with a concordance search on words for anger. Deena Grant, "Human Anger in Biblical Narrative," *Revue Biblique* 118 (2011) 339–61, similarly limits her analysis to anger words and finds the same result.

24  Therefore, this narrative does not form part of Schlimm's database of anger in Hebrew. Schlimm, *Fratricide to Forgiveness*. Schweers, "Uncovering Hidden Anger." Schweers is currently working on overlooked anger in narrative.

25  Schlimm, *Fratricide to Forgiveness*, 58–59. By Baloian's count, about three-fourths of all anger in the Old Testament is divine. Bruce Edward Baloian, *Anger in the Old Testament* (Lausane, CH: Peter Lang, 1992). Note his count is limited to anger words, which means he dramatically underestimates the number of anger episodes.

26  Schlimm, *Fratricide to Forgiveness*, 61.

27  Fruit appears in many different metaphors, and sometimes represents the result of actions (Prov 31:31; Jer 17:10). See Benjamin M. Austin, *Plant Metaphors in the Old Greek of Isaiah* (Atlanta, GA: Society of Biblical Literature, 2019), 110–14; Job Y. Jindo, *Biblical Metaphor Reconsidered: A Cognitive Approach to Poetic Metaphor in Biblical Prophecy in Jeremiah 1–24* (Leiden: Brill, 2010). The fruit-action blend is famous from Jesus's statement "by their fruits you shall know them." (Matt 7:20) See George Branch-Trevathan, *The Sermon on the Mount and Spiritual Exercises: The Making of the Matthean Self* (Leiden: Brill, 2020).

28 Chaney argues that the parable does not accuse the whole society but only the powerful elite. Marvin Chaney, "Whose Sour Grapes? The Addresees of Isaiah 5:1–7 in the Light of Political Economy," *Semeia* 87 (1999) 105–22. Walsh finds that viticulture was a widespread practice, including among small landholders. Walsh, *Fruit of the Vine*, 43–63. Both may be correct. Chaney's argument hinges on transformation of Judean economy and landholding precipitated by the rise in international trade in the 8th century that led to the expansion of rich estates condemned in Isaiah 5:8–10, immediately after the vineyard parable. Similarly, Isaiah 3:13–15 targets the elite who have plundered the poor. The vineyard parable, therefore, appears to be directed at these misbehaving elites rather than the entire society indiscriminately.

29 The vineyard song elicits the experience of anger through the misleading way it is narrated. The audience would likely understand from the beginning that the story is not simply a literal narrative about a vineyard, but something more. The audience might at first expect a love song, which then transitions into a complaint about infertility. The shift to first person in verse 3 requires further reinterpretation from a third person to the speaker himself. Only the end of the passage clarifies its final interpretation. The parable thereby includes a literary device that frustrates the interpretive goals of the audience in ways that mimic the frustrated goal of the vintner. In this way, the audience experiences anger in two dimensions: they sympathize with the anger of the vintner over his frustrated goal, and they experience their own frustration as an audience striving to understand where the story is going. See Gary R. Williams, "Frustrated Expectations in Isaiah v 1–7: A Literary Interpretation," *Vetus Testamentum* 35 (1985) 459–65.

30 On the state of discussion on moral disgust, see Roger Giner-Sorolla, "The Paradox of Moral Disgust and Three Possible Resolutions," in *The Handbook of Disgust Research: Modern Perspectives and Applications* (Cham: Springer Nature Switzerland, 2021), 139–57. The paradox in the title reflects the author's view that moral means rational and disgust is irrational. He thereby mischaracterizes both morality and disgust, but his discussion of how various research traditions have tried to account for the expansion of disgust to the moral realm is helpful.

31 Incest evokes disgust. Genesis 19:30–38 stigmatizes Moabites and Ammonites by depicting them as descendants of father-daughter incest. Cultures vary in what relationships are incestuous. Westerners find cousin marriage disgusting, but it has been common in many parts of the world including Europe before the Catholic Church prohibited

it. Heinrich argues that this prohibition made Westerners unusual outliers on several psychological metrics compared to the rest of the world. See Joseph Henrich, *The Weirdest People in the World: How the West Became Psychologically Peculiar and Particularly Prosperous* (London: Penguin UK, 2020). Heinrich coined the acronym WEIRD to characterize most psychology research subjects as Western, Educated, Industrialized, Rich, and Developed. Joseph Henrich, Steven J. Heine, and Ara Norenzayan, "The Weirdest People in the World," *Behavioral and Brain Sciences* 33 (2010) 1–75. Academic psychologists use college students as convenient research subjects, leading to research bias based on unrepresentative samples. Research on the mental health effects of time spent in nature suffers from this lack of diversity in research subjects. See Carlos Andres Gallegos-Riofrío et al., "Chronic Deficiency of Diversity and Pluralism in Research on Nature's Mental Health Effects: A Planetary Health Problem," *Current Research in Environmental Sustainability* 4 (2022) 1–11.

32 Brent A. Strawn, "On Vomiting: Leviticus, Jonah, Ea(a)rth," *The Catholic Biblical Quarterly* 74 (2012) 445–64.

33 In Leviticus 18, the abominable practices focus mostly around sexual acts, especially incest.

34 Kazen, *Emotions in Biblical Law*, 20–31; 71–94.

35 College-educated Westerners, by contrast, typically seek not to condemn behaviors they see as disgusting as immoral. Jonathan Haidt, *The Righteous Mind: Why Good People Are Divided By Politics and Religion* (New York, NY: Vintage, 2013), 3–83.

36 Modified from NABRE, which has *the Israelites were fruitful and prolific. They multiplied.* I divided the sentence differently based on sense and verb forms and consistently use *swarm* to render the disgusting aspect of the verb שׁרץ.

37 Kazen, *Emotions in Biblical Law*, 80. On fecundity as a general disgust elicitor, see Miller, *Disgust*, 47–57; Aurel Kolnai, *On Disgust* (Chicago, IL: Open Court, 2004), 56–58. Unclean quadrupeds do not appear as disgusting in the Priestly material.

38 William Henry Propp, *Exodus 1–18: A New Translation With Introduction and Commentary* (New Haven, CT: Yale University Press, 1999), 129–30.

39 Commentators note how these verbs profile excessive reproduction and repeat the verbs used in creation (Gen 1:20, 22, 28; 8:17; 9:1, 7; 17:2; 28:14), but tend to overlook how this excessive fecundity disgusts Pharaoh. On the connections to creation, see Victor H. Matthews, *Exodus:*

*An Exegetical Commentary* (Grand Rapids, MI: Baker Academic, 2011), 45–46; Christopher J. H. Wright, *Exodus* (Grand Rapids, MI: Zondervan Academic, 2021), 45–46. Moshe Greenberg, *Understanding Exodus: A Holistic Commentary on Exodus 1–11* (Eugene, OR: Cascade Books, 2013), 16, notes that the verb שׁרץ profiles "exuberant animal proliferation" used of "swarming and subhuman creatures," but does not develop this theme of disgust.

40 Modified from NABRE, which renders *the Egyptians began to loathe the Israelites*.

41 For example, Propp, *Exodus*, 133, glosses it as "fear and loathing," a translation that works if one understands the English expression to mean disgust. The title of the novel *Fear and Loathing in Las Vegas* (1971) by Hunter S. Thompson uses "fear and loathing" to profile moral disgust. English shows some overlap in terms for hatred and disgust. Since moral disgust can evoke anger, Hebrew may have similar overlap. I prefer to highlight the disgust evident in this passage because interpreters have largely overlooked the theme of disgust in Exodus. The verb קוט and its byform קוץ profile disgust. Interpreters have misunderstood the role of disgust in several narratives, so HALOT glosses the construction קוץ מפני of person as *dread* in Exodus 1:12; Numbers 22:3; Isaiah 7:16. The excessive fecundity of the Hebrews makes them disgusting to the Egyptians. The Moabites have the same reaction to the multitude of swarming Israelites in Numbers 22:3. King Ahaz may have a disgust reaction to the Ephraimites and Syrians during the seige of Jerusalem in Isaiah 7:16 both because of their swarming multitude and because of their treasonous purpose of killing him and rebelling against Assyria.

42 Terence E. Fretheim, *Exodus* (Louisville, KY: Westminster John Knox Press, 2010), 25. For fuller documentation of this promise in Genesis, see David J. A. Clines, *Theme of the Pentateuch* (2nd ed.; Sheffield: Sheffield Academic Press, 1997). The language also points to Hebrew obedience to the command to be fruitful and multiply from Genesis 1:28; 9:1,7. Carol Meyers, *Exodus* (Cambridge: Cambridge University Press, 2005), 33.

43 Modified from NABRE, which has *They are robust*. The MT reads an otherwise unattested form that may mean *lively* or *strong*. A repointing of the consonants yields *animals*. LXX omits the expression entirely. For a defense of the MT, see Propp, *Exodus*, 140–41. Even with the MT pointing, the term may evoke the animality of the Hebrew women. Matthews, *Exodus*, 92, notes that the MT pointing shows the

midwives speaking of the Hebrew women in a complimentary way (they are stronger than the Egyptians), but the reading *animal* shows the midwives speaking in a degrading way. I propose that they suited their speech to their audience, saying *animal* to placate Pharaoh by playing to his prejudices.

44   On excrement as disgust elicitor, see Thomas Staubli, "Feces: The Primary Disgust Elicitor in the Hebrew Bible and in the Ancient Near East," in *Sounding Sensory Profiles in the Ancient Near East*, ed. Annette Schellenberg and Thomas Krüger (Atlanta, GA: Society of Biblical Literature, 2019), 119–43.

45   On the psychological importance of maintaining a nature–culture divide, see Immo Fritsche and Annedore Hoppe, "We Supernaturals Terror Management and People's Ambivalent Relationship With Nature," in *Handbook of Terror Management Theory*, ed. Clay Routledge and Matthew Vess (London: Academic Press, 2019), 157–78.

46   For a full discussion of animal reminder disgust and application to biblical contexts, see Isaac Alderman, *The Animal At Unease With Itself: Death Anxiety and the Animal-Human Boundary in Genesis 2–3* (Lanham, MD: Lexington Books/Fortress Academic, 2020).

47   The Hebrew term glossed as *lazy* is נדפים, which may mean "to grow slack," profiling failure of courage in the Qal and used only in Exodus 5:8, 17 in the Niphal where it seems to mean "lazy" or "indifferent." Proverbs 18:9 employs the Hithpael: גם מתרפה במלאכתו אח הוא לבעל משחית.

48   Fretheim, *Exodus*, 84–85.

49   Modified from NABRE, which has *you have made us offensive to Pharaoh.*

50   The expression draws attention to the olfactory sense with ריח *odor*. The Hiphil verb הבאשתם *you have made stink* then takes ריחנו *our odor* as the object that is made stinky, like the fly spoils the scent of the ointment in Ecclesiastes 10:1: "Dead flies make the perfumer's ointment stink (יביע) and ferment." In other narrative examples of this verb profiling moral disgust, the Hiphil verb appears with a personal suffix without ריח *odor* (see below). The inclusion of ריח *odor* emphasizes the olfactory sense of the verb even as the preposition בעיני *in the eyes of* draws attention to the visual sense, which is also missing in other narrative examples that instead use the simpler preposition ב to indicate who is disgusted.

51   Pharaoh punishes those who are lazy as YHWH punishes those whose moral courage is wanting (Prov 24:10–12). Moral disgust may motivate attack.

52 Modified from NABRE which has *making me repugnant to the inhabitants*. Hebrew reads עכרתם אתי להבאישני בישב הארץ; LXX reads μισετόν, *hateful*.

53 The culturally accepted solution to rape in this ancient context was marriage (Deut 22:28–29). Shechem and his people go to great lengths to accommodate their demands (circumcision), making their treasonous genocide all the more horrific.

54 Modified from NABRE, which had *odious*. Hebrew reads נבאש *stinky*; LXX reads ᾐσχύνθησαν, *ashamed*.

55 Jonathan strikes נציב, which may profile a pillar (Gen 19:26), a garrison (1 Sam 10:5; 2 Sam 8:6, 14;), or maybe the leader of the garrison (1 Kgs 4:19). In this context, Jonathan's attack must include killing Philistines.

56 Modified from NABRE which has *His people Israel must surely detest him*. Hebrew: הבש הביש בעמו בישראל. LXX reads ᾔσχυνται αἰσχθνόμενος, *shameful*.

57 Modified from NABRE which has *in bad odor with David*. Hebrew: ויראו בני עמון כי נבאשו בדוד. LXX reads κατῃσχυνθησαν, *shameful*, but identifies the people of David as shamed, not themselves as disgusting. This may be due to confusion of בוש *be ashamed* and באש *be stinky*. See A. Graeme Auld, *I & II Samuel* (Louisville, KY: Westminster John Knox, 2011), 442.

58 Modified from NABRE, which has *odious*. Hebrew: כי נבאשת את אביך ושמע כל ישראל. LXX reads κατῃσχυνας, *shame*. LXX construes the action as something done to David rather than focusing on David's reaction.

59 Only Exodus 5:21 mentions the noun for odor and uses בעיני instead of ב to mark the person offended by the smell. Greek lacks this smell idiom, so LXX translators drew on the concepts of hatred and shame to conceptualize how the offended party perceives the smelly one. In Exodus 5:21, however, the Greek captures better the sense of the Hebrew with ἐβδελύξατε τὴν ὀσμην ἡμῶν *you have made detestable our odor*.

60 All other examples mark the disgusted person with the preposition ב.

61 Nicole L. Tilford, *Sensing World, Sensing Wisdom: The Cognitive Foundation of Biblical Metaphors* (Atlanta, GA: Society of Biblical Literature Press, 2017), notes that in this expression, "physical stench is not envisioned" but the bad smell signals negative moral judgment (146). The wording in Exodus 5:21, however, makes the physical smell a salient part of the meaning of the idiom. The expression lost its metaphorical

force by frequency of use, although we cannot be sure in the absence of native speakers to interview. Such so-called dead metaphors can be revived by novel expressions that revitalize the root metaphor. See Cornelia Müller, *Metaphors Dead and Alive, Sleeping and Waking: A Dynamic View* (Chicago, IL: University of Chicago Press, 2009).

62 Scholars have overlooked the extensive disgust in the exodus narrative despite extensive scholarship on this book. The lack of attention to this theme may reflect a longer tradition of inattention to emotion.

63 Blood triggers disgust across cultures. Note, however, that Mesopotamian cooking involved using animal blood as a cooking medium or basis for sauce, and modern Germans appreciate blood sausage. Still, the ancient Mesopotamians might have been disgusted if the Euphrates or Rhine turned to blood. Jean Bottéro, *Textes Culinaires Méesopotamiens / Mesopotamian Culinary Texts* (Winona Lake, IN: Eisenbrauns, 1995).

64 Propp, *Exodus*, 325: "For Israelite readers, the image of a land bleeding from its main artery would be particularly disturbing."

65 Food may be the basis of disgust in humans. See Paul Rozin, Jonathan Haidt, and Clark R. McCauley, "Disgust," in *Handbook of Emotions*, ed. Michael Lewis, Jeannette M. Haviland-Jones, and Lisa Feldman Barrett (New York, NY: Guilford, 2008), 757–76.

66 The frogs do not simply return to the Nile but die and make the whole land stink, making escape from the stench impossible. Werner Schmidt, *Exodus* (Göttingen: Vandenhoeck & Ruprecht, 2019), 394.

67 Propp thinks the verbal identity between the Hebrews and the frogs is humorous. He also notes that both Hebrews and frogs "go up" (1:10; 7:28, 29; 8:1, 2, 3) and that the fecundity (שׁרץ) of the frogs may evoke the term for unclean (שׁקץ) animals (Lev 11:20, 23). Propp, *Exodus*, 326. He also identifies the plague of frogs as "more of a prank than an attack." (349) Similarly, Wright thinks the abundance of frogs in the wrong place is comic, but also clearly identifies the frogs as disgusting. See Wright, *Exodus*, 211. The biblical text does not clarify whether the intent of the similarity is humorous or not. Disgusting topics can evoke laughter (e.g., bathroom humor). An Israelite audience likely took some pride in the fecundity attributed to their ancestors, but had a disgust reaction to the frogs. Davies remarks that "the sheer unpleasantness and discomfort of frogs crawling everywhere is sufficient to justify their presence being seen as a plague." Graham I. Davies, *Exodus 1–18* (Bloomsbury, 2020), 523.

68 Modified from NABRE *gnats*. This plague, like turning the water into blood, involves transformation. The dust *becomes* (היה) something else. Schmidt, *Exodus*, 396.

69 The Hebrew כנם has been variously understood as lice, mosquitos, ticks, sandflies, and gnats. Both Propp and Davies argue that the philological evidence points to lice. C. Houtman and Cornelis Houtman, *Exodus*, trans. Johan Rebel and Sierd Woudstra (Kampen: Kok, 1993), 138–39; Propp, *Exodus*, 327–28; Davies, *Exodus 1–18*, 536. Schmidt, *Exodus*, 396. The word appears in slightly different forms in 8:12 and 8:13.

70 The term ערב in Exodus 8:17 appears also in Psalms 78:45 where these creatures *devour* people, suggesting they are some kind of biting insect. Houtman and Houtman, *Exodus*, 139; Propp, *Exodus*, 328. Davies suggests it profiles worms on the basis of the Akkadian cognate *urbartu* II. Davies, *Exodus 1–18*, 549. Despite the uncertainty of the creature intended, commentators agree that the list of possibilities involves disgusting creatures (flies, stinging insects, worms).

71 Schmidt, *Exodus*, 402.

72 Vitaly Naumkin and Victor Porkomovsky, "Insects in Socotran Language and Culture," *Proceedings of the Seminar for Arabian Studies* 29 (1999) 111–14; Edward Neufeld, "Insects as Warfare Agents in the Ancient Near East (Exod 23:28; Deut 7:20; Josh 24:12; Isa 7:18–20)," *Orientalia* 49 (1980) 30–57; Francesco Saracino, "Ras Ign Hani78/20 and Some Old Testament Connections," *Vetus Testamentum* 32 (1982) 361–64.

73 Modified from NABRE, which has *Dead flies corrupt and spoil.*

74 Propp, *Exodus*, 331.

75 The word אבעבעת appears only here in the Bible. The cognate Akkadian *bubutu* profiles a pustule or boil. The term שחין profiles a kind of ulcer, boil, or rash that may occur on the skin. Propp, *Exodus*, 332; Davies, *Exodus 1–18*, 580–81.

76 Modified from NABRE *malignant boils.*

77 David J. A. Clines, *Job 1–20* (Waco, TX: Thomas Nelson, 1989), 47–49.

78 Davies, *Exodus 1–18*, 641–42.

79 Auld, *I & II Samuel*, 79; P. Kyle McCarter, *I Samuel* (Garden City, NJ: Doubleday, 1980), 118–26. Maeir proposes based on archeological evidence that עפלים profile penises as the organs afflicted. Philistine material culture includes penis-like vessels that may reflect a cultural concern with phalluses known from Greek culture (the Philistines may

have come from the Aegean). See Aren M. Maeir, "A New Interpretation of the Term ʿopalim (עפלים) in the light of recent Archeological Finds from Philistia," *Journal for the Study of the Old Testament* 32 (2007) 23–40.

80 The verb רמם appears only in Exodus 16:20, but verse 24 has the noun רמם *maggot*. In both verses, באש occurs to profile the disgusting and inedible nature of the rotten manna.

## Chapter 4

1 Jessica L. Tracy and Richard W. Robins, "The Self in Self-Conscious Emotions: A Cognitive Appraisal Approach," in *The Self-Conscious Emotions*, ed. Jessica L. Tracy, Richard W. Robins, and June Price Tangney (New York, NY: Guilford, 2007), 3–20.

2 Since William James, theorizing about the self has maintained the distinction between the "I-self" and the "me-self." We represent the me-self (known) to the I-self (knower). See James, William James, *The Principles of Psychology* (New York, NY: Henry Holt, 1890), 291–401. For his own abridgment of this work for classroom use, see William James, *Psychology* (Cleveland, OH: World Publishing, 1948), 176–216. For commentary, see David E. Leary, *The Routledge Guidebook to James's* Principles of Psychology (London: Routledge, 2018), esp. 228–55. For summaries of recent research, see Susan Harter, *The Construction of the Self: Developmental and Sociocultural Foundations* (2nd ed.; New York, NY: Guilford, 2015), 3; Hubert J. M. Hermans, "The Dialogical Self: A Process of Positioning in Space and Time," in *The Oxford Handbook of the Self*, ed. Shaun Gallagher (Oxford: Oxford University Press, 2011), 654–80.

3 For an excellent introduction to research on the self in developmental perspective, see Harter, *Construction of the Self*. She finds that the evidence steers between the extremes of "modern" and "post-modern" views of the self, which are driven more by ideology than data. See also Shaun Gallagher, *The Oxford Handbook of the Self* (Oxford: Oxford University Press, 2011); Anthony Elliott, *Concepts of the Self* (4th ed.; Cambridge: Polity, 2020). The emergent sense of self corresponds with the emergence of joint and group intentionality. When infants learn that other people have intentions and they can share an intention with another person, they form partnerships that make language learning possible. This capacity for shared intentionality emerges at the nine-month revolution. Around four years of age, children scale

the joint intention up to a collective intentionality, meaning they understand shared intentions across a cultural group. The capacity for collective intentionality makes culture possible. It also makes self-conscious emotions possible, which shape conduct along culturally acceptable lines. See Tomasello's trilogy for fascinating details on intentionality and the evolved psychological infrastructure that makes language and culture possible: Michael Tomasello, *A Natural History of Human Thinking* (Cambridge, MA: Harvard University Press, 2014); Michael Tomasello, *A Natural History of Human Morality* (Cambridge, MA: Harvard University Press, 2016); Michael Tomasello, *Becoming Human: A Theory of Ontogeny* (Cambridge, MA: Harvard University Press, 2019).

4  Harter, *Construction of the Self*, 210–11.

5  Jessica L. Tracy and Richard W. Robbins, "The Nature of Pride," in *The Self-Conscious Emotions*, ed. Jessica L. Tracy, Richard W. Robins, and June Price Tangney (New York, NY: Guilford, 2007), 263–81.

6  Dweck does not focus on emotion but studies how different ways of understanding success (and failure) impact performance. Authentically proud people perform better and improve over time. Carol S. Dweck, *Mindset: The New Science of Success* (Updated ed.; New York, NY: Random House, 2016).

7  Prakasam argues that both Zion and Babylon in Isaiah manifest hubristic pride, but the servant of YHWH shows authentic pride. Antony Dhas Prakasam, "Pride of Babylon and Zion in Isaiah in Light of the Theory of Self-Conscious Emotions," diss. (The Catholic University of America, 2018).

8  Klopfenstien argues that the major shame words have no clear antonyms except קלל (*light*), which has כבד (*heavy*) as its opposite. Martin A. Klopfenstein, *Scham und Schande nach dem Alten Testament: Eine Begriffsgeschichtliche Untersuchung Zu Den Hebräischen Wurzeln* Bôš, Klm, *und* Hpr (Zürich: Theologischer Verlag, 1972), 195. The vertical mapping of pride and shame suggests a conceptualization of these self-conscious emotions as opposites. Furthermore, evidence regarding shame from Isaiah implicates it in a contrastive relationship with pride. Terms for pride appear positively in reference to YHWH, but negatively in reference to humans. See Johanna Stiebert, *The Construction of Shame in the Hebrew Bible: The Prophetic Contribution* (New York, NY: Sheffield Academic Press, 2002).

9  These words include גבהות, גאות, גאון, and גוה, all derived from the root גאה *to be high*, גדל *to boast; arrogance, to be large/tall*, and שחץ *pride,*

*conspicuous height.* An additional term that can profile pride includes תפארת *glory, pride*. This term does not also profile height, but it does profile awe or wonder, which involves a sense of vastness (see chap. 5). Prakasam, "Pride of Babylon"; William Osborne, *Trees and Kings: A Comparative Analysis of Tree Imagery in Israels' Prophetic Tradition and the Ancinet Near East* (University Park, PA: Eisenbrauns, 2018), 116–17.

10 Similarly, the patient person has long breath and an impatient person short breath. On these emotional and cognitive metaphors for רוח, see Nicole L. Tilford, *Sensing World, Sensing Wisdom: The Cognitive Foundation of Biblical Metaphors* (Atlanta, GA: Society of Biblical Literature Press, 2017), 142–43.

11 For an introduction to image schemas with application to biblical studies, see Philip D. King, *Surrounded By Bitterness: Image Schemas and Metaphors for Conceptualizing Distress in Classical Hebrew* (Eugene, OR: Pickwick, 2012). See 99–139 on the verticality schema and distress as down. For a general cognitive linguistic introduction to image schemas, see Vyvyan Evans, *Cognitive Linguistics: A Complete Guide* (Edinburgh: Edinburgh Universtiy Press, 2019), 221–240; Raymond W. Gibbs, "Embodiment," in *The Cambridge Handbook of Cognitive Linguistics*, ed. Barbara Dancygier (Cambridge: Cambridge University Press, 2017), 449–62; Jordan Zlatev, "Embodied Intersubjectivity," in *The Cambridge Handbook of Cognitive Linguistics*, ed. Barbara Dancygier (Cambridge: Cambridge University Press, 2017), 172–87. Experimental studies find "image schemas have important psychological validity in several linguistic and non-linguistic domains." Gibbs, "Embodiment," 453. Karen Sullivan, "Conceptual Metaphor," in *The Cambridge Handbook of Cognitive Linguistics*, ed. Barbara Dancygier (Cambridge: Cambridge University Press, 2017), 385–406.

12 King, *Surrounded By Bitterness*, 100–110.

13 For emotional expression as a key to conceptualization, see Zoltán Kövecses, *Emotion Concepts* (New York, NY: Springer-Verlag, 1990), esp. 88–108 on pride; Zoltán Kövecses, *Metaphors of Anger, Pride, and Love: A Lexical Approach to the Structure of Concepts* (Philadelphia, PA: John Benjamins, 1986), esp. 39–60. Prakasam, "Pride of Babylon," notes the consilience between conceptual metaphorical approaches to pride and the theory of self-conscious emotions.

14 On the social origins of the self, see David A. Bosworth, *House of Weeping: The Motif of Tears in Akkadian and Hebrew Prayers* (Atlanta, GA: SBL Press, 2019), 3–20. Tomasello has developed a compelling

description of how humans develop shared intention (between two people) and collective intention (shared intention at a societal scale). This shared intentionality makes language and culture possible and desirable. It also accounts for how pride and shame emerge around four years of age, when children develop collective intentionality, or an ability to regulate their behavior according to social norms. See his trilogy Tomasello, *Natural History of Human Thinking*; Tomasello, *Natural History of Human Morality*; Tomasello, *Becoming Human*. See also Philippe Rochat, *Others in Mind: Social Origins of Self-Consciousness* (Cambridge: Cambridge University Press, 2009). Research related to place attachment and place identity accentuates how people form a sense of self in the context of a physical ecology. James long ago observed the material self includes the body, family, home, and possessions. James, *The Principles of Psychology*, 1.292–93. More recently, scholars investigate place identity, or how our home place shapes our sense of self and personal identity. It is closely related to place attachment, or the affective bonds between person and place. Leila Scannell and Robert Gifford, "Defining Place Attachment: A Tripartite Organizing Framework," *Journal of Environmental Psychology* 30 (2010) 1–10; Toru Ishikawa, *Human Spatial Cognition and Experience: Mind in the World, World in the Mind* (London: Routledge, 2021), 210–11.

15 One illustration of the self as a social reality emerges in the inner voice. Most people have an inner voice that they experience as intimate, private, and individual. But this voice derives from the social environment. See Bosworth, *House of Weeping*, 15–20; Charles Fernyhough, *The Voices Within: The History and Science of How We Talk to Ourselves* (New York, NY: Basic Books, 2016); Lev Vygotsky, *Thought and Language,* trans. Regina Hanfmann, Gertrude Vakar, and Alex Kozulin (Cambridge, MA: MIT Press, 2012); René van der Veer and Jaan Valsinger, eds. *The Vygostsky Reader* (Oxford: Blackwell, 1994); Hermans, "The Dialogical Self: A Process of Positioning in Space and Time." For analysis of the self with specific attention to agency in biblical literature, see Carol A. Newsom, *The Spirit Within Me: Self and Agency in Ancient Israel and Second Temple Judaism* (New Haven, CT: Yale University Press, 2021). She speaks of a "neurophysiologic self" that various cultures construct differently but has very little to say about what this neurophysiologic self is. She does not make overly broad claims about people unavailable for interviews, and notes the limitations of ancient literature as a source for reconstructing an Israelite understanding of the self.

16 J. J. M. Roberts, *First Isaiah* (Minneapolis, MN: Fortress Press, 2015), 207–8. Early Christian commentators claimed that the language was so hyperbolic, that it could not apply to any historical human and must therefore be about the devil. Origen, *On First Principles,* trans. G. W. Butterworth (Boston, MA: Peter Smith, 1973), 49–51. The name "Lucifer" derives from Jerome's Latin rendering of verse 12.

17 מדהבה is a hapax of uncertain meaning, but 1QIsaA reads מרהבה from the root רהב *to oppress, assault* (Qal), which is supported by Symmachus, Theodotian, Peshitta, and Targums. The term continues the theme of the king of Babylon as an oppressive and despotic tyrant. Joseph Blenkinsopp, *Isaiah 1–39* (New Haven, CT: Yale University Press, 2000), 284; Roberts, *First Isaiah*, 205.

18 Interpreters have disagreed about whether the trees here are literal trees or metaphors for minor kings conquered by the king of Babylon. The historical reality of the great forests and their exploitation by empires lends itself to both literal and metaphorical use. Osborne, *Trees and Kings*, 123–25. Kirsten Nielsen, *There is Hope for a Tree: The Tree as Metaphor in Isaiah* (Sheffield: JSPT Press, 1989), 162, sees the trees as vassal kings.

19 Osborne, *Trees and Kings*, 50–54.

20 On the identification of this tree in LXX and beyond, see Jacobus A. Naude and Cynthia L. Miller-Naude, "Lexicography and the translation of 'cedars of Lebanon' in the Septuagint," *HTS Teologiese Studies / Theological Studies* 74 (2018).

21 John Pairman Brown, *Israel and Hellas: The Legacy of Iranian Imperialism and the Individual* (Berlin: Walter de Gruyter, 2001), 119–51.

22 Philip S. Johnston, *Shades of Sheol: Death and Afterlife in the Old Testament* (Downers Grove, IL: InterVarsity Press, 2002); Wayne Horowitz, *Mesopotamian Cosmic Geography* (Winona Lake, IN: Eisenbrauns, 2011), 348–62. Some ancient tales tell of heroes who went to the underworld and returned.

23 For other personifications of Sheol, see Isa 5:14; 28:14–22; Hos 13:14; Hab 2:5; Jon 2:2; Pss 49:16; 69:16; Prov 1:12; 27:20; Job 18:13–14; 26:6; 28:22.

24 The *rephaim* are dead and divine or semi-divine ancestors, like the heroes of ancient Greek lore. Mark S. Smith, *Poetic Heroes: Literary Commemorations of Warriors and Warrior Culture in the Early Biblical World* (Grand Rapids, MI: Eisenbrauns, 2014), 137–62; Brian R. Doak, *The Last of the Rephaim: Conquest and Cataclysm in the Heroic Ages of Ancient Israel* (Boston, MA: Ilex Foundation, 2012).

25 Slightly modified from NABRE, which has *pomp* instead of *pride*.

26 NABRE has *worms* for all but the last of these examples. The Hebrew in all cases has רמה *maggot*.

27 NABRE ends the verse with *you who conquered nations*. The expression *lying on your back* interprets גוי as *back*. See Raymond C. Van Leeuwen, "Isa 14: 12, *ḥôlēš al gwym* and Gilgamesh XI, 6," *Journal of Biblical Literature* (1980) 173–84, followed by Roberts, *First Isaiah*, 206.

28 Jeffrey L. Cooley, *Poetic Astronomy in the Ancient Near East* (Winona Lake, IN: Eisenbrauns, 2013), 241–45. Schipp argues that the term profiles a star. R. Mark Shipp, *Of Dead Kings and Dirges: Myth and Meaning in Isaiah 14:4b-21* (Atlanta, GA: Society of Biblical Literature, 2002), 67–79.

29 On the similarities between this myth and Isaiah 14, see Cooley, *Poetic Astronomy in the Ancient Near East*, 244. Robert Miller, *The Dragon, the Mountain, and the Nations: An Old Testament Myth, Its Origins, and Its Afterlives* (University Park, PA: Explorations in Ancient Near E, 2018), 213–14. Isaiah 14:12–15 and KTU 1.6 I. 57–65 use cognate vocabulary for all these concepts. On ארץ *land* as *underworld* in Hebrew and Ugaritic, see Mark S. Smith, "Baal in the Land of Death," *Ugaritische Forshung* 17 (1986) 311–14.

30 Lambert denies that ancient Israelites had an interior life or inner voice, so he does not think the expression "to say in the heart" profiles inner speech or plans. David A. Lambert, "Refreshing Philology: James Barr, Supersessionism, and the State of Biblical Words," *Biblical Interpretation* 24 (2016) 332–56, esp. 341–49. He has influenced other scholars who likewise imagine that the interior–exterior distinction did not apply in ancient Israel. For example, Anthony I. Lipscomb, "'They Shall be Clothed in Shame': Is Shame an Emotion in the Hebrew Bible?," *Journal for the Study of Ancient Judaism* 12 (2021) 313–59; David A. Lambert, "Mourning Over Sin/affliction and the Problem of "Emotion" as a Category in the Hebrew Bible," in *Mixed Feelings and Vexed Passions*, ed. F. Scott Spencer (Atlanta, GA: Society of Biblical Literature Press, 2017), 139–60. All humans have a need to discern the thoughts and motives of others in order to maintain relationships and navigate the social world. This work of mind reading (or mentalization, or theory of mind) is a necessary part of human life that requires a distinction between interior and exterior self. One line of cross-cultural research finds that the body–mind distinction appears across cultures, but cultures differ in how they further subdivide the mind. Kara Weisman et al., "Similarities and Differences in Concepts of Mental

Life among Adults and Children in Five Cultures," *Nature Human Behaviour* 5 (2021) 1358–68.

31 Slightly modified from NABRE.

32 This traditional translation of עליון captures its association with height. It is an old term for the Canaanite God El that has been adopted and applied to YHWH. See Mark S. Smith, *The Origins of Biblical Monotheism: Israel's Polytheistic Background and The Ugaritic Texts* (Oxford: Oxford University Press, 2001), 48–49, 156–57.

33 Reading אדני, *foundations* instead of MT אבני *stones*. See Blenkinsopp, *Isaiah 1–39*, 285. NABRE renders *depths*.

34 Reading נפל *miscarriage* on the basis of LXX, Targ, and Aquila. Thus Hans Wildberger, *Isaiah 13–27*, trans. Thomas H. Trapp (Minneapolis, MN: Fortress, 1997), 46; Blenkinsopp, *Isaiah 1–39*, 285. נצל *corpse* is also possible and yields a similar meaning involving decayed flesh that triggers disgust. Roberts, *First Isaiah*, 206. The MT reads נצר *sprout*. For various solutions to this issue, see Wildberger, *Isaiah 13–27*, 46. Beuken reads MT as a reference to progeny like the plant references in 14:20, 22. See Willem A. M. Beuken, *Jesaja 13–27*, trans. Ulrich Berges (Freiburg: Herders, 2007), 50, 96. NABRE captures the disgust of the expression by rendering *loathsome carrion*.

35 Posner notes the occurrences and distribution of shame terms in the Psalter: בוש (occurs 42 times), הרף (33 times), כלם (13 times), חפר (7 times), and קלה (twice). Those with more than two words are: Psalms 24 (4 words); 31 (4); 35 (7); 40 (4); 44 (6); 69 (11); 70 (4); 71 (6); 109 (4); 119 (9). She notes that Psalms 69–71 form a minicollection of shame psalms. Ruth Poser, "'Ja, Auf Die Armen Hört Die Lebendige, Ihre Gefangenen Verachtet Sie Nicht': (Ps 69,34): Beschämung Und Anerkennung in Ausgewählten Psalmen," in *Die verborgene Macht der Scham: Ehre, Scham und Schuld im alten Israel, in seinem Umfeld und in der gegenwärtigen Lebensvelt* (Göttingen: Vandenhoek & Ruprecht, 2018), 112–38; Ruth Poser, "Scham in Der Hebräischen Bible," in *Verstrickt in Schuld, gefangen von Scham?* (Neukirchen-Vluyn: Neukirchener Theologie, 2015), 137–54, esp. 148–54.

36 Alphonso Groenewald, "Psalm 69: A Composition-Critical Contribution," in *One Text, A Thousand Methods: Studies in Memory of Sjef van Tilborg*, ed. Ulrich Berges and Patrick Chatelion Counet (Leiden: Brill, 2005), 77–96; Frank-Lothar Hossfeld et al., *Psalms 2: A Commentary on Psalms 51–100* (2005), 184.

37 He may be one of those who publicly mourn the loss of the temple and agitate for its restoration in Isaiah 61:2–3 and Zechariah 7:3–5.

See Alphonso Groenewald, *Psalm 69: Its Structure, Redaction and Composition* (Münster: Lit Verlag, 2003); Hans-Joachim Kraus, *Psalmen I* (Neukirchen: Neukirchener Verlag, 1972), 482–83; Adele Berlin, "Psalms and the Literature of Exile: Psalms 137, 44, 69, and 78," in *The Book of Psalms: Composition and Reception*, ed. Patrick D. Miller, Peter W. Flint, and Aaron Brunell (Leiden: Brill, 2005), 65–86.

38   On the distinction in general, see Jennifer Jacquet, *Is Shame Necessary? New Uses for an Old Tool* (New York, NY: Pantheon, 2015), 11–19, 28–32; Julien A. Deonna, Raffaele Rodogno, and Fabrice Teroni, *In Defense of Shame: The Faces of an Emotion* (Oxford: Oxford University Press, 2012), 44–57, 73–88. For an application of the distinction to Psalm 51, see Lesley DiFransico, "Distinguishing Emotions of Guilt and Shame in Psalm 51," *Biblical Theology Bulletin* 48 (2018) 180–87. Steibert critiques the distinction between shame cultures and guilt cultures because they create a series of contrast that implicitly present guilt cultures (like the modern West) as superior to shame cultures. Also, the contrasts may hinge on the Western pretense that shame is not important in the West. Scheff argues persuasively that shame is ubiquitous in social interactions in the West as elsewhere. Thomas J. Scheff, *Microsociology: Discourse, Emotion, and Social Structure* (Chicago: University of Chicago Press, 1990). For further evidence of this claim, see Cathy O'Neil, *The Shame Machine: Who Profits in the New Age of Humiliation* (New York, NY: Crown, 2022); Jon Ronson, *So You've Been Publicly Shamed* (New York, NY: Riverhead, 2015).

39   Daniel M. T. Fessler, "Shame in Two Cultures: Implications for Evolutionary Approaches," *Journal of Cognition and Culture* 4 (2004) 207–62. There is no cross-cultural research on guilt and shame in young children, but extensive research in adults. From the evidence of adults, Fessler argues that shame is universal but guilt is not.

40   Stiebert rightly notes that the subjective experience of shame as an emotion is not the same as objective shaming. Johanna Stiebert, "Shame and the Body in Psalms and Lamentations of the Hebrew Bible and in Thanksgiving Hymns from Qumran," *Old Testament Essays* 20 (2007) 798–829. Some recent work has confused matters by arguing that the ancient Israelites had no interior self and therefore Stiebert's helpful distinction does not apply. See Lipscomb, "'They Shall be Clothed in Shame': Is Shame an Emotion in the Hebrew Bible?" Steibert and Lipscomb agree that the honor-shame model of Mediterranean societies has no value for biblical studies. Anthropologists have come to believe that it has no value for the modern communities it purports

to describe, but some biblical scholars still invoke it as if it had value, such as Zeba Crook, "Honor, Shame, and Social Status Revisited," *Journal of Biblical Literature* 128 (2009) 591–611. Earlier efforts to understand Hebrew shame vocabulary, see Klopfenstein, *Sham und Shande*; Lyn M. Bechtel, "The Biblical Experience of Shame/shaming: The Social Experience of Shame/shaming in Biblical Israel in Relation to Its Usage as Religious Metaphor," diss., Drew University, 1983.

41 The inexpensiveness of shame makes it an appealing form of punishment. Shaming others imposes no costs on the community but can mean serious costs to the one shamed, whether they concur with the community's negative evaluation or not. Jacquet, *Is Shame Necessary? New Uses for an Old Tool.* She recalls J. Bruce Ismay, the owner of the *Titanic*, who escaped the doomed ship on a lifeboat (149–51). He never admitted any wrongdoing and insisted he felt no shame. The shaming of the public, however, led to a highly constricted life in hiding. Similarly, people shamed online often delete their social media accounts in an effort to hide.

42 The waters do not evoke the forces of chaos; no chaos, combat, or creation appears. Denise Dombkowski Hopkins, *Psalms: Books 2–3* (Collegeville, MN: Liturgical Press, 2016), 203.

43 Groenewald, *Psalm 69*, 44.

44 William P. Brown, *Seeing the Psalms: A Theology of Metaphor* (Louisville, KY: Westminster John Knox, 2002), 114.

45 Modified from NABRE *let your saving help protect me, God.* The NABRE obfuscates the upward movement of the Hebrew verb שׂגב *to make high or inaccessible* (and thereby protect).

46 Boyle argues that broken hearts in Hebrew do not profile psychological suffering but willful violation of God's law. That meaning does not fit Psalm 69 at all and seems improbable elsewhere. See Marjorie O'Rourke Boyle, "Broken Hearts: The Violation of Biblical Law," *Journal of the American Academy of Religion* 73 (2005) 731–57. See the critique of Boyle in Stiebert, "Shame and the Body," 809, n. 27.

47 Ronson, *So You've Been Publicly Shamed* relates the experiences of several people who endured public shaming in social media. Shamed individuals suffer emotional pain, reputation damage, and sometimes loss of livelihood. Shame has been implicated in suicides, including ritual suicides in traditional Japan.

48 Christiane de Vos and Gert Kwakkel, "Psalm 69: The Petitioner's Understanding of Himself, His God, and His Enemies," in *Psalms and Prayers: Papers Read at the Joint Meeting of the Society of Old Testament*

*and Het Oudtestamentlische werkgezelschap in Nederland en België, Appledoorn, August 2006* (Leiden: Brill, 2007), 159–79. Contra Fredrik Lindström, *Suffering and Sin: Interpretations of Illness in the Individual Complaint Psalms* (Stockholm: Almqvist and Wiksell, 1994), who thinks the drowning images must involve physical danger in addition to shame because shame is not serious enough to motivate this image (326, 338, 340, 346–47). Those who think being shamed is not a serious problem should read Ronson, *So You've Been Publicly Shamed*; Jacquet, *Is Shame Necessary? New Uses for an Old Tool*; O'Neil, *The Shame Machine: Who Profits in the New Age of Humiliation.*

49  Ronson, *So You've Been Publicly Shamed*. O'Neil recounts instances of public shaming and argues that individuals are often shamed for systemic problems that are not their fault. O'Neil, *The Shame Machine: Who Profits in the New Age of Humiliation*. For more academic accounts of shame in contemporary society, see Deonna, Rodogno, and Teroni, *In Defense of Shame*; Jacquet, *Is Shame Necessary? New Uses for an Old Tool.*

50  NABRE renders *his pride will be brought low.*

51  The idea follows the oath formula that invites punishment for misbehavior. Blane Conklin, *Oath Formulas in Biblical Hebrew* (University Park, PA: Pennsylvania State University Press, 2011).

52  Lipscomb, "'They Shall be Clothed in Shame': Is Shame an Emotion in the Hebrew Bible?"

53  On ancient seafaring and ship design, see Lionel Casson, *The Ancient Mariners: Seafarers and Sea Fighters of the Mediterranean in Ancient Times* (2nd ed.; Princeton, NJ: Princeton University Press, 1991).

54  The terms profile animals, but their identification remains elusive. The MT לחפר פרות is a corruption of 1QIsaᵃ לחפרפרים that may profile *moles*. See Hans Wildberger, *Isaiah 1–12*, trans. Thomas H. Trapp (Minneapolis, MN: Fortress, 1990), 101–102, 120.

55  The Hebrew expressions indicate that Israelites breathed through their noses. Habitually breathing through the mouth has a range of negative consequences. See James Nestor, *Breath: The New Science of a Lost Art* (New York, NY: Riverhead, 2020).

56  On breathing as a way of construing cognition and emotion, see Tilford, *Sensing World*, 137–47.

57  Gary V. Smith, *Isaiah 1–39* (Nashville, TN: B&H Publishing Group, 2007), 141, identifies the reaction in this verse as "fear and shame."

58  The term לבנה appears ony here and in Song of Songs 6:10. See Wildberger, *Isaiah 13–27*, 509–10.

59 The term חמה profiles the sun in poetry, but with emphasis on its heat/light based on its use in Psalm 19:7 where that nothing is hidden from the חמה of the sun (שׁמשׁ). Several commentators seek to unnecessarily emend Job 30:28, but Job uses חמה to say that he walks around darkened "but not by the sun (חמה)." Unlike the maiden of Song of Songs 1:5, 6, 7, Job's face is made dark by his suffering, not the sun (Jer 8:22; 14:2; Pss 35:14; 38:7; Job 5:11). See Robert Gordis, *The Book of Job: Commentary, New Translation, Special Studies* (New York, NY: Jewish Theological Seminary, 1978), 337; Édouard Dhorme, *A Commentary on the Book of Job*, trans. Harold Knight (Nashville: Thomas Nelson, 1967), 447.

60 J. Cheryl Exum, *Song of Songs: A Commentary* (Louisville, KY: Westminster John Knox, 2005), 222.

61 The NABRE rendering of חפר as *blush* captures the sense that the light of the moon will grow dim. Similarly, Beuken, *Jesaja 13–27*, 317. Wildberger, *Isaiah 13–27*, 504 has *the moon will be red with shame and the sun will be white with humiliation.*

# Chapter 5

1 Research on negative emotions has exceeded that on positive emotions because the survival advantages of negative emotions are clearer. We can also more easily differentiate negative emotions from one another than positive emotions, which makes them easier to study. For example, anger and fear correspond to widely divergent behaviors, but joy and gratitude seem similar. Many mental health problems involve negative emotions, so research focuses more on negative emotions for therapeutic purposes. Michelle N. Shiota, "The Evolutionary Perspective in Positive Emotion Research," in *Handbook of Positive Emotions*, ed. Michele M. Tugade, Michelle N. Shiota, and Leslie D. Kirby (New York, NY: Guilford, 2014), 44–59.

2 Michele M. Tugade, Hillary C. Devlin, and Barbara L. Frederickson, "Infusing Positive Emotions Into Life: The Broaden-and-build Theory and a Dual-Process Model of Resilience," in *Handbook of Positive Emotions*, ed. Michele M. Tugade, Michelle N. Shiota, and Leslie D. Kirby (New York, NY: Guilford, 2014), 28–43; Barbara L. Frederickson, "The Role of Positive Psychology: The Broaden-and-Build Theory of Positive Emotions," *American Psychologist* 56 (2001) 218–26.

3 Barbara L. Frederickson et al., "The Undoing Effect of Positive Emotions," *Motivation and Emotion* 42 (2000) 237–58.

4 Recovery and resilience are not the same thing. Recovery assumes significant symptoms of trauma or grief that disrupt normal functioning. Recovery is the process of returning to good functioning. Resilience means not experiencing significant symptoms of trauma or grief following events that might be expected to impede functioning. See George A Bonanno, "Loss, Trauma, and Human Resilience: Have We Underestimated the Human Capacity to Thrive after Extremely Aversive Events?," *American Psychologist* 59 (2004) 101–13; George A. Bonanno, *The Other Side of Sadness: What the New Science of Bereavement Tells Us About Life After Loss* (Rev. ed.; New York, NY: Basic Books, 2019); George A. Bonanno, *The End of Trauma: How the New Science of Resilience Is Changing How We Think About PTSD* (New York, NY: Basic Books, 2021).

5 The Israelites may have conceptualized rainwater as returning to heaven through the channel that connects water below the earth to water above the earth. Genesis 1:6 distinguished water above and below the dome of the sky/heaven. One narrative explains the flood of Noah as the result of opening the floodgates in the dome, and the waters somehow recede, presumably ultimately returning to their place above the dome. On limited evidence for Mesopotamian beliefs about water and precipitation, see Wayne Horowitz, *Mesopotamian Cosmic Geography* (Winona Lake, IN: Eisenbrauns, 2011), 262–63, 344–47.

6 On these dimensions of joy, see Chris Meadows, *A Psychological Perspective on Joy and Emotional Fulfillment* (New York, NY: Routledge, 2013).

7 In English, *joy* is a generic term that can be further specified by a range of other words like *exultant* and *gleeful* that profile high activation joy, in contrast to *serene* and *contented* that profile low activation joy. Insufficient data prohibits a comparably rich analysis of Hebrew lexemes, but שמחה appears to be the most basic term. See Gary A. Anderson, *A Time to Mourn, a Time to Dance: The Expression of Grief and Joy in Israelite Religion* (Penn State University Press, 1991). Other terms profile related experiences like high-activation rejoicing (שׂושׂ) and exulting (עלז and עלץ), and several terms can profile low-activation joy, including pleasure (נעים), happy (אשׁר), happy (טוב), blessed (ברך), peace (שׁלם). Further words profile specific behaviors related to joy, such as singing (רנן and זמר), shouting (גיל and צהל), praising (הלל), leaping (דלג), dancing (מחול), laughing (שׂחק), and hand-clapping (מחא). While some seek to differentiate as many emotions as there are words, word meaning depends on both a profile and a base, and several Hebrew

terms appear to profile different aspects of joy. Words and concepts do not exist in a one-on-one relationship, and linguistic expressions are not limited to single words.

8 Young teens from a Native American tribe in the Sonoran desert responded with exuberant joy when they saw the ocean for the first time. The response of the children reflects the expectation that people living in arid environments will be especially sensitive to the joy water can inspire. In cultures with easier access to water, the presence of water sill exerts an emotional pull, although it may be less dramatic or obvious high-activation joy. Even in well-watered regions, people pay more money for a hotel room with a view of water and homes near water sell for more money than those just a few blocks from the shore, sometimes much more. Wallace J. Nichols, *Blue Mind: The Surprising Science That Shows How Neing Near, in, on, or Under Water Can Make You Happier, More Connected, and Better At What You Do* (New York, NY: Back Bay Books, 2014), 19–20.

9 Hilary Marlow, *Biblical Prophets and Contemporary Environmental Ethics: Re-Reading Amos, Hosea, and First Isaiah* (Oxford: Oxford University Press, 2009), 134–38.

10 John Pairman Brown, *Israel and Hellas: The Legacy of Iranian Imperialism and the Individual* (Berlin: Walter de Gruyter, 2001), 119–50.

11 Joseph Blenkinsopp, *Isaiah 1–39* (New Haven, CT: Yale University Press, 2000), 407–9.

12 Isaiah 27:19 employs שמחה, which does not specify the various dimensions of joy, and the word גיל *rejoice,* indicating the high-activation joy of the lowly.

13 The Hebrew אשרי *happy* appears to profile serene joy rather than high-energy rejoicing (Ps 1:1; 34:9; 127:5).

14 The terms שקט *quiet,* בטח *trust,* שלום *peace,* מנוחה *rest,* שאנן *ease* evoke serene joy in Isaiah 32:17–18.

15 Adrian Curtis, *Oxford Bible Atlas* (4th ed.; Oxford: Oxford University Press, 2009), 27. The NABRE rendering as *Arabian Sea* is misleading.

16 This flower has not been securely identified and appears only here and in Song of Songs 2:1 in parallel with a term that likely profiles the lily. J. J. M. Roberts, *First Isaiah* (Minneapolis, MN: Fortress Press, 2015), 440.

17 The Hebrew verb בקע in the Niphal profiles a *cleaving* or *breaking* that is often sudden or definitive, such as YHWH splitting the waters at the exodus (Exod 14:21), splitting a mountain in two (Zech 14:4), the earth opening up to swallow rebels (Num 16:31), or an egg hatching (Isa 59:5).

18 The root שׂושׂ *rejoice* appears in 35:1, 10, שׂמחה *joy* in 35:10, גיל *rejoice* in 35:1, 2 (twice), רנן *sing for joy* in 35:2, 6, 10, and דלג *leap* in 35:6. The passage mentions negative emotions as absent: the anxious of heart should take courage and fear not (35:4) and sorrow and mourning will flee (35:10). The passage depicts joy through the transformation of the natural and human worlds.

19 Hebrew terms זרע *seed* appears often with the sense of descendants. The similar term צאצא profiles the *produce* of the earth. The text develops the plant-people blend by describing how these seeds grow into trees.

20 On the emergence and development of the reading of a second exodus even in places where the reference is not explicit, see Øystein Lund, *Way Metaphors and Way Topics in Isaiah 40–55* (Tübingen: Mohr Siebeck, 2007), 4–21.

21 Humans generally prefer landscapes with water, and this preference appears to be more pronounced in those from arid environments. See Rachel Kaplan and Stephen Kaplan, *The Experience of Nature: A Psychological Perspective* (Cambridge: Cambridge University Press, 1989); Äsa Ode Sang and Caroline M. Hagerhall, "Scenic Beauty: Visual Landscape Assessment and Human Landscape Perception," in *Environmental Psychology: An Introduction* (Hoboken, NJ: Wiley, 2019), 45–54; Matthew P. White et al., "Blue Landscapes and Public Health," in *Oxford Textbook of Nature and Public Health*, ed. Matilda van den Bosch and William Bird (Oxford: Oxford University Press, 2018), 154–59; Simon Bell, *Landscape: Pattern, Perception and Process* (2nd ed.; New York, NY: Taylor & Francis, 2013); Nichols, *Blue Mind*.

22 The texts use various Hebrew terms profiling joy and joyful behaviors: גיל in 49:13; רנה in 44:23; 49:13; 55:12; רנן in 42:11; 44:23; 49:13; שׂמחה in 52:12.

23 The term שׂושׂ has arid land as a subject in Isaiah 35:1, but this verb does not appear at all in Isaiah 40–55.

24 The luminaries (sun, moon, stars) may be unique among these elements of creation. Cooley argues that Hebrews regarded them as fully alive personalities. See Jeffrey L. Cooley, *Poetic Astronomy in the Ancient Near East* (Winona Lake, IN: Eisenbrauns, 2013).

25 This verse inspired Joerstad's dissertation, published as Mari Joerstad, *The Hebrew Bible and Environmental Ethics: Humans, Nonhumans, and the Living Landscape* (Cambridge: Cambridge University Press, 2019).

26 Joerstad, *Hebrew Bible and Environmental Ethics*, 39–40. Joerstad says she might attribute happiness to a tree "if it is flourishing or bearing

fruit," but "it would not occur to me to talk about trees rejoicing at the end of World War II." Biblical writers, however, do speak this way and "this is what I want to understand! How do they view trees, how do they interact with them, to make such language sensible and important?" (p. 40). She draws on animism to explain these texts. Animists, however, do not attribute personhood to all nature indiscriminately. Hallowell describes an encounter in which an animist explains that only some rocks are alive. A. Irving Hallowell, "Ojibwa Ontology, Behavior, and Worldview," in *Readings in Indigenous Religions*, ed. Graham Harvey (London: A&C Black, 2002), 18–49. See discussion in Graham Harvey, *Animism: Respecting the Living World* (2nd ed.; London: Hurst and Co., 2017), 31–48. The new animism in anthropology rejects the Western misunderstanding of animist societies as generously, indiscriminately, and naively ascribing life to everything. See Istvan Praet, *Animism and the Question of Life* (London: Routledge, 2014). If we look for animism in Isaiah, we are more likely to find it in passages like Isaiah 1:29–31; 57:3–13; 65:3 than in personifications of nature writ large. These passages condemn practices associated with idolatry that seem to involve some affection for specific trees, which some Israelites may or may not have conceptualized as persons. Groves of trees may have elicited place attachment and been conceptualized as an appropriate place to offer worship to deities, much as mountains similarly appeared as appealing places to offer sacrifice throughout the ancient Mediterranean. The trees may have served as symbols of divinity without themselves being invested with human-like qualities. Large trees serve as landmarks (e.g., Gen 12:6; Deut 11:30) and attract cultural meanings that may become contested in a community. For more on animism, see Philippe Descola, *Beyond Nature and Culture,* trans. Janet Lloyd (Chicago, IL: University of Chicago Press, 2013); Graham Harvey, ed. *The Handbook of Contemporary Animism* (London: Routledge, 2014); Eduardo Kohn, *How Forests Think: Toward an Anthropology Beyond the Human* (Berkeley, CA: University of California Press, 2013).

27  Robert Murray, *The Cosmic Covenant: Biblical Themes of Justice, Peace and the Integrity of Creation* (London: Sheed and Ward, 1992); Richard J. Clifford and John Joseph Collins, *Creation in the Biblical Traditions* (Washington, DC: Catholic Biblical Association of America, 1992); Richard J. Clifford, *Creation Accounts in the Ancient Near East and in the Bible* (Washington, DC: Catholic Biblical Association of America, 1994); Christopher J. H. Wright, *Old Testament Ethics for the People of*

*God* (Downers Grove, IL: InterVarsity, 2004); Ronald Simkins, *Creator and Creation: Nature in the Worldview of Ancient Israel* (Peabody, MA: Hendrickson, 1994); William P. Brown, *The Ethos of the Cosmos: The Genesis of Moral Imagination in the Bible* (Wm. B. Eerdmans Publishing, 1999); Terence E. Fretheim, *God and World in the Old Testament: A Relational Theology of Old Testament* (Nashville, TN: Abingdon, 2010).

28  The last two chapters of Isaiah recapitulate the theme of joy within the book. Miguel Ángel Garzón Moreno, *La Alegría En Isaías: La Legría Como Unidad Y Estructura Del Libro a Partir De Su Epílogo (is 65–66)* (Estella: Editorial Verbo Divino, 2011). See his appendix 4 for detailed data on the distribution of joy-related vocabulary in Isaiah.

29  Dacher Keltner and Jonathn Haidt, "Approaching Awe, a Moral, Spiritual, and Aesthetic Emotion," *Cognition and Emotion* (2003) 297–314, here 303.

30  We all navigate the world with a variety of knowledge structures that help us make sense of experience. These structures include categorizes we use for objects and experiences, scripts for navigating familiar routines, and concepts that articulate knowledge about specific domains. Awe can upset these settled structures. Yang Bai et al., "Awe, the Diminished Self, and Collective Engagement: Universals and Cultural Cariations in the Small Self," *Journal of Personality and Social Psychology* 113 (2017) 185–209; Alice Chirico and David B. Yaden, "Awe: A Self-Transcendent and Sometimes Transformative Emotion," in *The Function of Emotions: When and Why Emotions Help Us*, ed. Heather C. Lench (Cham, Switzerland: Springer Nature Switzerland, 2018), 221–33; Michelle N. Shiotta et al., "Transcending the Self: Awe, Elevation, and Inspiration," in *Handbook of Positive Emotions*, ed. Michele M. Tugade, Michelle N. Shiota, and Leslie D. Kirby (New York, NY: Guilford, 2014), 362–77.

31  Shiota, "Transcending the Self: Awe, Elevation, and Inspiration", 366.

32  Keltner and Haidt, "Approaching Awe", 305–306. Keltner and Haidt review survey evidence and find five major types of awe based on what elicits the experience: threat, beauty, ability, virtue, supernatural causality. Threat involves vastness allied with fear, elicited by social or natural phenomena (e.g., charismatic leader or thunderstorm). Beauty can elicit awe, especially beautiful people and natural scenes. Ability can evoke awe when it appears exceptional, such as extreme feats of athleticism. Virtue similarly elicits awe, as when we see acts of mercy or sacrifice. They also list supernatural causality to refer to the perception

of divinity manifesting itself, although this category is vague and may overlap with all the above. For example, an act of sacrifice or special talent may seem divine.

33 Chirico and Yaden, "Awe," 222–27.

34 Chirico and Yaden, "Awe," esp. 225–27. They postulate that awe originated as a response to nature that later became generalized to the social order. Keltner and Haidt, "Approaching Awe" had postulated an origin in social hierarchy, but early humans did not have social stratification.

35 Researchers find that awe reduces dependence on schemas, stereotypes, and other knowledge structures, while other positive emotions like joy and pride increase dependence on these knowledge structures. For example, most positive emotions increase susceptibility to weak but repeated persuasive messages, while awe has the opposite effect. Similarly, awe leads to reduced dependence on stereotypes. Studies also find that awe reduces the sense of self and leads to a tendency to orient the self toward transcendent realities. Shiota, "Transcending the Self: Awe, Elevation, and Inspiration," 366.

36 Hebrew vocabulary of awe appears related to terms for fear. Likely candidates for Hebrew words that can profile awe include the noun מורא and the Niphal participle of ירא (HALOT glosses as *awe* and *awesome*, respectively). Lasater draws attention to the use of the Niphal participle to refer to God but severs it from the experience of fear without connecting it to awe. Context clarifies meaning. When fear words appear in contexts that indicate awe (grandeur, smallness of self, and need for accommodation), then translators may be correct to render the words as "awe" or "awesome." For example, the NRSV includes the word "awe" twenty-two times, mostly translating words related to fear (e.g., ירא in Ps 5:5; גור in Ps 22:24; חתת in Mal 2:5; ערץ in Isa 29:23). Other translations likewise translate fear words with "awe," but there is significant variety among specific contexts where awe appears in various translations. This variety may be due in part to a lack of clarity among English speakers about what awe is, as hearers may associate the term with fear, joy, wonder, or surprise depending on the context of the Hebrew word and the translator's prior experience of the English word. Recent scholarship has brought some clarity to the concept, but few English speakers know this scholarship or align their daily speech with it if they do. The evidence from physiology and facial expression suggests that awe might be an emotion separate from surprise, joy, and fear, yet potentially related to these emotions. See Shiota, "Transcending the Self: Awe, Elevation, and Inspiration."

37 The repeated expression "I am, there is no other" may or may not indicate monotheistic belief. For a summary of scholarship, see Matthias Albani, "Monotheism in Isaiah," in *The Oxford Handbook of Isaiah*, ed. Lena-Sofia Tiemeyer (Oxford: Oxford University Press, 2020), 219–48.

38 Norman C. Habel, *The Book of Job: A Commentary* (Philadelphia, PA: Westminster, 1985), 533–35; Michael V. Fox, "God's Answer and Job's Response," *Biblica* (2013) 1–23.

39 Habel, *Job*, 102–106; C. L. Seow, *Job 1–21: Interpretation and Commentary* (Grand Rapids, MI: Eerdmans, 2013), 319–28; J. Gerald Janzen, *Job* (Louisville, KY: Westminster John Knox, 1985), 61–63; Samuel E. Balentine, *Job* (Macon, GA: Smyth & Helwys, 2006), 86–88; Víctor Morla Asensio, *Libro De Job* (Estella: Verbo Divino, 2007), 147–48.

40 Carol A. Newsom, *The Book of Job: A Contest of Moral Imaginations* (Oxford: Oxford University Press, 2003), 241–56, describes the divine speeches as sublime, which is another way of saying that they evoke awe. The speeches evoke an "overwhelming force that scatters the self-presence of the hearer" (254).

41 Jörg Jeremias, *Theophanie: Die Geschichte Einer Alttestamentlichen Gattung* (Neukirchener-Vluyn: Neukirchener Verlag, 1965).

42 The divine name YHWH occurs only in the frame narrative and the frame around YHWH's speeches (Job 38:1; 40:1, 3; 42:1). The appearance of YHWH in 12:9 is likely an error. See David J. A. Clines, *Job 38–42* (Waco, TX: Thomas Nelson, 2011), 1095.

43 James A. Wharton, *Job* (Louisville, KY: Westminster John Knox, 1999), 164–65, 169–70; T. C. Ham, "The Gentle Voice of God in Job 38," *Journal of Biblical Literature* 132 (2013) 527–41, here 529.

44 Eric Ortlund, "God's Joy in Creation in the Book of Job," *Presbyterion* 47 (2021) 5–15, here 11.

45 Ortlund notes that Psalm 25:12 expresses awe at a group of humans and Saul arguably expresses awe at David in 1 Sam 17:55–56. Ortlund, "God's Joy," 11; Ham, "Gentle Voice of God," 532.

46 גבר profiles *man* and connotes strength and courage. See Robert Gordis, *The Book of Job: Commentary, New Translation, Special Studies* (New York, NY: Jewish Theological Seminary, 1978), 442–43. On girding loins, see, Clines, *Job 38–42*, 1096–97; Katherine Low, "Implications Surrounding Girding the Loins in Light of Gender, Body, and Power," *Journal for the Study of the Old Testament* 36 (2011) 3–30. Here it is not a call to physical combat but mental contest. YHWH calls Job to pay attention.

47 Thus NABRE. *Please* is too strong a translation but captures the soft-
ening quality of the particle נא. See Ham, "Gentle Voice of God," 534.

48 Fox claims that Job can answer all the questions YHWH asks with three
exceptions (Job 38:19 on the dwelling place of light and darkness;
38:24 on where light and the east wind emerge; 39:1–3 on the gesta-
tion period of the gazelle). Fox underestimates how the questions that
Job can answer still point to realities that he does not understand. He
may know that the earth is founded on the void, but he does not know
how anything can be founded on nothing. Fox, "God's Answer and
Job's Response," 14.

49 Fox, "God's Answer and Job's Response," 13.

50 Michael Fishbane, "Jeremiah IV 23–26 and Job III 3–13: A Recovered
Use of the Creation Pattern," *Vetus Testamentum* 21 (1971) 151–67,
followed by Habel, *Job*, 104–106; Balentine, *Job*, 82–88. Clines, *Job
38–42*, 81, thinks Job's indictment of creation is limited to the elements that impact his personal fate, but it is not clear how this limits
the indictment.

51 Ortlund, "God's Joy," 12.

52 In Schneider's several interviews, many people pointed to nature as
triggering awe, and awe as critical to resilience and recovery. See Kirk
J. Schneider, *Awakening to Awe: Personal Stories of Profound Transformation* (Lanham, MD: Jason Aronson, 2009). Williams provides an
accessible and engaging journalistic summary of research on the power
of nature to evoke awe and well-being. Florence Williams, *The Nature
Fix: Why Nature Makes Us Happier, Healthier, and More Creative* (New
York, NY: Norton, 2017), 187–201. Most of her work details the
abundant research on the positive effects of time spent in nature independent of experiences of awe.

53 "The experience of trauma is paradoxically similar to the awe-inspiring personal experiences of the vastness of nature, i.e., one is rendered
humble, small, and insignificant." John P. Wilson, "Trauma and Transformation of the Self: Restoring Meaning and Wholeness to Personality," in *The Posttraumatic Self: Restoring Meaning and Wholeness to
Personality*, ed. John P. Wilson (New York, NY: Routledge, 2006), 399–
423, quote 409. Wilson notes that people who recover from trauma
show openness to new ideas, ability to acknowledge mistakes, and an
appreciation of the value of everything. YHWH's speeches to Job seek to
cultivate these qualities in the suffering Job. On the value of awe and
positive emotion for enhancing resilience and facilitating recovery, see
John P. Wilson, "Transformational Principles: Healing and Recovery
From Psychic Trauma," in *The Posttraumatic Self: Restoring Meaning*

*and Wholeness to Personality*, ed. John P. Wilson (New York, NY: Routledge, 2006), 425–57, esp 444–49; John P. Wilson, "Trauma, Optimal Experiences, and Integrative Psychological States," in *The Posttraumatic Self: Restoring Meaning and Wholeness to Personality*, ed. John P. Wilson (New York, NY: Routledge, 2006), 211–53; Elliott D. Ihm et al., "Awe as a Meaning-Making Emotion: On the Evolution of Awe and the Origin of Religions," in *The Evolution of Religion, Religiosity and Theology: A Multilevel and Multidisciplinary Approach*, ed. Jay R. Feierman and Lluis Oviedo (London: Routledge, 2020), 139–53; Michael F. Steger and Crystal L. Park, "The Creation of Meaning Following Trauma: Meaning Making and Trajectories of Distress and Recovery," in *Trauma Therapy in Context: The Science and Craft of Evidence-Based Practice*, ed. Robert A. McMackin et al. (Washington, DC: American Psychological Association, 2012), 171–91. On meaning making, see Elizabeth M. Altmaier, ed. *Reconstructing Meaning After Trauma: Theory Research, and Practice* (Amsterdam: Elselvier, 2017); Crystal L. Park, "Religion and Meaning," in *Handbook of Psychology of Religion and Spirituality*, ed. Raymond F. Paloutzian and Crystal L. Park (New York, MY: Guilford, 2013), 357–79. For work on trauma recovery in the biblical field, see Brent A Strawn, "Trauma, Psalmic Disclosure, and Authentic Happiness," in *Bible through the Lens of Trauma*, ed. Elizabeth Boase and Christopher G. Frechette (Atlanta, GA: Society of Biblical Literature, 2016), 143–60. See related research on post-traumatic growth and its application to the Bible in Xi Li, "Posttraumatic Growth in Psalms of Laments, Jeremiah, and Lamentations," diss., (The Catholic University of America, 2022).

54  Fishbane, "Jeremiah IV 23–26 and Job III 3–13: A Recovered Use of the Creation Pattern"; followed by Habel, *Job*, 103–106; Balentine, *Job*, 79, 82–88; Seow, *Job 1–21*, 313–15; Asensio, *Libro De Job*, 147–48.

55  On the effects of positive emotion on physical and mental health, see Judith Tedlie Moskowitz and Laura R. Saslow, "Health and Psychology: The Importance of Positive Affect," in *Handbook of Positive Emotions*, ed. Michele M. Tugade, Michelle N. Shiota, and Leslie D. Kirby (New York, NY: Guilford, 2014), 413–31. See also Ingrid Fetell Lee, *Joyful: The Surprising Power of Ordinary Things to Create Extraordinary Happiness* (New York, NY: Little, Brown Spark, 2018), esp. 189–216 on awe. On hope and gratitude, see Jennifer S. Cheavens and Lorie A. Ritschel, "Hope Theory," in *Handbook of Positive Emotions*, ed. Michele M. Tugade, Michelle N. Shiota, and Leslie D. Kirby

(New York, NY: Guilford, 2014) 398–410; Anthony H. Ahrens and Courtney N. Forbes, "Gratitude," in *Handbook of Positive Emotions*, ed. Michele M. Tugade, Michelle N. Shiota, and Leslie D. Kirby (New York, NY: Guilford, 2014), 324–61.

56 On the joy of wisdom in Proverbs 8, see Richard J. Clifford, *Proverbs* (Louisville, KY: Westminster John Knox, 1999), 97. Michael V. Fox, *Proverbs 1–9* (New York, NY: Doubleday, 2000), 285–89; Gerlinde Baumann, *Die Weisheitsgestalt in Proverbien 1–9: Traditionsgeschichtliche Und Theologische Studien* (Tübingen: Mohr Seibeck, 1996), 139–40.

57 Janzen notes that the ambiguity of YHWH's relationship to the sea appears also in YHWH's relationship with the Satan whom YHWH similarly supports and constrains. See Janzen, *Job*, 134–35. The mighty forces of chaos in human imagination become harmless in comparison to YHWH (sea, wild animals, Behemoth, Leviathan). Habel, *Job*, 138–39. Brian R. Doak, *Consider Leviathan: Narratives of Nature and Self in Job* (Minneapolis, MN: Fortress, 2014), 193: the sea is "demythologized and radically *personalized* under God's own care."

58 Lance R Hawley, *Metaphor Competition in the Book of Job* (Göttingen: Vandenhoeck & Ruprecht, 2018), 189.

59 Habel, *Job*, 544, The questions imply YHWH's care for the lion and raven and lead Job to reevaluate the role of wild animals in creation. Job and his culture tend to devalue wild creatures as useless or dangerous, but YHWH seeks to use these creatures to evoke wonder and awe by seeing YHWH's care for marginal animals as parallel to concern for marginal land in 38:26–27. See Hawley, *Metaphor Competition*, 189–91.

60 The hind might here be a female mountain goat. See Clines, *Job 38–42*, 1120.

61 The animal is not the wild ass but more likely the larger and stronger onager. See. H. H. Shugart, *Foundations of the Earth: Global Ecological Change and the Book of Job* (New York, NY: Columbia University Press, 2014), 71–72.

62 The onager laughs at the bonds of domestic life. Job likens his scoffers to onagers in 30:1. Hawley rightly notes that these scoffers do not literally live in the wilderness in Job 30:1–8. Rather, these humans resemble lowly and marginalized creatures that do live in the wilderness outside human civilization. See Hawley, *Metaphor Competition*, 193–95.

63 On the extinct auroch, see Shugart, *Foundations of the Earth*, 36–69.

64 YHWH asks if the aurochs would *be willing* or *agree* (אבה) to serve him. The assumed answer is no.

65 The two verses use the words בטח *trust* and אמן *trust* to characterize Job's potential relationship with the aurochs. This wild animal was too strong and too wild to be tamed and trusted among people.

66 In rare cases, some thoroughbred horses have briefly achieved 45mph, and the world record is 55mph. Ostriches avoided extinction in the Near East for a long time through their speed and residence in the wilderness. With the introduction of rifles, this subspecies of ostrich was hunted to extinction. For information about ostriches, see Edgar Williams, *Ostrich* (London: Reaktion, 2013). Walker-Jones argues that רנן does not profile the ostrich hen, but another ground-nesting bird like a sandgrouse that escapes horses through flight. See Arthur Walker-Jones, "The So-Called Ostrich in the God Speeches of the Book of Job (Job 39, 13–18)," *Biblica* (2005) 494–510. Followed by Hawley, *Metaphor Competition*, 196–99, who insists that the bird cannot be an ostrich. Ostrich fits the context well, and biblical literature elsewhere shows significant interest in the ostrich, profiling the cock and hen with יענה (Isa 13:21; 34:13; 43:20; Jer 50:39; Mic 1:9; Job 30:29). Furthermore, there are several strategies for hunting ground-nesting birds that can fly, but galloping after them on horseback is not one of them. For ostrich hunting, however, a horse is indispensable as ancient iconography attests. The vignette fits the ostrich well.

67 Deborah O'Daniel Cantrell, *The Horsemen of Israel: Horses and Chariotry in Monarchic Israel (Ninth-Eighth Centuries B.c.e.)* (Winona Lake, IN: Eisenbrains, 2011), 11–34.

68 Hippos kill hundreds of people per year, some estimate thousands, by trampling or biting them. The bite of the hippos exerts more force than any other animal with the exception of the crocodile (the crocodile is the evident basis for Leviathan). By contrast, sharks kill about five people per year. The only creature more dangerous are pathogens carried by various vectors, such as the plasmodium bacteria carried by mosquitos who infect people with malaria.

69 Modified from NABRE, which has *Look, I am of little account.*

70 Habel, *Job*, 549.

71 Job's sense of smallness is not the same as the painful sting of humiliation. The questions make him feel small (awed), but do not make him feel ashamed or humiliated like the king of Babylon cast down from heaven to Sheol. In Isaiah 14, yhwh's wrath against human hubris punishes the king. In Job, yhwh's questions do not humiliate but remind Job of his smallness and instill awe as a way to reverse Job's grief. Asensio, *Libro De Job*, 1463, captures the sense by noting that "the verb קלל

does not here denote lightness language nor lend itself to a moral sense, but rather refers the reader to the smallness of human worth [*no denota aquí ligereza de lenguaje ni se presta a interpretaciones de tipo moral, sino que remite al lector a la escasez de valía humana*]." Other commentators have partially misunderstood these words. Balentine, *Job*, 667–68, attributes shame to Job in this moment and thinks Job concedes that he is of little importance to YHWH. But YHWH's appearance to Job and boast in Job 1:8 indicates that Job is important to YHWH. Similarly, Clines, *Job 38–42*, 1138–39, thinks that Job has interpreted YHWH's questions as humiliating, although YHWH does not intend to humiliate him. Clines rejects any notion of human smallness compared to the divine, but that contrast is exactly the point. Janzen, *Job*, 243, overreads Job's statement as a clever response to YHWH: "If I am of no account, what shall I answer you." The translation "if" (a possible but unlikely meaning of הֵן, which is here a mirative particle expressing Job's surprise) implies Job's disagreement with the proposition that he is small as YHWH has tried to make him feel. Habel, *Job*, 549, sees that the verb indicates that Job has been reduced to smallness through the speech of YHWH, yet he also misreads this smallness as humiliation.

72 This gesture has been read as conveying shame or awe. For a discussion of possible interpretations, see G. Yuri Glazov, "The Significance of the 'Hand on the Mouth' Gesture in Job XL 4," *Vetus Testamentum* 42 (2002) 30–41.

73 The choice of the word מְזִמָּה profiles a plan or purpose similar to מַחֲשָׁבָה in Isaiah 55:9. Neither term denotes wickedness, although both appear in context describing the wicked schemes of humans. See Clines, *Job 38–42*, 1205, contra Habel, *Job*, 581.

74 The Niphal participle נִפְלָא profiles awe (Ps 139:14; Prov 30:18), often used of YHWH's wondrous acts (Exod 30:20; 34:10; Josh 3:5; Judg 6:13; Ps 40:6; 106:22). Together with Job's acknowledgment that he is small in Job 40:2, this term profiles Job's experience of awe, or his experience of the vastness of creation and the creator. NABRE renders *marvelous*.

75 Translation from Roland E. Murphy, *The Book of Job: A Short Reading* (New York, NY: Paulist, 1999), 100. Murphy notes that Job 42:6 "cannot be translated with certainty, due to the obscurity of the Hebrew text." (99) Three expressions create most of the ambiguities: מאס (reject, despise; melt); נחם (repent, be consoled); dust and ashes (a reference to the ashes and dust in Job 2:8 and 12, Job's mourning, or his mortality). Most possibilities cohere with the interpretation of Job as overawed

by YHWH. The verb נחם need not imply previous wrongdoing, only a change of mind (Exod 13:17; Jer 4:28; Jon 3:9). Perhaps Job changes his mind about dust and ashes, meaning that he turns away from his lament and resumes normal life (Habel, *Job*, 575). Since נחם may mean *be comforted*, perhaps Job accepts the comfort offered by YHWH, understanding that he is dust and ashes, small and mortal (Clines, *Job 38–42*, 1218–23). Or perhaps he changes his mind about the human condition (Janzen, *Job*, 255–59; Leo G. Perdue, *Wisdom in Revolt: Metaphorical Theology in the Book of Job* (Sheffield: Sheffield Academic Press, 1991), 232). By any of these interpretations, Job's experience of awe changes him. He ceases his mourning and complaint because they are no longer sustained by his prior understanding. NABRE renders *I disown what I have said, and repent in dust and ashes.*

76   YHWH becomes angry at Job's friends because they have not spoken rightly about God as Job has (Job 42:7). Job has spent most of the book attacking God's character, while his friends consistently praised God and condemned Job. At the end, Job expresses a change of heart and concludes his complaint. Nam identifies three ways in which Job's speeches differ from the friends that may explain the distinction God makes between them. Duck-Woo Nam, *Talking About God: Job 42:7–9 and the Nature of God in the Book of Job* (New York, NY: Peter Lang, 2003). First, Job often speaks directly to God, which the friends never do. Second, these speeches to God seek an encounter and YHWH responds favorably. Third, YHWH's speeches respond to the prior dialogue in ways that correct both Job and the friends, but the friends' worldview requires more correction because they hold an ossified and simplified view of moral order unresponsive to experience. Along similar lines, Immanuel Kant argued that Job's speeches come from an honesty lacking in his friends. Job speaks sincerely, but his friends flatter God. Immanuel Kant, "On the Miscarriage of All Philosophical Trials in Theodicy (1791)," in *Religion and Rational Theology*, ed. Allen Wood and George di Giovanni (Cambridge: Cambridge University Press, 2013), 19–37.

# BIBLIOGRAPHY

Adolphs, Ralph and David J. Anderson. *The Neuroscience of Emotion: A New Synthesis*. Princeton, NJ: Princeton University Press, 2018.

Ahrens, Anthony H. and Courtney N. Forbes. "Gratitude." In *Handbook of Positive Emotions*, edited by Michele M. Tugade, Michelle N. Shiota, and Leslie D. Kirby, 324–61. New York, NY: Guilford, 2014.

Albani, Matthias. "Monotheism in Isaiah." In *The Oxford Handbook of Isaiah*, edited by Lena-Sofia Tiemeyer, 219–48. Oxford: Oxford University Press, 2020.

Albrecht, Glenn A. *Earth Emotions: New Words for a New World*. Ithaca, NY: Cornell University Press, 2019.

Alderman, Isaac. *The Animal at Unease with Itself: Death Anxiety and the Animal-Human Boundary in Genesis 2–3*. Lanham, MD: Lexington Books/Fortress Academic, 2020.

Altmaier, Elizabeth M., ed. *Reconstructing Meaning after Trauma: Theory Research, and Practice*. Amsterdam: Elsevier, 2017.

Andersen, Francis I. and David Noel Freedman. *Amos: A New Translation with Introduction and Commentary*. New York, NY: Doubleday, 1989.

Anderson, Bernhard W. *From Creation to New Creation*. Minneapolis: Fortress, 1994.

Anderson, David. *The Nature of the Beast: How Emotions Guide Us*. New York, NY: Basic Books, 2022.

Anderson, Gary A. *A Time to Mourn, a Time to Dance: The Expression of Grief and Joy in Israelite Religion*. Penn State University Press, 1991.

Asensio, Víctor Morla. *Libro de Job*. Estella: Verbo Divino, 2007.

Astington, Janet Wilde and Jodie A. Baird. *Why Language Matters for Theory of Mind*. Oxford: Oxford University Press, 2005.

Atkins, Peter Joshua. "Mythology or Zoology?: A Study of the Impact of Translation History in Isaiah 13:21." *Biblical Interpretation* 24 (2016): 48–59.

Auld, A. Graeme. *I & II Samuel*. Louisville, KY: Westminster John Knox, 2011.

Austin, Benjamin M. *Plant Metaphors in the Old Greek of Isaiah*. Atlanta, GA: Society of Biblical Literature, 2019.

Austin, Elizabeth. *Treading on Thin Air: Atmospheric Physics, Forensic Meteorology, and Climate Change: How Weather Shapes Our Everyday Lives*. New York: Pegasus, 2016.

Bai, Yang, Lauren A. Maruskin, Serena Chen, Amie M. Gordon, Jennifer E. Stellar, Galen D. McNeil, Kaiping Peng, and Dacher Keltner. "Awe, the Diminished Self, and Collective Engagement: Universals and Cultural Variations in the Small Self." *Journal of Personality and Social Psychology* 113 (2017): 185–209.

Balentine, Samuel E. *Job*. Macon, GA: Smyth & Helwys, 2006.

Baloian, Bruce Edward. *Anger in the Old Testament*. Lausane, CH: Peter Lang, 1992.

Baron-Cohen, Simon. *Mindblindness: An Essay on Autism and Theory of Mind*. Cambridge: MIT Press, 1997.

Barr, James. *The Semantics of Biblical Language*. Eugene, OR: Wipf and Stock, 2004.

Barrett, Lisa Feldman. *How Emotions Are Made: The Secret Life of the Brain*. Boston: Houghton Mifflin Harcourt, 2017.

Barrett, Lisa Feldman and James A. Russell. *The Psychological Construction of Emotion*. New York, NY: Guilford, 2014.

Barrett, Michael. "The Danger of Heartless Religion: An Exposition of Isaiah 1:2–18." *Puritan Reformed Journal* 6 (2014): 5–15.

Barton, John. "Ethics in Isaiah of Jerusalem." *Journal of Theological Studies* 32 (1981): 1–18.

Barton, John. *Joel and Obadiah: A Commentary*. Louisville, KY: Westminster John Know, 2001.

Basson, Alec. "People are Plants: A Conceptual Metaphor in the Hebrew Bible." *Old Testament Essays* 19 (2006): 573–83.

Baumann, Gerlinde. *Die Weisheitsgestalt in Proverbien 1–9: Traditionsgeschichtliche und theologische Studien*. Tübingen: Mohr Seibeck, 1996.

Bechtel, Lyn M. "The Biblical Experience of Shame/Shaming: The Social Experience of Shame/Shaming in Biblical Israel in Relation to Its Usage as Religious Metaphor," diss., Drew University, 1983.

Becker, Ernest. *The Denial of Death*. New York, NY: Simon and Schuster, 1973.

Bell, Simon. *Landscape: Pattern, Perception and Process*. 2nd ed. New York, NY: Taylor & Francis, 2013.

Bergen, Benjamin. "Embodiment." In *Cognitive Linguistics: Foundations of Language*, edited by Ewa Dąbrowska and Dagmar Divjak, 11–35. Berlin: Walter de Gruyter, 2019.

Berges, Ulrich. "Personifications and Prophetic Voices of Zion in Isaiah and Beyond." In *The Elusive Prophet: The Prophet as Historical Person, Literary Character and Annonymous Artist*, edited by Johannes Cornelis De Moor, 54–82. Leiden: Brill, 2001.

Bergmann, Claudia D. *Childbirth as a Metaphor for Crisis: Evidence from the Ancient Near East, the Hebrew Bible, and 1QH XI, 1–18*. Berlin: Walter de Gruyter, 2008.

Berlin, Adele. "Psalms and the Literature of Exile: Psalms 137, 44, 69, and 78." In *The Book of Psalms: Composition and Reception*, edited by Patrick D. Miller, Peter W. Flint, and Aaron Brunell, 65–86. Leiden: Brill, 2005.

Berman, Joshua. "What does the Ox Know in Isa 1:3a." *Vetus Testamentum* 64 (2014): 382–88.

Beuken, Willem A. M. *Jesaja 13–27*. Translated by Ulrich Berges. Freiburg: Herders, 2007.

Black, Fiona C. and Jennifer L. Koosed, eds. *Reading with Feeling: Affect Theory and the Bible*. Atlanta, GA: Society of Biblical Literature, 2019.

Blenkinsopp, Joseph. *Isaiah 1–39*. New Haven, CT: Yale University Press, 2000.

Blenkinsopp, Joseph. *Isaiah 56–66*. New Haven, CT: Yale University Press, 2003.

Boda, Mark J., Carol J. Dempsey, and LeAnn Snow Flesher. *Daughter Zion: Her Portrait, Her Response*. Atlanta, GA: Society of Biblical Literature, 2012.

Bonanno, George A. "Loss, Trauma, and Human Resilience: Have We Underestimated the Human Capacity to Thrive after Extremely Aversive Events?" *American Psychologist* 59 (2004): 101–13.

Bonanno, George A. *The Other Side of Sadness: What the New Science of Bereavement Tells Us about Life after Loss*. Rev. ed. New York, NY: Basic Books, 2019.

Bonanno, George A. *The End of Trauma: How the New Science of Resilience Is Changing How We Think About PTSD*. New York, NY: Basic Books, 2021.

Bosch, Matilda van den and William Bird. *Oxford Textbook of Nature and Public Health*. Oxford: Oxford University Press, 2018.

Bosman, H. L. "Jeremiah 8:8: Why are Scribes Accused of Corrupting the Torah?" *Acta Theologica Supplementum* 26 (2018): 118–35.

Bosworth, David A. "Daughter Zion and Weeping in Lamentations 1–2." *Journal for the Study of the Old Testament* 38 (2013): 217–37.

Bosworth, David A. *House of Weeping: The Motif of Tears in Akkadian and Hebrew Prayers*. Atlanta, GA: Society of Biblical Literature Press, 2019.

Bottéro, Jean. *Textes culinaires Méesopotamiens / Mesopotamian Culinary Texts*. Winona Lake, IN: Eisenbrauns, 1995.

Boyle, Marjorie O'Rourke. "Broken Hearts: The Violation of Biblical Law." *Journal of the American Academy of Religion* 73 (2005): 731–57.

Branch-Trevathan, George. *The Sermon on the Mount and Spiritual Exercises: The Making of the Matthean Self*. Leiden: Brill, 2020.

Brown, Brené. *Atlas of the Heart: Mapping Meaningful Connection and the Language of Human Experience*. New York, NY: Random House, 2021.

Brown, John Pairman. *Israel and Hellas: The legacy of Iranian Imperialism and the Individual*. Berlin: Walter de Gruyter, 2001.

Brown, William P. *The Ethos of the Cosmos: The Genesis of Moral Imagination in the Bible*. Grand Rapids, MI: Eerdmans, 1999.

Brown, William P. *Seeing the Psalms: A Theology of Metaphor*. Louisville, KY: Westminster John Knox, 2002.

Broyles, Craig C. *Psalms*. Peabody, MA: Hendrickson, 1999.

Busch, Fredric N., ed. *Mentalization: Theoretical Considerations, Research Findings, and Clinical Implications*. London: Routledge, 2011.

Bybee, Joan. *Frequency of Use and the Organization of Language*. Oxford: Oxford University Press, 2006.

Bybee, Joan. *Language, Usage and Cognition*. Cambridge: Cambridge University Press, 2010.

Cantrell, Deborah O'Daniel. *The Horsemen of Israel: Horses and Chariotry in Monarchic Israel (Ninth-Eighth Centuries B.C.E.)*. Winona Lake, IN: Eisenbrains, 2011.

Carasik, Michael. *Theologies of the Mind in Biblical Israel*. New York, NY: Peter Lang, 2006.

Carr, David M. *The Formation of the Hebrew Bible: A New Reconstruction*. Oxford: Oxford University Press, 2011.

Carroll, Robert P. *Jeremiah: A Commentary*. Philadelphia, PA: Westminster, 1986.

Cassidy, Jude and Phillip R. Shaver. *Handbook of Attachment*. 3rd ed. New York, NY: Guilford, 2016.

Casson, Lionel. *The Ancient Mariners: Seafarers and Sea Fighters of the Mediterranean in Ancient Times*. 2nd ed. Princeton, NJ: Princeton University Press, 1991.

Catholic Committee of Appalachia. *The Telling Takes Us Home: Taking Our Place in the Stories that Shape Us; A People's Pastoral from the Catholic Committee of Appalachia*. Spencer, WV: Catholic Committee of Appalachia, 2015.

Chaney, Marvin. "Whose Sour Grapes?: The Addressees of Isaiah 5:1–7 in the Light of Political Economy." *Semeia* 87 (1999): 105–22.

Cheavens, Jennifer S. and Lorie A. Ritschel. "Hope Theory." In *Handbook of Positive Emotions*, edited by Michele M. Tugade, Michelle N. Shiota, and Leslie D. Kirby, 398–410. New York, NY: Guilford, 2014.

Childs, Brevard S. *Isaiah*. Louisville, KY: Westminster John Knox Press, 2001.

Chirico, Alice and David B. Yaden. "Awe: A Self-Transcendent and Sometimes Transformative Emotion." In *The Function of Emotions: When and Why Emotions Help Us*, edited by Heather C. Lench, 221–33. Cham, Switzerland: Springer Nature Switzerland, 2018.

Clifford, Richard J. "The Hebrew Scriptures and the Theology of Creation." *Theological Studies* 46 (1985): 507–23.

Clifford, Richard J. *Creation Accounts in the Ancient Near East and in the Bible*. Washington, DC: Catholic Biblical Association of America, 1994.

Clifford, Richard J. *Proverbs*. Louisville, KY: Westminster John Knox, 1999.

Clifford, Richard J. *Psalms 73–150*. Nashville, TN: Abingdon, 2003.

Clifford, Richard J. and John Joseph Collins. *Creation in the Biblical Traditions*. Washington, DC: Catholic Biblical Association of America, 1992.

Clines, David J. A. *Job 1–20*. Waco, TX: Thomas Nelson, 1989.

Clines, David J. A. "Was there an 'BL II 'Be Dry' in Classical Hebrew?" *Vetus Testamentum* 42 (1992): 1–10.

Clines, David J. A. *Theme of the Pentateuch*. 2nd ed. Sheffield: Sheffield Academic Press, 1997.

Clines, David J. A. *Job 38–42*. Waco, TX: Thomas Nelson, 2011.

Conklin, Blane. *Oath Formulas in Biblical Hebrew*. University Park, PA: Pennsylvania State University Press, 2011.

Cooley, Jeffrey L. *Poetic Astronomy in the Ancient Near East*. Winona Lake, IN: Eisenbrauns, 2013.

Cornelius, Randolph R. *The Science of Emotion: Research and Tradition in the Psychology of Emotion*. Upper Saddle River, NJ: Prentice Hall, 1996.

Counted, Victor and Fraser Watts. "Place Attachment in the Bible: The Role of Attachment to Sacred Places in Religious Life." *Journal of Psychology and Theology* 45 (2017): 218–32.

Crenshaw, James L. *Joel: A New Translation with Introduction and Commentary*. New York, NY: Doubleday, 1995.

Croft, William and D. Alan Cruse. *Cognitive Linguistics*. Cambridge: Cambridge University Press, 2004.

Crook, Zeba. "Honor, Shame, and Social Status Revisited." *Journal of Biblical Literature* 128 (2009): 591–611.

Crozier, W. Ray and Peter J. de Jong, eds. *The Psychological Significance of the Blush*. Cambridge: Cambridge University Press, 2012.

Curtis, Adrian. *Oxford Bible Atlas*. 4th ed. Oxford: Oxford University Press, 2009.

Curtis, Valerie. *Don't Look, Don't Touch, Don't Eat: The Science Behind Revulsion*. Chicago, IL: University of Chicago Press, 2013.

Dąbrowska, Ewa and Dagmar Divjak. *Cognitive Linguistics: A Survey of Linguistic Subfields*. Berlin: Walter de Gruyter, 2019.

Dąbrowska, Ewa and Dagmar Divjak. *Cognitive Linguistics: Foundations of Language*. Berlin: Walter de Gruyter, 2019.

Dąbrowska, Ewa and Dagmar Divjak. *Cognitive Linguistics: Key Topics*. Berlin: Walter de Gruyter, 2019.

Dancygier, Barbara. *The Cambridge Handbook of Cognitive Linguistics*. Cambridge: Cambridge University Press, 2017.

Davies, Graham I. *Exodus 1–18*. Bloomsbury, 2020.

de Vos, Christiane and Gert Kwakkel. "Psalm 69: The Petitioner's Understanding of Himself, His God, and His Enemies." In *Psalms and Prayers: Papers Read at the Joint Meeting of the Society of Old Testament and Het Oudtestamentlische werkgezelschap in Nederland en België, Appledoorn, August 2006*, 159–79. Leiden: Brill, 2007.

Deonna, Julien A., Raffaele Rodogno, and Fabrice Teroni. *In Defense of Shame: The Faces of an Emotion*. Oxford: Oxford University Press, 2012.

Descola, Philippe. *Beyond Nature and Culture*. Translated by Janet Lloyd. Chicago, IL: University of Chicago Press, 2013.

Devlin, Ann Sloan. "Concepts, Theories and Research Approaches." In *Environmental Psychology and Human Well-Being: Effects of Built and Natural Settings*, edited by Ann Sloan Devlin, 1–28. London: Academic Press, 2018.

Devlin, Ann Sloan. *Environmental Psychology and Human Well-Being*. Cambridge, MA: Academic Press, 2018.

Dhorme, Édouard. *A Commentary on the Book of Job*. Translated by Harold Knight. Nashville: Thomas Nelson, 1967.

Di Masso, Andrés, John Dixon, and Kevin Durrheim. "Place Attachment as Discursive Practice: The Role of Language, Affect, Space, Power, and Materiality in Person-Place Bonds." In *Place Attcahment: Advances in Theory, Methods and*

*Applications*, edited by Lynne C. Manzo and Patrick Devine-Wright, 77–92. London: Routledge, 2021.

Di Masso, Andrés, John Dixon, and Kevin Durrheim. "Place Attachment as Discursive Practice." In *Place Attachment: Advances in Theory, Methods and Application*, edited by Lynne Manzo and Patrick Devine-Wright, 75–86. London: Routledge, 2013.

DiFransico, Lesley. "Distinguishing Emotions of Guilt and Shame in Psalm 51." *Biblical Theology Bulletin* 48 (2018): 180–87.

Divjak, Dagmar and Catherine L. Caldwell-Harris. "Frequency and Entrenchment." In *Cognitive Linguistics: Foundations of Language*, edited by Ewa Dąbrowska and Dagmar Divjak, 61–86. Berlin: Walter de Gruyter, 2019.

Dixon, Thomas M. *Weeping Britannia: Portrait of a Nation in Tears*. New York: Oxford University Press, 2015.

Doak, Brian R. *The Last of the Rephaim: Conquest and Cataclysm in the Heroic Ages of Ancient Israel*. Boston, MA: Ilex Foundation, 2012.

Doak, Brian R. *Consider Leviathan: Narratives of Nature and Self in Job*. Minneapolis, MN: Fortress, 2014.

Dow, Lois K. Fuller. *Images of Zion: Biblical Antecedents for the New Jerusalem*. Sheffield: Sheffield Phoenix, 2010.

Driver, G. R. "Confused Hebrew Roots." In *Occident and Orient: Being Studies in Semitic Philology and Literature, Jewish History and Philosophy and Folklore in the Widest Sense, in Honour of Haham Dr. M. Gaster's 80th Birthday*, edited by Bruno Schindler and Arthur Marmorstein, 73–82. London: Taylor's Foreign Press, 1936.

Duhm, Bernhard. *Das Buch Jesaia*. Göttingen: Vandenhoeck and Ruprecht, 1922.

Dweck, Carol S. *Mindset: The New Science of Success*. Updated ed. New York, NY: Random House, 2016.

Ekman, Paul. *Darwin and Facial Expression: A Century of Research in Review*. Cambridge, MA: Malor Books, 2006.

Ekman, Paul. *Emotions Revealed: Recognizing Faces and Feelings to Improve Communication and Emotional Life*. Rev. ed. New York, NY: Holt, 2007.

Elliott, Anthony. *Concepts of the Self*. 4th ed. Cambridge: Polity, 2020.

Epley, Nicholas. *Mindwise: Why We Misunderstand What Others Think, Believe, Feel, and Want*. New York, NY: Vintage, 2015.

Evans, Vyvyan. *The Language Myth: Why Language is Not an Instinct*. Cambridge: Cambridge University Press, 2014.

Evans, Vyvyan. *The Crucible of Language: How Language and Mind Create Meaning*. Cambridge: Cambridge University Press, 2015.

Evans, Vyvyan. *Cognitive Linguistics: A Complete Guide*. Edinburgh: Edinburgh University Press, 2019.

Exum, J. Cheryl. *Song of Songs: A Commentary*. Louisville, KY: Westminster John Knox, 2005.

Fauconnier, Gilles. *Mappings in Thought and Language*. Cambridge: Cambridge University Press, 1997.

Fauconnier, Gilles and Mark Turner. *The Way We Think*. New York, NY: Basic Books, 2008.

Faust, Avraham. "Society and Culture in the Kingdom of Judah during the Eighth Century." In *Archaeology and History of Eighth-Century Judah*, edited by Zev I. Farber and Jacob L. Wright, 179–204. Atlanta, GA: Society of Biblical Literature, 2018.

Fernyhough, Charles. *The Voices Within: The History and Science of How We Talk to Ourselves*. New York, NY: Basic Books, 2016.

Fessler, Daniel M. T. "Shame in Two Cultures: Implications for Evolutionary Approaches." *Journal of Cognition and Culture* 4 (2004): 207–62.

Firth-Godbehere, Richard. *A Human History of Emotion: How the Way We Feel Built the World We Know*. New York, NY: Little, Brown Spark, 2021.

Fishbane, Michael. "Jeremiah IV 23–26 and Job III 3–13: A Recovered Use of the Creation Pattern." *Vetus Testamentum* 21 (1971): 151–67.

Fohrer, Georg. *Das Buch Jasaja: Kapitel 24–39*. Zürich: Zwingli, 1962.

Fonagy, Peter, Gyorgy Gergely, and Elliot L. Jurist. *Affect Regulation, Mentalization, and the Development of the Self*. New York, NY: Other Press, 2004.

Fox, Elaine. *Emotion Science: Cognitive and Neuroscientific Approaches to Understanding Human Emotions*. London: Palgrave Macmillan, 2008.

Fox, Michael V. *Proverbs 1–9*. New York, NY: Doubleday, 2000.

Fox, Michael V. "God's Answer and Job's Response." *Biblica* (2013): 1–23.

Frederickson, Barbara L. "The Role of Positive Psychology: The Broaden-and-Build Theory of Positive Emotions." *American Psychologist* 56 (2001): 218–26.

Frederickson, Barbara L., Roberta A. Mancuso, Christine Branigan, and Michele M. Tugade. "The Undoing Effect of Positive Emotions." *Motivation and Emotion* 42 (2000): 237–58.

Fretheim, Terence E. *Exodus*. Louisville, KY: Westminster John Knox Press, 2010.

Fretheim, Terence E. *God and World in the Old Testament: A Relational Theology of Old Testament*. Nashville, TN: Abingdon, 2010.

Fritsche, Immo and Annedore Hoppe. "We Supernaturals: Terror Management and People's Ambivalent Relationship With Nature." In *Handbook of Terror Management Theory*, edited by Clay Routledge and Matthew Vess, 157–78. London: Academic Press, 2019.

Fullilove, Mindy Thompson. "'The Frayed Knot': What Happens to Place Attachment in the Context of Serial Forced Displacement?" In *Place Attachment: Advances in Theory, Methods and Applications*, edited by Lynne C. Manzo and Patrick Devine-Wright, 141–53. London: Routledge, 2013.

Galambush, Julie. *Jerusalem in the Book of Ezekiel: The City as Yahweh's Wife*. Atlanta, GA: Society of Biblical Literature, 1992.

Gallagher, Shaun. *The Oxford Handbook of the Self*. Oxford: Oxford University Press, 2011.

Gallegos-Riofrío, Carlos Andres, Hassan Arab, Amaya Carrasco-Torrontegui, and Rachelle K. Gould. "Chronic Deficiency of Diversity and Pluralism in Research on Nature's Mental Health Effects: A Planetary Health Problem." *Current Research in Environmental Sustainability* 4 (2022): 1–11.

Galor, Katharina and Hanswulf Bloedhorn. *The Archaeology of Jerusalem from the Origins to the Ottoman*. New Haven, CT: Yale University Press, 2013.

Geeraerts, Dirk and Hubert Cuyckens. *The Oxford Handbook of Cognitive Linguistics*. Oxford: Oxford University Press, 2007.

Gibbs, Raymond W. "Embodiment." In *The Cambridge Handbook of Cognitive Linguistics*, edited by Barbara Dancygier, 449–62. Cambridge: Cambridge University Press, 2017.

Gillmayr-Bucher, Susanne. "Metaphors of Space and Time: Imagining Stability in the Fourth Book of the Psalms." In *Networks of Metaphors in the Hebrew Bible*, edited by Danilo Verde and Antje Labahn, 215–32. Leuven: Peeters, 2020.

Giner-Sorolla, Roger. "The Paradox of Moral Disgust and Three Possible Resolutions." In *The Handbook of Disgust Research: Modern Perspectives and Applications*, 139–57. Cham: Springer Nature Switzerland, 2021.

Glazov, G. Yuri. "The Significance of the 'Hand on the Mouth' Gesture in Job XL 4." *Vetus Testamentum* 42 (2002): 30–41.

Goldberg, Adele E. *Constructions at Work: The Nature of Generalization in Language*. Oxford: Oxford University Press, USA, 2006.

Goldberg, Adele E. *Explain Me This: Creativity, Competition, and the Partial Productivity of Constructions*. Princeton, NJ: Princeton University Press, 2019.

Goldhagen, Sarah Williams. *Welcome to Your World*. New York, NY: HarperCollins, 2017.

Goldingay, John. *Psalms*. Grand Rapids, MI: Baker Academic, 2006.

Goldingay, John and David Payne. *Isaiah 40–55 Vol 1*. London: Bloomsbury, 2006.

Goldingay, John and David Payne. *Isaiah 40–55 Vol 2*. London: Bloomsbury, 2006.

Goldingay, John and David Payne. *Isaiah 56–66*. London: Bloomsbury, 2014.

Gordis, Robert. *The Book of Job: Commentary, New Translation, Special Studies*. New York, NY: Jewish Theological Seminary, 1978.

Grant, Deena. "Human Anger in Biblical Narrative." *Revue Biblique* 118 (2011): 339–61.

Grant, Deena E. *Divine Anger in the Hebrew Bible*. Washington, DC: Catholic Biblical Association, 2014.

Green, Stefan. "Zion as Mother in the Restored Relationship Between God and God's People: A Study of Isaiah 66:7–14A," 266–97. Sheffield: Sheffield Phoenix, 2019.

Greenberg, Moshe. *Understanding Exodus: A Holistic Commentary on Exodus 1–11*. Eugene, OR: Cascade Books, 2013.

Grillon, Christian, Mark Pellowski, Kathleen R. Merikangas, and Michael Davis. "Darkness Facilitates the Acoustic Startle Reflex in Humans." *Biological Psychiatry* 42 (1997): 453–60.

Groenewald, Alphonso. *Psalm 69: Its Structure, Redaction and Composition*. Münster: Lit Verlag, 2003.

Groenewald, Alphonso. "Psalm 69: A Composition-Critical Contribution." In *One Text, A Thousand Methods: Studies in Memory of Sjef van Tilborg*, edited by Ulrich Berges and Patrick Chatelion Counet, 77–96. Leiden: Brill, 2005.

Groenewald, Alphonso. "Isaiah 1:2–3, Ethics and Wisdom. Isaiah 1:2–3 and the Song of Moses (Dt 32): Is Isaiah a Prophet like Moses?" *Hervormde Teologiese Studies* 67 (2011): 1–6.

Habel, Norman C. *The Book of Job: A Commentary.* Philadelphia, PA: Westminster, 1985.

Hägerhäll, Caroline, Richard Taylor, Gunnar Cerwén, Greg Watts, Matilda van den Bosch, Daniel Press, and Steven Minta. "Biological Mechanisms and Neurophysiological Responses to Sensory Input from Nature." In *Oxford Textbook of Nature and Public Health*, edited by Matilda van den Bosch and William Bird, 79–88. Oxford: Oxford University Press, 2018.

Haidt, Jonathan. *The Righteous Mind: Why Good People are Divided by Politics and Religion.* New York, NY: Vintage, 2013.

Hallowell, A. Irving. "Ojibwa Ontology, Behavior, and Worldview." In *Readings in Indigenous Religions*, edited by Graham Harvey, 18–49. London: A&C Black, 2002.

Ham, T. C. "The Gentle Voice of God in Job 38." *Journal of Biblical Literature* 132 (2013): 527–41.

Hamawand, Zeki. *Semantics: A Cognitive Account of Linguistic Meaning.* Sheffield: Equinox, 2016.

Harmon-Jones, Eddie and Cindy Harmon-Jones. "Anger." In *Handbook of Emotions*, edited by Lisa Feldman Barrett, Michael Lewis, and Jeannette M. Haviland-Jones, 774–91. New York, NY: Guilford, 2018.

Hart, Christopher. "Discourse." In *Cognitive Linguistics: A Survey of Linguistic Subfields*, edited by Ewa Dąbrowska and Dagmar Divjak, 81–107. Berlin: Walter de Gruyter, 2019.

Hart, Christopher and Dominik Lukeš. *Cognitive Linguistics in Critical Discourse Analysis.* Newcastle upon Tyne: Cambridge Scholars Publishing, 2009.

Harter, Susan. *The Construction of the Self: Developmental and Sociocultural Foundations.* 2nd ed. New York, NY: Guilford, 2015.

Harvey, Graham, ed. *The Handbook of Contemporary Animism* London: Routledge, 2014.

Harvey, Graham. *Animism: Respecting the Living World.* 2nd ed. London: Hurst and Co., 2017.

Hawley, Lance R. *Metaphor Competition in the Book of Job.* Göttingen: Vandenhoeck & Ruprecht, 2018.

Hayes, Katherine Murphey. *The Earth Mourns: Prophetic Metaphor and Oral Aesthetic.* Leiden: Brill, 2002.

Headland, T. N. and H. W. Greene. "Hunter-Gatherers and Other Primates as Prey, Predators, and Competitors of Snakes." *Proceedings of the National Academy of Sciences* 108 (2011): E1470–4.

Healey, John F. "Ancient Agriculture and the Old Testament (with special reference to Isaiah XXVIII 23–29)." In *Prophets, Worship, and Theodicy: Studies in Prophetism, Biblical Theology, and Structural and Rhetorical Analysis, and on the*

*Place of Music in Worship: Papers Read at the Joint British-Dutch Old Testament Conference held at Woudschoten, 1982*, 108–19. Leiden: Brill, 1984.

Henrich, Joseph. *The Weirdest People in the World: How the West Became Psychologically Peculiar and Particularly Prosperous*. London: Penguin UK, 2020.

Henrich, Joseph, Steven J. Heine, and Ara Norenzayan. "The Weirdest People in the World." *Behavioural Brain Sciences* 33 (2010): 1–75.

Hermans, Hubert J. M. "The Dialogical Self: A Process of Positioning in Space and Time." In *The Oxford Handbook of the Self*, edited by Shaun Gallagher, 654–80. Oxford: Oxford University Press, 2011.

Hester, Randolph T. "Do Not Detach!: Instructions From and For Community Design." In *Place Attachment: Advances in Theory, Methods and Application*, edited by Lynne Manzo and Patrick Devine-Wright, 191–206. London: Routledge, 2013.

Hester, Randolph T. "Reattach!: Practicing Endemic Design." In *Place Attcahment: Advances in Theory, Methods and Applications*, edited by Lynne C. Manzo and Patrick Devine-Wright, 208–25. London: Routledge, 2021.

Hoehl, S., K. Hellmer, M. Johansson, and G. Gredebäck. "Itsy Bitsy Spider . . . : Infants React with Increased Arousal to Spiders and Snakes." *Frontiers of Psychology* 8 (2017): 1710.

Hogan, Patrick Colm and Bradley J. Irish. "Introduction: Literary Feelings: Understanding Emotions." In *The Routledge Companion to Literature and Emotion*, edited by Patrick Colm Hogan, Bradley J. Irish, and Lalita Pandit Hogan, 1–11. London: Routledge, 2022.

Holladay, William L. *The Root ŠUBH in the Old Testament with Particular Reference to Its Usage in Covenant Contexts*. Leiden: Brill, 1958.

Holladay, William L. *Jeremiah 1*. Philadelphia: Fortress, 1986.

Hopkins, Denise Dombkowski. *Psalms: Books 2–3*. Collegeville, MN: Liturgical Press, 2016.

Hoppe, Leslie J. *The Holy City: Jerusalem in the Theology of the Old Testament*. Collegeville, MN: Liturgical Press, 2000.

Horowitz, Wayne. *Mesopotamian Cosmic Geography*. Winona Lake, IN: Eisenbrauns, 2011.

Hossfeld, Frank-Lothar, Erich Zenger, Linda M. Maloney, and Klaus Baltzer. *Psalms 2: A Commentary on Psalms 51–100*. 2005.

Houtman, Cornelis. *Exodus*. Translated by Johan Rebel and Sierd Woudstra. Kampen: Kok, 1993.

Houtman, Cornelis. *Der Himmel im Alten Testament: Israels Weltbild und Weltanschauung*. Leiden: Brill, 1993.

Huffmon, Herbert B. "The Covenant Lawsuit in the Prophets." *Journal of Biblical Literature* (1959): 285–95.

Ihm, Elliott D., Raymond F. Paloutzian, Michael van Elk, and Jonathan W. Schooler. "Awe as a Meaning-Making Emotion: On the Evolution of Awe and the Origin of Religions." In *The Evolution of Religion, Religiosity and Theology: A*

*Multilevel and Multidisciplinary Approach*, edited by Jay R. Feierman and Lluis Oviedo, 139–53. London: Routledge, 2020.

Immordino-Yang, Mary Helen. "Embodied Brains, Social Minds: Towards a Cultural Neuroscience of Social Emotion." In *The Oxford Handbook of Cultural Neuroscience*, edited by Joan Y. Chiao, Shu-Chen Li, Rebecca Seligman, and Robert Turner, 129–42. Oxford: Oxford University Press, 2016.

Ishikawa, Toru. *Human Spatial Cognition and Experience: Mind in the World, World in the Mind*. London: Routledge, 2021.

Jacquet, Jennifer. *Is Shame Necessary? New Uses for an Old Tool*. New York, NY: Pantheon, 2015.

James, Thomas. *Aesop's Fables*. London: John Murray, 1887.

James, William. *The Principles of Psychology*. New York, NY: Henry Holt, 1890.

James, William. *Psychology*. Cleveland, OH: World Publishing, 1948.

Janzen, J. Gerald. *Job*. Louisville, KY: Westminster John Knox, 1985.

Jaynes, Julian. *The Origin of Consciousness in the Breakdown of the Bicameral Mind*. Boston: Houghton Mifflin, 1976.

Jensen, Joseph. *The Use of* Tôrâ *by Isaiah: His Debate with the Wisdom Tradition*. Washington, DC: Catholic Biblical Association, 1973.

Jeremias, Jörg. *Theophanie: Die Geschichte einer alttestamentlichen Gattung*. Neukirchener-Vluyn: Neukirchener Verlag, 1965.

Jindo, Job Y. *Biblical Metaphor Reconsidered: A Cognitive Approach to Poetic Metaphor in Biblical Prophecy in Jeremiah 1–24*. Leiden: Brill, 2010.

Joaquin, Anna Dina L. and John H. Schumann. *Exploring the Interactional Instinct*. Oxford: Oxford University Press, 2013.

Joerstad, Mari. *The Hebrew Bible and Environmental Ethics: Humans, Nonhumans, and the Living Landscape*. Cambridge: Cambridge University Press, 2019.

Johnson, Eric. "A Phenomenological Investigation of Fear of the Dark." *Journal of Phenomenological Psychology* 19 (1988): 179–94.

Johnson, Mark. *The Body in the Mind: The Bodily Basis of Meaning, Imagination, and Reason*. Chicago, IL: University of Chicago Press, 1987.

Johnson, Mark. *Embodied Mind, Meaning, and Reason*. Chicago, IL: University of Chicago Press, 2017.

Johnston, Elizabeth and Leah Olson. *The Feeling Brain: The Biology and Psychology of Emotions*. New York, NY: Norton, 2015.

Johnston, Philip S. *Shades of Sheol: Death and Afterlife in the Old Testament*. Downers Grove, IL: InterVarsity Press, 2002.

Joshua, J. Van Ee. "Wolf and Lamb as Hyperbolic Blessing: Reassessing Creational Connections in Isaiah 11:6–8." *Journal of Biblical Literature* 137 (2018): 319–37.

Jouon, Paul and Tamitsu Muraoka. *A Grammar of Biblical Hebrew*. Rome: Gregorian Biblical BookShop, 2006.

Kahneman, Daniel. *Thinking, Fast and Slow*. New York, NY: Farrar, Straus and Giroux, 2011.

Kant, Immanuel. "On the Miscarriage of All Philosophical Trials in Theodicy (1791)." In *Religion and Rational Theology*, edited by Allen Wood and George di Giovanni, 19–37. Cambridge: Cambridge University Press, 2013.

Kaplan, Rachel and Stephen Kaplan. *The Experience of Nature: A Psychological Perspective*. Cambridge: Cambridge University Press, 1989.

Kaplan, Stephen. "The Restorative Benefits of Nature: Toward an Integrative Framework." *Journal of Environmental Psychology* 15 (1995): 169–82.

Kaplan, Stephen and Marc G. Berman. "Directed Attention as a Common Resource for Executive Functioning and Self-Regulation." *Perspectives on Psychological Science* 5 (2010): 43–57.

Karen, Robert. *Becoming Attached: First Relationships and How They Shape Our Capacity to Love*. Oxford: Oxford University Press, 1998.

Kawai, Nobuyuki. *The Fear of Snakes: Evolutionary and Psychobiological Perspectives on Our Innate Fear*. Singapore: Springer, 2019.

Kazen, Thomas. *Emotions in Biblical Law: A Cognitive Science Approach*. Sheffield: Sheffield Phoenix Press, 2011.

Kazen, Thomas. "Disgust in Body, Mind, and Language: The Case of Impurity in the Hebrew Bible." In *Mixed Feelings and Vexed Passions: Exploring Emotions in Biblical Literature*, edited by F. Scott Spencer, 177–95. Atlanta, GA: Society of Biblical Literature, 2017.

Keel, Othmar. *Die Geschichte Jerusalems und die Entstehung des Monotheismus*. Vandenhoeck & Ruprecht, 2007.

Kellert, Stephen R. *The Biophilia Hypothesis*. Washington, DC: Island Press, 1995.

Kellert, Stephen R. *Kinship to Mastery: Biophilia in Human Evolution and Development*. Washington, DC: Island Press, 1997.

Kellert, Stephen R. *Birthright: People and Nature in the Modern World*. New Haven: Yale University Press, 2012.

Kellert, Stephen R. *Nature by Design: The Practice of Biophilic Design*. New Haven, CT: Yale University Press, 2018.

Keltner, Dacher and Jonathn Haidt. "Approaching Awe, a Moral, Spiritual, and Aesthetic Emotion." *Cognition and Emotion* (2003): 297–314.

Kessler, Rainer. "'Söhne habe ich grossgezogen und emporgebracht . . . ': Gott als Mutter in Jes 1,2." In *"Ihr Völker, klatscht in die Hände!" Festschrift für Erhard S. Gerstenberger zum 65. Geburtstag*, edited by Raiiner Kessler et al., 134–47. Munich: Lit, 1997.

Kim, Brittany. *"Lengthen Your Tent-Cords": The Metaphorical World of Israel's Household in the Book of Isaiah*. University Park, PA: Eisenbrauns, 2018.

King, Philip D. *Surrounded by Bitterness: Image Schemas and Metaphors for Concetualizing Distress in Classical Hebrew*. Eugene, OR: Pickwick, 2012.

Klopfenstein, Martin A. *Scham und Schande nach dem Alten Testament: Eine begriffsgeschichtliche Untersuchung zu den hebräischen Wurzeln* bôš, klm, *und* hpr. Zürich: Theologischer Verlag, 1972.

Knowles, Melody D. *Centrality Practiced: Jerusalem in the Religious Practice of Yehud and teh Diaspora in the Persian Period*. Atlanta, GA: Society of Biblical Literature, 2006.

Kohn, Eduardo. *How Forests Think: Toward an Anthropology Beyond the Human*. Berkeley, CA: University of California Press, 2013.

Kolnai, Aurel. *On Disgust*. Chicago, IL: Open Court, 2004.

Koole, Jan Leunis. *Isaiah: Isaiah 40–48*. Kampen: Pharos, 1997.

Kopcsó, Krisztina and András Láng. "Uncontrolled Thoughts in the Dark? Effects of Lighting Conditions and Fear of the Dark on Thinking Processes." *Imagination, Cognition, Personality: Consciousness in Theory, Research and Clinical Practice* 39 (2019): 97–108.

Korsmeyer, Carolyn. *Savoring Disgust: The Foul and the Fair in Aesthetics*. Oxford: Oxford University Press, 2011.

Kövecses, Zoltán. *Metaphors of Anger, Pride, and Love: A Lexical Approach to the Structure of Concepts*. Philadelphia, PA: John Benjamins, 1986.

Kövecses, Zoltán. *Emotion Concepts*. New York, NY: Springer-Verlag, 1990.

Kövecses, Zoltán. *Metaphor: A Practical Introduction*. 2nd ed. Oxford: Oxford University Press, 2010.

Kövecses, Zoltán. *Where Metaphors Come From: Reconsidering Context in Metaphor*. Oxford: Oxford University Press, 2015.

Kozlova, Ekaterina E. *Maternal Grief in the Hebrew Bible*. Oxford: Oxford University Press, 2017.

Kraus, Hans-Joachim. *Psalmen I*. Neukirchen: Neukirchener Verlag, 1972.

Kurschner, Alan E. "James Barr on the 'Illegitimate Totality Transfer' Word-Concept Fallacy." In *James Barr Assessed: Evaluating His Legacy over the Last Sixty Years*, edited by Stanley E. Porter, 70–114. Leiden: Brill, 2021.

Kynes, Will. *An Obituary for "Wisdom Literature": The Birth, Death, and Intertextual Reintegration of a Biblical Corpus*. Oxford: Oxford University Press, 2019.

Lakoff, George and Mark Johnson. *Metaphors We Live By*. Chicago, IL: University of Chicago Press, 2008.

Lambert, David A. "Refreshing Philology: James Barr, Supersessionism, and the State of Biblical Words." *Biblical Interpretation* 24 (2016): 332–56.

Lambert, David A. "Mourning over Sin/Affliction and the Problem of 'Emotion' as a Category in the Hebrew Bible." In *Mixed Feelings and Vexed Passions*, edited by F. Scott Spencer, 139–60. Atlanta, GA: Society of Biblical Literature Press, 2017.

Lancaster, Mason D. "Metaphor Research and the Hebrew Bible." *Currents in Biblical Research* 19 (2021): 235–85.

Langacker, Ronald W. *Cognitive Grammar: A Basic Introduction*. Oxford: Oxford University Press, 2008.

Lasater, Phillip Michael. "'The Emotions' in Biblical Anthropology? A Genealogy and Case Study with ירא." *Harvard Theological Review* 110 (2017): 520–40.

Lasater, Phillip Michael. *Facets of Fear: The Fear of God in Exilic and Post-Exilic Contexts*. Tübingen: Mohr Siebeck, 2019.

Leary, David E. *The Routledge Guidebook to James's* Principles of Psychology. London: Routledge, 2018.

LeDoux, Joseph. *The Emotional Brain: The Mysterious Underpinnings of Emotional Life*. New York, NY: Simon and Schuster, 1996.

LeDoux, Joseph. *Synaptic Self: How Our Brains Become Who We Are*. New York, NY: Penguin, 2003.

LeDoux, Joseph. *Anxious: Using the Brain to Understand and Treat Fear and Anxiety*. New York, NY: Penguin, 2016.

LeDoux, Joseph. *The Deep History of Ourselves: The Four-Billion-Year Story of How We Got Conscious Brains*. New York, NY: Penguin, 2019.

Lee, Ingrid Fetell. *Joyful: The Surprising Power of Ordinary Things to Create Extraordinary Happiness*. New York, NY: Little, Brown Spark, 2018.

Lee, Namhee, Lisa Mikesell, Anna Dina L. Joaquin, Andrea W. Mates, and John H. Schumann. *The Interactional Instinct: The Evolution and Acquisition of Language*. Oxford: Oxford University Press, 2009.

Leopold, Aldo. *A Sand County Almanac with Essays on Conservation from Round River*. New York, NY: Ballantine Books, 1984.

Lessing, R. Reed. "Yahweh Versus Marduk: Creation Theology in Isaiah 40–55." *Concordia Journal* 36 (2010): 234–44.

Levenson, Jon D. *Sinai and Zion: An Entry into the Jewish Bible*. New York, NY: Harper One, 1985.

Levin, Ted. *America's Snake: The Rise and Fall of the Timber Rattlesnake*. Chicago, IL: University of Chicago Press, 2016.

Levos, Joshua and Tammy Lowery Zacchilli. "Nyctophobia: From Imagined to Realistic Fears of the Dark." *Psy Chi Journal of Psychological Research* 20 (2015): 102–10.

Lewicka, Maria. "Place Attachment: How Far have We Come in the Last 40 Years?" *Journal of Environmental Psychology* 31 (2011): 207–30.

Lewicka, Maria. "In Search of Roots: Memory as Enabler of Place Attachment." In *Place Attachment: Advances in Theory, Methods and Applications*, edited by Lynne C. Manzo and Patrick Devine-Wright, 49–60. London: Routledge, 2013.

Li, Xi. "Posttraumatic Growth in Psalms of Laments, Jeremiah, and Lamentations," diss., The Catholic University of America, 2022.

Lieberman, Matthew D. *Social: Why Our Brains Are Wired to Connect*. New York, NY: Crown, 2013.

Lindström, Fredrik. *Suffering and Sin: Interpretations of Illness in the Individual Complaint Psalms*. Stockholm: Almqvist and Wiksell, 1994.

Lipscomb, Anthony I. "'They Shall be Clothed in Shame': Is Shame an Emotion in the Hebrew Bible?" *Journal for the Study of Ancient Judaism* 12 (2021): 313–59.

Littlemore, Jeannette and John R. Taylor. *The Bloomsbury Companion to Cognitive Linguistics*. London: Bloomsbury, 2014.

Løland, Hanne. *Silent or Salient Gender?: The Interpretation of Gendered God-Language in the Hebrew Bible, Exemplified in Isaiah 42, 46, and 49*. Tübingen: Mohr Seibeck, 2008.

Lombardo, Thomas J. *The Reciprocity of Perceiver and Environment: The Evolution of James J. Gibson's Ecological Psychology*. London: Routledge, 1987.

Louv, Richard. *Last Child in the Woods: Saving Our Children from Nature-Deficit Disorder*. Chapel Hill, NC: Algonquin Books, 2008.

Low, Katherine. "Implications Surrounding Girding the Loins in Light of Gender, Body, and Power." *Journal for the Study of the Old Testament* 36 (2011): 3–30.

Low, Maggie. *Mother Zion in Deutero-Isaiah: A Metaphor for Zion Theology*. New York, NY: Peter Lang, 2013.

Luck, C. C., R. R. Patterson, and O. V. Lipp. "'Prepared' Fear or Socio-Cultural learning? Fear Conditioned to Guns, Snakes, and Spiders is Eliminated by Instructed Extinction in a Within-Participant Differential Fear Conditioning Paradigm." *Psychophysiology* 57 (2020): e13516.

Lund, Øystein. *Way Metaphors and Way Topics in Isaiah 40–55*. Tübingen: Mohr Siebeck, 2007.

Lundgren, Erick, Daniel Ramp, Juliet C. Stromberg, Jianguo Wu, Nathan C. Nieto, Martin Sluk, Karla T. Moeller, and Arian D. Wallach. "Equids Engineer Desert Water Availability." *Science* 372 (2021): 491–95.

Maeir, Aren M. "A New Interpretation of the Term *'opalim* (עפלים) in the light of recent Archeological Finds from Philistia." *Journal for the Study of the Old Testament* 32 (2007): 23–40.

Maier, Christl M. *Daughter Zion, Mother Zion: Gender, Space, and the Sacred in Ancient Israel*. Minneapolis: Fortress, 2008.

Marlow, Hilary. *Biblical Prophets and Contemporary Environmental Ethics: Re-Reading Amos, Hosea, and First Isaiah*. Oxford: Oxford University Press, 2009.

Matthews, Victor H. *Exodus: An Exegetical Commentary*. Grand Rapids, MI: Baker Academic, 2011.

Mays, James Luther. *Amos: A Commentary*. Louisville, KY: Westminster John Knox Press, 1969.

McCarter, P. Kyle. *I Samuel*. Garden City, NJ: Doubleday, 1980.

McGinn, Colin. *The Meaning of Disgust*. Oxford: Oxford University Press, 2011.

McKane, William. *Jeremiah*. Edinburgh: T & T Clark, 1986.

Meadows, Chris. *A Psychological Perspective on Joy and Emotional Fulfillment*. New York, NY: Routledge, 2013.

Menninghaus, Winfried. *Disgust: Theory and History of a Strong Sensation*. Translated by Howard Eiland and Joal Golb. Albany, NY: SUNY Press, 2012.

Meyers, Carol. *Exodus*. Cambridge: Cambridge University Press, 2005.

Mihaylov, Nikolay and Douglas D. Perkins. "Community Place Attachment and Its Role in Social Capital Development." In *Place Attachment: Advances in Theory, Methods and Application*, edited by Lynne Manzo and Patrick Devine-Wright, 61–74. London: Routledge, 2013.

Mihaylov, Nikolay, Douglas D. Perkins, and Richard C. Stedman. "Community Responses to Environmental Threat: Place Cognition, Attachment, and Social Action." In *Place Attachment: Advances in Theory, Methods and Applications*, edited by Lynne Manzo and Patrick Devine-Wright, 161–76. London: Routledge, 2021.

Mikulincer, Mario and Phillip R. Shaver. *Attachment in Adulthood: Structure, Dynamics, and Change.* New York, NY: Guilford, 2010.

Mikulincer, Mario and Phillip R. Shaver. "Adult Attachment and Emotion Regulation." In *Handbook of Attachment,* edited by Jude Cassidy and Phillip R. Shaver, 507–33. New York, NY: Guilford, 2016.

Miller-Naudé, Cynthia and C. H. J. van der Merwe. "הנה and Mirativity in Biblical Hebrew." *Hebrew Studies* 52 (2011): 53–81.

Miller, Robert. *The Dragon, the Mountain, and the Nations: An Old Testament Myth, Its Origins, and Its Afterlives.* University Park, PA: Explorations in Ancient Near E, 2018.

Miller, Susan Beth. *Disgust: The Gatekeeper Emotion.* Hillsdale, NJ: Analytic Press, 2004.

Mirguet, Françoise. "What is an 'Emotion' in the Hebrew Bible?: An Experience that Exceeds Most Contemporary Concepts." *Biblical Interpretation* (2016): 442–65.

Mirguet, Françoise. "The Study of Emotions in Early Jewish Texts: Review and Perspectives." *Journal for the Study of Judaism* 50 (2019): 557–603.

Moreno, Miguel Ángel Garzón. *La Alegría en Isaías: La legría como unidad y estructura del libro a partir de su epílogo (Is 65–66).* Estella: Editorial Verbo Divino, 2011.

Moskowitz, Judith Tedlie and Laura R. Saslow. "Health and Psychology: The Importance of Positive Affect." In *Handbook of Positive Emotions,* edited by Michele M. Tugade, Michelle N. Shiota, and Leslie D. Kirby, 413–31. New York, NY: Guilford, 2014.

Müller, Cornelia. *Metaphors Dead and Alive, Sleeping and Waking: A Dynamic View.* Chicago, IL: University of Chicago Press, 2009.

Murphy, Roland E. *The Book of Job: A Short Reading.* New York, NY: Paulist, 1999.

Murray, Robert. *The Cosmic Covenant: Biblical Themes of Justice, Peace and the Integrity of Creation.* London: Sheed and Ward, 1992.

Nabhan, Gary Paul and Stephen Trimble. *The Geography of Childhood: Why Children Need Wild Places.* Boston, MA: Beacon, 1994.

Nam, Duck-Woo. *Talking About God: Job 42:7–9 and the Nature of God in the Book of Job.* New York, NY: Peter Lang, 2003.

Naude, Jacobus A. and Cynthia L. Miller-Naude. "Lexicography and the translation of 'cedars of Lebanon' in the Septuagint." *HTS Teologiese Studies / Theological Studies* 74 (2018):

Naumkin, Vitaly and Victor Porkomovsky. "Insects in Socotran Language and Culture." *Proceedings of the Seminar for Arabian Studies* 29 (1999): 111–14.

Nestor, James. *Breath: The New Science of a Lost Art.* New York, NY: Riverhead, 2020.

Neufeld, Edward. "Insects as Warfare Agents in the Ancient Near East (Ex. 23:28; Deut. 7:20; Josh. 24:12; Isa. 7:18–20)." *Orientalia* 49 (1980): 30–57.

Newsom, Carol A. *The Book of Job: A Contest of Moral Imaginations*. Oxford: Oxford University Press, 2003.

Newsom, Carol A. *The Spirit within Me: Self and Agency in Ancient Israel and Second Temple Judaism*. New Haven, CT: Yale University Press, 2021.

Nichols, Wallace J. *Blue Mind: The Surprising Science that Shows How Being Near, In, On, or Under Water Can Make You Happier, More Connected, and Better at What You Do*. New York, NY: Back Bay Books, 2014.

Nielsen, Kirsten. "Das Bild des Gerichts (*rib*-pattern) in Jes i–xii." *Vetus Testamentum* 29 (1979): 309–24.

Nielsen, Kirsten. *Yahweh as Prosecutor and Judge: An Investigation of the Prophetic Lawsuit (rîb-pattern)*. Sheffield, UK: JSOT Press, 1981.

Nielsen, Kirsten. *There is Hope for a Tree: The Tree as Metaphor in Isaiah*. Sheffield: JSPT Press, 1989.

O'Keeffe, Anne and Michael McCarthy. *The Routledge Handbook of Corpus Linguistics*. 2nd ed. London: Routledge, 2022.

O'Neil, Cathy. *The Shame Machine: Who Profits in the New Age of Humiliation*. New York, NY: Crown, 2022.

Oakley, Todd and Esther Pascual. "Conceptual Blending Theory." In *The Cambridge Handbook of Cognitive Linguistics*, edited by Barbara Dancygier, 423–48. Cambridge: Cambridge University Press, 2017.

Öhman, Arne. "Fear and Anxiety: Overlaps and Dissociations." In *Handbook of Emotions*, edited by Michael Lewis, Jeannette M. Haviland-Jones, and Lisa Feldman Barrett, 709–29. New York, NY: Guilford Press, 2008.

Öhman, Arne and Susan Mineka. "Fears, Phobias, and Preparedness: Toward an Evolved Module of Fear and Fear Learning." *Psychological Review* 108 (2001): 483–522.

Öhman, Arne and Susan Mineka. "The Malicious Serpent: Snakes as a Prototypical Stimulus for an Evolved Module of Fear." *Current Directions in Psychological Science* 12 (2003): 5–9.

Olatunji, Bunmi O. and Dean McKay, eds. *Disgust and Its Disorders: Theory, Assessment, and Treatment Implications*. Washington, DC: American Psychological Association, 2009.

Olyan, Saul M. *Biblical Mourning: Ritual and Social Dimensions*. Oxford; New York: Oxford University Press, 2004.

Origen. *On First Principles*. Translated by G. W. Butterworth. Boston, MA: Peter Smith, 1973.

Ortlund, Eric. "God's Joy in Creation in the Book of Job." *Presbyterion* 47 (2021): 5–15.

Osborne, William. *Trees and Kings: A Comparative Analysis of Tree Imagery in Israels' Prophetic Tradition and the Ancinet Near East*. University Park, PA: Eisenbrauns, 2018.

Panksepp, Jaak and Lucy Biven. *The Archaeology of Mind: Neuroevolutionary Origins of Human Emotions*. New York, NY: Norton, 2012.

Pantoja, Jennifer Metten. *The Metaphor of the Divine as Planter of the People: Stinking Grapes or Pleasant Planting?* Leiden: Brill, 2017.

Paquot, Magali and Stefan Th. Gried. *A Practical Handbook of Corpus Linguistics.* Cham: Springer Nature Switzerland, 2020.

Park, Crystal L. "Religion and Meaning." In *Handbook of Psychology of Religion and Spirituality,* edited by Raymond F. Paloutzian and Crystal L. Park, 357–79. New York, NY: Guilford, 2013.

Perdue, Leo G. *Wisdom in Revolt: Metaphorical Theology in the Book of Job.* Sheffield: Sheffield Academic Press, 1991.

Polaski, Donald C. *Authorizing an End: The Isaiah Apocalypse and Intertextuality.* Leiden; Boston: Brill, 2001.

Poser, Ruth. "Scham in der Hebräischen Bible." In *Verstrickt in Schuld, gefangen von Scham?,* 137–54. Neukirchen-Vluyn: Neukirchener Theologie, 2015.

Poser, Ruth. "'Ja, auf die Armen hört die Lebendige, ihre Gefangenen verachtet sie nicht': (Ps 69,34): Beschämung und Anerkennung in ausgewählten Psalmen." In *Die verborgene Macht der Scham: Ehre, Scham und Schuld im alten Israel, in seinem Umfeld und in der gegenwärtigen Lebensvelt,* 112–38. Göttingen: Vandenhoek & Ruprecht, 2018.

Potegal, Michael and Gerhard Stemmler. "Cross-Disciplinary Views of Anger: Consensus and Controversy." In *International Handbook of Anger: Constituent and Concomitant Biological, Psychological, and Social Processes,* edited by Michael Potegal, Gerhard Stemmler, and Charles Spielberger, 3–8. New York: Springer Science & Business Media, 2010.

Poulsen, Frederik. *Representing Zion: Judgment and Salvation in the Old Testament.* London: Taylor and Francis, 2014.

Praet, Istvan. *Animism and the Question of Life.* London: Routledge, 2014.

Prakasam, Antony Dhas. "Pride of Babylon and Zion in Isaiah in Light of the Theory of Self-Conscious Emotions," diss., The Catholic University of America, 2018.

Propp, William Henry. *Exodus 1–18: A New Translation with Introduction and Commentary.* New Haven, CT: Yale University Press, 1999.

Reich, Ronny and Eli Shukron. "The Urban Development of Jerusalem in the Late Eighth Century B.C.E." In *Jerusalem in Bible and Archaeology: The First Temple Period,* edited by Andrew G. Vaughn and Ann E. Killebrew, 209–18. Atlanta, GA: Society of Biblical Literature, 2003.

Rimé, Bernard. "Mental Rumination, Social Sharing, and the Recovery from Emotional Exposure." In *Emotion, Disclosure, and Health,* edited by James Pennebaker. Washington, DC: American Psychological Association, 1995.

Rimé, Bernard. "Interpersonal Emotion Regulation." In *Handbook of Emotion Regulation, First Edition,* edited by James J. Gross, 466–85. New York, NY: Guilford, 2007.

Rimé, Bernard. "Emotion Elicits the Social Sharing of Emotion: Theory and Empirical Review." *Emotion Review* 1 (2009): 60–85.

Rimé, Bernard. *Le partage social des émotions*. Paris: Presses Universitaires de France - PUF, 2009.

Rimé, Bernard and Véronique Christophe. "How Individual Emotional Episodes Feed Collective Memory." In *Collective Memory of Political Events*, edited by James Pennebaker, Dario Paez, and Bernard Rimé, 131–46. Mahwah, NJ: Lawrence Earlbaum, 1997.

Rimé, Bernard, Susanna Corsini, and Gwénola Herbette. "Emotion, Verbal Expression, and the Social Sharing of Emotion." In *The Verbal Communication of Emotions: Interdisciplinary Perspectives*, edited by Susan R. Fussel, 185–208. Mahwah, NJ: Lawrence Erlbaum, 2002.

Rimé, Bernard, Gwénola Herbette, and Susanna Corsini. "The Social Sharing of Emotion: Illusory and Real Benefits of Talking about Emotional Experiences." In *Emotional Expression and Health: Advances in Theory, Assessment, and Clinical Applications*, edited by Ivan Nyklíček, Lydia Temoshok, and Ad Vingerhoets, 29–42. New York, NY: Brunner-Routledge, 2004.

Rimé, Bernard, Dario Paez, Patrick Kanyangara, and Vincent Yzerbyt. "The Social Sharing of Emotions in Interpersonal and in Collective Situations: Common Psychosocial Consequences." In *Emotion Regulation and Well-Being*, edited by Ivan Nyklíček, Ad Vingerhoets, and Marcel Zeelenberg, 147–63. New York, NY: Springer, 2011.

Roberts, J. J. M. "The Davidic Origin of the Zion Tradition." In *The Bible and the Ancient Near East: Collected Essays*, 313–30. Winona Lake, IN: Eisenbrauns, 2002.

Roberts, J. J. M. "Zion in the Theology of the Davidic-Solomonic Empire." In *The Bible and the Ancient Near East: Collected Essays*, 331–47. Winona Lake, IN: Eisenbrauns, 2002.

Roberts, J. J. M. *First Isaiah*. Minneapolis, MN: Fortress Press, 2015.

Robertson, S. Ian. *Human Thinking: The Basics*. London: Routledge, 2021.

Rochat, Philippe. *Others in Mind: Social Origins of Self-Consciousness*. Cambridge: Cambridge University Press, 2009.

Rohrer, Tim. "Embodiment and Experientialism." In *The Oxford Handbook of Cognitive Linguistics*, edited by Dirk Geeraerts and Hubert Cuyckens, 25–47. Oxford: Oxford University Press, 2007.

Ronson, Jon. *So You've Been Publicly Shamed*. New York, NY: Riverhead, 2015.

Routledge, Clay and Matthew Vess. *Handbook of Terror Management Theory*. London: Academic Press, 2019.

Rozin, Paul, Jonathan Haidt, and Clark R. McCauley. "Disgust." In *Handbook of Emotions*, edited by Michael Lewis, Jeannette M. Haviland-Jones, and Lisa Feldman Barrett, 757–76. New York, NY: Guilford, 2008.

Rugoff, Barbara. *The Cultural Nature of Human Development*. Oxford: Oxford University Press, 2003.

Russaw, Kimberly D. *Daughters in the Hebrew Bible*. Lexington Books / Fortress: Fortress Academic, 2020.

Rüterswörden, Udo. "Ochs und Esel in Des 1,2–3." In *Die unwiderstehliche Wahrheit: Studien zur alttestamentlichen Prophetie, Festschrift für Arndt Meinhold*, edited by Rüdiger Lux, 382–88. Leipzig: Evangelische Verlagsanstalt, 2006.

Salters, R. B. *Lamentations*. London: T&T Clark, 2010.

Sang, Äsa Ode and Caroline M. Hagerhall. "Scenic Beauty: Visual Landscape Assessment and Human Landscape Perception." In *Environmental Psychology: An Introduction*, 45–54. Hoboken, NJ: Wiley, 2019.

Saracino, Francesco. "Ras Ign Hani78/20 and Some Old Testament Connections." *Vetus Testamentum* 32 (1982): 361–64.

Scannell, Leila and Robert Gifford. "Defining Place Attachment: A Tripartite Organizing Framework." *Journal of Environmental Psychology* 30 (2010): 1–10.

Scannell, Leila and Robert Gifford. "Comparing the Theories of Interpersonal and Place Attachment." In *Place Attachment: Advances in Theory, Methods and Application*, edited by Lynne Manzo and Patrick Devine-Wright, 23–36. London: Routledge, 2013.

Scannell, Leila, Elizabeth Williams, Robert Gifford, and Carmen Sarich. "Parallels between Interpersonal and Place Attachment: An Update." In *Place Attcahment: Advances in Theory, Methods and Applications*, edited by Lynne Manzo and Patrick Devine-Wright, 45–60. London: Routledge, 2021.

Scheff, Thomas J. *Microsociology: Discourse, Emotion, and Social Structure*. Chicago: University of Chicago Press, 1990.

Schimel, Jeff, Joseph Hayes, and Michael Sharp. "A Consideration of Three Critical Hypotheses." In *Handbook of Terror Management Theory*, edited by Clay Routledge and Matthew Vess, 1–30. London: Academic Press, 2019.

Schlimm, Matthew R. *From Fratricide to Forgiveness: The Language and Ethics of Anger in Genesis*. Winona Lake, IN: Eidenbrauns, 2011.

Schmid, Hans-Jörd. "Entenchment, Salience, and Basic Levels." In *The Oxford Handbook of Cognitive Linguistics*, edited by Dirk Geeraerts and Hubert Cuyckens, 117–38. Oxford: Oxford University Press, 2007.

Schmidt, Werner. *Exodus*. Göttingen: Vandenhoeck & Ruprecht, 2019.

Schneider, Kirk J. *Awakening to Awe: Personal Stories of Profound Transformation*. Lanham, MD: Jason Aronson, 2009.

Schweers, Katherine. "Uncovering Hidden Anger in the Psalms Using Psychological Models of Anger." *Biblical Theology Bulletin* (forthcoming):

Seow, C. L. *Job 1–21: Interpretation and Commentary*. Grand Rapids, MI: Eerdmans, 2013.

Seufert, Michael J. "A Walk They Remembered: Covenant Relationship as Journey in the Deuteronomistic History." *Biblical Interpretation* 25 (2017): 149–71.

Shiota, Michelle N. "The Evolutionary Perspective in Positive Emotion Research." In *Handbook of Positive Emotions*, edited by Michele M. Tugade, Michelle N. Shiota, and Leslie D. Kirby, 44–59. New York, NY: Guilford, 2014.

Shiota, Michelle N., Todd M. Thrash, Alexander F. Danvers, and John T. Dombrowski. "Transcending the Self: Awe, Elevation, and Inspiration." In

*Handbook of Positive Emotions*, edited by Michele M. Tugade, Michelle N. Shiota, and Leslie D. Kirby, 362–77. New York, NY: Guilford, 2014.

Shipp, R. Mark. *Of Dead Kings and Dirges: Myth and Meaning in Isaiah 14:4b-21.* Atlanta, GA: Society of Biblical Literature, 2002.

Shiraev, Eric B. and David A. Levy. *Cross-Cultural Psychology: Critical Thinking and Contemporary Applications.* 5th ed. London: Routledge, 2013.

Shugart, H. H. *Foundations of the Earth: Global Ecological Change and the Book of Job.* New York, NY: Columbia University Press, 2014.

Simkins, Ronald. *Yahweh's Activity in History and Nature in the Book of Joel.* Lewiston, NY: Edwin Mellen, 1991.

Simkins, Ronald. *Creator and Creation: Nature in the Worldview of Ancient Israel.* Peabody, MA: Hendrickson, 1994.

Smith, Gary V. *Isaiah 1–39.* Nashville, TN: B&H Publishing Group, 2007.

Smith, Gary V. *Isaiah 40–66.* Nashville, TN: B&H Publishing Group, 2009.

Smith, Mark S. "Baal in the Land of Death." *Ugaritische Forshung* 17 (1986): 311–14.

Smith, Mark S. *The Origins of Biblical Monotheism: Israel's Polytheistic Background and the Ugaritic Texts.* Oxford: Oxford University Press, 2001.

Smith, Mark S. *Poetic Heroes: Literary Commemorations of Warriors and Warrior Culture in the Early Biblical World.* Grand Rapids, MI: Eisenbrauns, 2014.

Smith, Tiffany Watt. *The Book of Human Emotions.* New York, NY: Little, Brown and Co., 2016.

Soares, S. C., D. Kessel, M. Hernández-Lorca, M. J. García-Rubio, P. Rodrigues, N. Gomes, and L. Carretié. "Exogenous Attention to Fear: Differential Behavioral and Neural Responses to Snakes and Spiders." *Neuropsychologia* 99 (2017): 139–47.

Solomon, Sheldon, Jeff Greenberg, and Tom Pyszczynski. *The Worm at the Core: On the Role of Death in Life.* London: Penguin, 2015.

Spencer, F. Scott. *Mixed Feelings and Vexed Passions.* Atlanta, GA: Society of Biblical Literature, 2017.

Staubli, Thomas. "Feces: The Primary Disgust Elicitor in the Hebrew Bible and in the Ancient Near East." In *Sounding Sensory Profiles in the Ancient Near East,* edited by Annette Schellenberg and Thomas Krüger, 119–43. Atlanta, GA: Society of Biblical Literature, 2019.

Steg, Linda and Judith J. M. de Groot. *Environmental Psychology: An Introduction.* 2nd ed. Hoboken, NJ: Wiley, 2019.

Steg, Linda and Judith I. M. de Groot, eds. *Place Attachment.* Hoboken, NJ: Wiley, 2019.

Steger, Michael F. and Crystal L. Park. "The Creation of Meaning Following Trauma: Meaning Making and Trajectories of Distress and Recovery." In *Trauma Therapy in Context: The Science and Craft of Evidence-Based Practice,* edited by Robert A. McMackin, Elana Newman, Jason M. Folger, and Terence M. Keane, 171–91. Washington, DC: American Psychological Association, 2012.

Steiner, Magreet L. "The Notion of Jerusalem as a Holy City." In *Reflection and Refraction: Studies in Biblical Historiography in Honor of A. Graeme Auld*, edited by Robert Rezetko, Timothy Henry Lim, and W. Brian Aucker, 447–58. Leiden: Brill, 2007.

Stiebert, Johanna. *The Construction of Shame in the Hebrew Bible: The Prophetic Contribution*. New York, NY: Sheffield Academic Press, 2002.

Stiebert, Johanna. "Shame and the Body in Psalms and Lamentations of the Hebrew Bible and in Thanksgiving Hymns from Qumran." *Old Testament Essays* 20 (2007): 798–829.

Stiebert, Johanna. *Fathers and Daughters in the Hebrew Bible*. Oxford: Oxford University Press, 2013.

Strawn, Brent A. *What is Stronger Than a Lion?: Leonine Image and Metaphor in the Hebrew Bible and Ancient Near East*. Göttingen: Vandenhoeck & Ruprecht, 2005.

Strawn, Brent A. "On Vomiting: Leviticus, Jonah, Ea(a)rth." *The Catholic Biblical Quarterly* 74 (2012): 445–64.

Strawn, Brent A. "Trauma, Psalmic Disclosure, and Authentic Happiness." In *Bible through the Lens of Trauma*, edited by Elizabeth Boase and Christopher G. Frechette, 143–60. Atlanta, GA: Society of Biblical Literature, 2016.

Stromberg, Jacob. *Isaiah After Exile: The Author of Third Isaiah as Reader and Redactor of the Book*. Oxford: Oxford University Press, 2011.

Stulac, Daniel J. *History and Hope: The Agrarian Wisdom of Isaiah 28–35*. University Park, PA: Eisenbrauns, 2018.

Sullivan, Karen. "Conceptual Metaphor." In *The Cambridge Handbook of Cognitive Linguistics*, edited by Barbara Dancygier, 385–406. Cambridge: Cambridge University Press, 2017.

Sweeney, Marvin A. *The Twelve Prophets: Hosea, Joel, Amos, Obadiah, Jonah*. Collegeville, MN: Liturgical Press, 2000.

Sweeney, Marvin Alan. *Isaiah 1–39*. Grand Rapids, MI: Eerdmans, 1996.

Syropoulos, Syriopoulos, Uri Lifshin, Jeff Greenberg, Dylan E. Horner, and Bernhard Leidner. "Bigotry and the Human-Animal Divide: (Dis)belief in Human Evolution and Bigoted Attitudes across Different Cultures." *Journal of Personality and Social Psychology* (2022): 1–29.

Tager-Flusberg, Helen and Michael Lombardo. *Understanding Other Minds: Perspectives from Developmental Social Neuroscience*. 3rd ed. Oxford: Oxford University Press, 2013.

Taylor, John R. *Linguistic Categorization*. 3rd ed. New York, NY: Oxford University Press, 2003.

Thompson, Ross A., Jeffry A. Simpson, and Lisa J. Berlin, eds. *Attachment: The Fundamental Questions* New York, NY: Guilford, 2021.

Tilford, Nicole L. *Sensing World, Sensing Wisdom: The Cognitive Foundation of Biblical Metaphors*. Atlanta, GA: Society of Biblical Literature Press, 2017.

Tomasello, Michael. *Constructing a Language: A Usage-Based Theory of Language Acquisition*. Cambridge, MA: Harvard University Press, 2003.

Tomasello, Michael. *Origins of Human Communication*. Cambridge, MA: MIT Press, 2010.

Tomasello, Michael. *A Natural History of Human Thinking*. Cambridge, MA: Harvard University Press, 2014.

Tomasello, Michael. *A Natural History of Human Morality*. Cambridge, MA: Harvard University Press, 2016.

Tomasello, Michael. *Becoming Human: A Theory of Ontogeny*. Cambridge, MA: Harvard University Press, 2019.

Tomasello, Michael and Hannes Rakoczy. "What Makes Human Cognition Unique? From Individual to Shared to Collective Intentionality." *Intellectica* 46–47 (2007): 25–48.

Tov, Emanuel. *Textual Criticism of the Hebrew Bible*. 3rd ed. Minneapolis, MN: Fortress, 2012.

Townsend, Mardie, Claire Henderson-Wilson, Haywantee Ramkissoon, and Rona Weerasuriya. "Therapuetic Landscapes, Restorative Environments, Place Attachment, and Well-Being." In *Oxford Textbook of Nature and Public Health*, edited by Matilda van den Bosch and William Bird, 57–62. Oxford: Oxford University Press, 2018.

Tracy, Jessica L. and Richard W. Robbins. "The Nature of Pride." In *The Self-Conscious Emotions*, edited by Jessica L. Tracy, Richard W. Robins, and June Price Tangney, 263–81. New York, NY: Guilford, 2007.

Tracy, Jessica L. and Richard W. Robins. "The Self in Self-Conscious Emotions: A Cognitive Appraisal Approach." In *The Self-Conscious Emotions*, edited by Jessica L. Tracy, Richard W. Robins, and June Price Tangney, 3–20. New York, NY: Guilford, 2007.

Tugade, Michele M., Hillary C. Devlin, and Barbara L. Frederickson. "Infusing Positive Emotions into Life: The Broaden-and-Build Theory and a Dual-Process Model of Resilience." In *Handbook of Positive Emotions*, edited by Michele M. Tugade, Michelle N. Shiota, and Leslie D. Kirby, 28–43. New York, NY: Guilford, 2014.

Tull, Patricia K. "Persistent Vegetative States: People as Plants and Plants as People in Isaiah." In *The Desert Will Bloom: Poetic Visions in Isaiah*, edited by A. Joseph Everson and Hyun Chul Paul Kim, 17–34. Atlanta, GA: Society of Biblical Literature, 2009.

Ulrich, Roger S. "Aesthetic and Affective Response to Natural Environment." In *Behavior and the Natural Environment*, 85–125. New York: Springer, 1983.

Ulrich, Roger S. "Biophilia, Biophobia, and Natural Landscapes." *The Biophilia Hypothesis* 7 (1993): 73–137.

Van den Berg, Agnes E. and Hank Staats. "Environmental Psychology." In *Oxford Textbook of Nature and Public Health*, edited by Matilda van den Bosch and William Bird, 51–56. Oxford: Oxford University Press, 2018.

Van Leeuwen, Raymond C. "Isa 14: 12, *hôlēš al gwym* and Gilgamesh XI, 6." *Journal of Biblical Literature* (1980): 173–84.

Vandaele, Jeroen. "Cognitive Poetics and the Problem of Metaphor." In *The Routledge Handbook of Cognitive Linguistics*, edited by Xu Wen and John R. Taylor, 450–83. New York, NY: Routledge, 2021.

van der Veer, René and Jaan Valsinger, eds. *The Vygostsky Reader*. Oxford: Blackwell, 1994.

Vygotsky, Lev. *Thought and Language*. Translated by Regina Hanfmann, Gertrude Vakar, and Alex Kozulin. Cambridge, MA: MIT Press, 2012.

Wagner, Eric J. *The Mountain's Shadow*. Tübingen: Mohr Siebeck, forthcoming.

Walker-Jones, Arthur. "The So-Called Ostrich in the God Speeches of the Book of Job (Job 39, 13–18)." *Biblica* (2005): 494–510.

Walsh, Carey Ellen. *The Fruit of the Vine: Viticulture in Ancient Israel*. Winona Lake, IN: Eisenbrauns, 1996.

Weisman, Kara, Cristine H. Legare, Rachel E. Smith, Vivian A. Dzokoto, Felicity Aulino, Emily Ng, John C. Dulin, Nicole Ross-Zehnder, Joshua D. Brahinsky, and Tanya Marie Luhrmann. "Similarities and Differences in Concepts of Mental Life among Adults and Children in Five Cultures." *Nature Human Behaviour* 5 (2021): 1358–68.

Wen, Xu and Canzhong Jiang. "Embodiment." In *The Routledge Handbook of Cognitive Linguistics*, edited by Xu Wen and John R. Taylor, 145–60. New York, NY: Routledge, 2021.

Wen, Xu and John R. Taylor, eds. *The Routledge Handbook of Cognitive Linguistics*. New York, NY: Routledge, 2021.

Wenkel, David H. "Wild Beasts in the Prophecy of Isaiah: The Loss of Dominion and Its Renewal through Israel as the New Humanity." *Journal of Theological Interpretation* (2011): 251–63.

Wharton, James A. *Job*. Louisville, KY: Westminster John Knox, 1999.

Whedbee, J. William. *Isaiah and Wisdom*. Nashville, TN: Abington, 1971.

White, Matthew P., Rebecca Lovell, Benedict W. Wheeler, Sabine Pahl, Sebastian Völker, and Michael H. Depledge. "Blue Landscapes and Public Health." In *Oxford Textbook of Nature and Public Health*, edited by Matilda van den Bosch and William Bird, 154–59. Oxford: Oxford University Press, 2018.

Wierzbicka, Anna. *Emotions Across Languages and Cultures: Diversity and Universals*. Cambridge: Cambridge University Press, 1999.

Wildberger, Hans. *Isaiah 1–12*. Translated by Thomas H. Trapp. Minneapolis, MN: Fortress, 1990.

Wildberger, Hans. *Isaiah 13–27*. Translated by Thomas H. Trapp. Minneapolis, MN: Fortress, 1997.

Wildberger, Hans. *Isaiah 28–39*. Translated by Thomas H. Trapp. Minneapolis, MN: Fortress, 2002.

Williams, Edgar. *Ostrich*. London: Reaktion, 2013.

Williams, Florence. *The Nature Fix: Why Nature Makes Us Happier, Healthier, and More Creative*. New York, NY: Norton, 2017.

Williams, Gary R. "Frustrated Expectations in Isaiah v 1–7: A Literary Interpretation." *Vetus Testamentum* 35 (1985): 459–65.

Williamson, H. G. M. "Isaiah 1 and the Covenant Lawsuit." In *Covenant as Context: Essays in Honor of E. W. Nicholson*, edited by Andrew David Hastings Mayes and Robert B. Salters, 393–406. Oxford: Oxford University Press, 2003.

Williamson, H. G. M. *Isaiah 1–5*. London: T & T Clark, 2006.

Williamson, H. G. M. *Isaiah 6–12*. London: Bloomsbury Publishing, 2018.

Willis, John T. "Isaiah 2:2–5 and the Psalms of Zion." In *Writing and Reading the Scroll of Isaiah: Studies of an Interpretive Tradition, Volume One*, edited by Craig C. Broyles and Craig A. Evans, 295–316. Leiden: Brill, 1997.

Wilson, Edward O. "Biophilia and the Conservation Ethic." In *Evolutionary Perspectives on Environmental Problems*, edited by Justin J. Penn and Ivan Mysterud, 263–72. London: Routledge, 2017.

Wilson, Edward O. *Biophilia*. Cambridge, MA: Harvard University Press, 1984.

Wilson, John P. "Transformational Principles: Healing and Recovery from Psychic Trauma." In *The Posttraumatic Self: Restoring Meaning and Wholeness to Personality*, edited by John P. Wilson, 425–57. New York, NY: Routledge, 2006.

Wilson, John P. "Trauma and Transformation of the Self: Restoring Meaning and Wholeness to Personality." In *The Posttraumatic Self: Restoring Meaning and Wholeness to Personality*, edited by John P. Wilson, 399–423. New York, NY: Routledge, 2006.

Wilson, John P. "Trauma, Optimal Experiences, and Integrative Psychological States." In *The Posttraumatic Self: Restoring Meaning and Wholeness to Personality*, edited by John P. Wilson, 211–53. New York, NY: Routledge, 2006.

Wilson, Sir Charles William. *Picturesque Palestine, Sinai, and Egypt*. London: J. S. Virtue, 1881.

Wischnowsky, Marc. *Tochter Zion: Aufname und Überwindung der Stadtklage in den Prophetenschrift des Alten Testament*. Neukirchen-Vluyn: Neukirchener Verlag, 2001.

Wolde, Ellen Van. *Reframing Biblical Studies: When Language and Text Meet Culture, Cognition, and Context*. Winona Lake, IN: Eisenbrauns, 2009.

Wright, Christopher J. H. *Old Testament Ethics for the People of God*. Downers Grove, IL: InterVarsity, 2004.

Wright, Christopher J. H. *Exodus*. Grand Rapids, MI: Zondervan Academic, 2021.

Zlatev, Jordan. "Embodied Intersubjectivity." In *The Cambridge Handbook of Cognitive Linguistics*, edited by Barbara Dancygier, 172–87. Cambridge: Cambridge University Press, 2017.

# SUBJECT INDEX

Cheavens, Jennifer S., 176n55, 184

childbirth, 9, 10, 29, 33, 59–60, 95, 96–97

children, 3, 8, 9–12, 24–25, 33, 34, 41–43, 49–50, 97

Childs, Brevard S., 135n60, 144n58, 184

Chirico, Alice, 172n30, 173n33, n44, 184

City of David, 12–13

city, 7–20, 25, 28, 35, 99, 106, *see also* Babylon, Zion, Jerusalem

Clifford, Richard J., 112n4, n7, 135n69, 171n27, 177n56, 184

Clines, David J. A., 132n42, 135n61, 152n42, 156n77, 174n42, n46

cognitive bias, 5–6, 123n35

cognitive linguistics, 111n2, 119n24, 121n28, 122n31, 123n34, 126n7, 127n11, 159n11, *see also* attention, blend, concepts, construal, embodiment, entrenchment, image schema, intentionality, language, memory, mentalization, mental space, metaphor, mind-body dualism, mind reading, personification, polysemy, profile, semantics, theory of mind, thinking, up/down, words

community, 8, 10, 13–15, 15, 22, 25, 29, 69, 70, 76–77, 78, 85, 88, 90–91, 102, 106

concepts, 1–3, 4–5, 9, 10, 17, 37, 39, 70, 75, 83, 101, 108

conceptual blend, *see* blend

Conklin, Blane, 166n51, 184

consciousness, 115n13, 116n14

construal, 5, 7, 8, 9, 13, 15, 22, 24, 33, 39, 43, 45, 58, 65, 73, 82, 83, 87, 89, 90, 93, 123n33

Cooley, Jeffrey L., 140n18, 162n28, n29, 170n24, 184

Cornelius, Randolph R., 113n9, 184

corpus linguistics, 5, 122n32

Counted, Victor, 124n3, 125n5, 129n19, 132n41, 185

creation, 1–2, 11, 27, 28, 30–31, 36, 41, 43, 44–48, 50–51, 53, 71, 74–75, 81, 82, 83, 87, 89, 90–92, 93, 94, 96–97, 98, 101–3, 105–8, 112n4, n7, 113n8

Crenshaw, James L., 133n49, 185

crocodile, 101, 178n68

Croft, William D., 119n25, 185

Crook, Zeba, 165n40, 185

Cruse, Alan, 119n25, 185

culture, 1, 2, 3, 4, 46, 47, 51, 53, 56, 57, 60, 67, 69, 90, 112n6, 117n15, 118n20, 119n21, 121n27, 153n45, 158n3, 160n14, 162n30, 164n38

Curtis, Adrian, 131n33, 169n15, 185

Curtis, Valerie, 148n18, n19, 149n22, 185

Dąbrowska, Ewa, 111n2, 120n24, 123n34, 126n7, 182, 185, 186, 189

Dancygier, Barbara, 111n2, 120n24, 127n11, 159n11, 185, 188, 197, 202, 205

darkness, 1, 31–32, 36–37, 65, 66, 83, 87, 97, 140n19

daughter Zion, 12

David, 12–13, 16, 48, 57, 61–62

Davies, Graham I., 155n67, 156n69, n70, n75, n78, 185

day of YHWH, 28, 29–30, 32, 33, 34, 35–37, 65, 81–82, 105, 106, 107

de Jong, Peter J., 139n12, 185

de Vos, Christiane, 165n48, 185

demon, 33

Dempsey, Carol J., 130n25, 183

Wilson, Sir Charles William, 131n36, 205

wind, 23, 24, 28, 65, 93, 107, 175n48

Wischnowsky, Marc, 129n23, 205

Wolde, Ellen Van, 120n24, 205

wolf, 48–50, 146n65

words, 3–5, 8, 28, 38, 44, 55, 57, 70, 74, 81, 82, 87, 117n16, 121n29, 122n30, 127n9, 132n42, 138n6, 146n2, 149n23, n25, 158n8, n9, 163n35, 168n7, 169n7, 173n36, 179n71, *see also* semantics, polysemy

Wright, Christopher J. H., 152n39, 155n67, 171n27, 205

Zaphon, 14–15, 73–74

Zenger, Erich, 190

Zion, 7–16, 19, 28, 30, 80, 82, 86, 87, 105, 126n8, 127n9, n10, n11, 128n13, 129n18, 25, 130n27, 158n7, *see also* Jerusalem

Zion theology, 13

Zlatev, Jordan, 159n11, 205

# SCRIPTURE INDEX